TEACHER'S EDITION

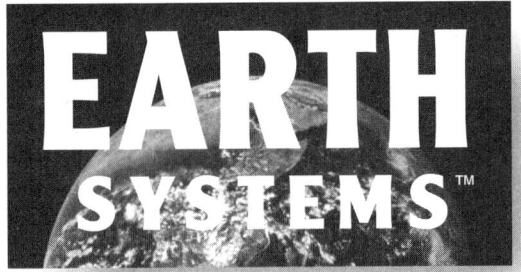

AN INQUIRY EARTH SCIENCE PROGRAM

INVESTIGATING FOSSILS

Michael J. Smith Ph.D.
American Geological Institute

John B. Southard Ph.D.
Massachusetts Institute of Technology

Colin Mably
Curriculum Developer

Developed by the American Geological Institute
Supported by the National Science Foundation and
the American Geological Institute Foundation

Published by
It's About Time Inc., Armonk, NY

It's About Time, Inc.
84 Business Park Drive, Armonk, NY 10504
Phone (914) 273-2233 Fax (914) 273-2227
Toll Free (888) 698-TIME
www.Its-About-Time.com

President
Laurie Kreindler

Project Editor	**Contributing Writer**	**Creative/Art Director**
Ruta Demery	William Jones Matthew Smith	John Nordland
Studio Manager	**Production Manager**	**Associate Editor**
Jon Voss	Joan Lee	Al Mari

Design/Production
Kathleen Bowen
Kadi Sarv

All student activities in this textbook have been designed to be as safe as possible, and have been reviewed by professionals specifically for that purpose. As well, appropriate warnings concerning potential safety hazards are included where applicable to particular activities. However, responsibility for safety remains with the student, the classroom teacher, the school principals, and the school board.

Investigating Earth Systems™ is a registered trademark of the American Geological Institute. Registered names and trademarks, etc., used in this publication, even without specific indication thereof, are not to be considered unprotected by law.

It's About Time® is a registered trademark of It's About Time, Inc. Registered names and trademarks, etc., used in this publication, even without specific indication thereof, are not to be considered unprotected by law.

© Copyright 2002: American Geological Institute

All rights reserved. No part of this publication may be reproduced, stored in a retrieval system, or transmitted, in any form or by any means, electronic, mechanical, photocopying, recording, or otherwise, without the prior written permission of the copyright owner.

Care has been taken to trace the ownership of copyright material contained in this publication. The publisher will gladly receive any information that will rectify any reference or credit line in subsequent editions.

Printed and bound in the United States of America

ISBN #1-58591-096-1

1 2 3 4 5 QC 06 05 04 03 02

This project was supported, in part, by the
National Science Foundation (grant no. 9353035)

Opinions expressed are those of the authors and not necessarily those of the National Science Foundation or the donors of the American Geological Institute Foundation.

Teacher's Edition

Student's Edition Illustrations and Photos

Cover photo, courtesy of the Smithsonian Institution; Border photo, Doug Sherman, Geo File Photography

F9, F10, F21, F23, F30, F43, F44, technical art by Burmar Technical

F47 (top photo), Caitlin Callahan; F19, Digital Vision Royalty Free Image (North American Scenics)

F8, James Edmunds; Fvii, Fxiv, F2, F12, F20, F29, F42, F51, F52, F59, illustrations by Dennis Falcon

F54 (diagram modified from "Fossil Horses in Cyberspace") with permission of the Florida Museum of Natural History

Fxiii (upper left), Geological Survey of Western Australia

F35, Bruce S. Grant; F6, Albert M. Hines; F39, Micromass UK LTD

F5, F47, Bruce Molnia; F15, NASA

F26, OAR/National Undersea Research Program; Fxiii (upper right), Fxiv, F17 (top), F28, Paleontological Research Institution

F1, Peabody Museum of Natural History; F36, F48, (photograph montage) F51, F53, PhotoDisc

Fxiii, (lower right), Fxiii (lower left), F4, F17 (top), F25, F32, F37, F58, Doug Sherman, Geo File Photography

F16, F41, F46, F57, Smithsonian Institution

F22 (map), F61 (map), US Geological Survey

F55, Washington State University, College of Veterinary Medicine

Taking Full Advantage of Investigating Earth Systems Through Professional Development

Implementing a new curriculum is challenging. That is why It's About Time, Inc. has partnered with the American Geological Institute, developers of *Investigating Earth Systems (IES)*, to provide a full range of professional development services. The sessions described below were designed to help you deepen your understanding of the content, pedagogy, and assessment strategies outlined in this Teacher's Edition, and adapt the program to suit the needs of your students and your local and state standards and curriculum frameworks.

Professional Development Services Available

Implementation Workshops
Two to five-day sessions held at your site that prepare you to implement the inquiry, systems, and community-based approach to learning Earth Science featured in *IES*. These workshops can be tailored to serve the needs of your school district, with chapters selected from the modules based on local or state curricula and framework criteria.

Program Overviews
One to three-day introductory sessions that provide a complete overview of the content and pedagogy of the *IES* program, as well as hands-on experience with activities from specific chapters. Program overviews are designed in consultation with school districts, counties, and SSI organizations.

Regional New-Teacher Summer Institutes
Two to five-day sessions that are designed to deepen your Earth Science content knowledge, and to prepare you to teach through inquiry. Guidance is provided in the gathering and use of appropriate materials and resources and specific attention is directed to the assessment of student learning.

Leadership Institutes
Six-day summer sessions conducted by the American Geological Institute that are designed to prepare current users for professional development leadership and mentoring within their districts or as consultants for It's About Time.

Follow-up Workshops
One to two-day sessions that provide additional Earth Science content and pedagogy support to teachers using the program. These workshops focus on identifying and solving practical issues and challenges to implementing an inquiry-based program.

Mentoring Visits
One-day visits that can be tailored to your specific needs that include class visits, mentoring teachers of the program, and in-service sessions.

Please fill in the form below to receive more information about participating in one of these Professional Development Services. The form can be directly faxed to our Professional Development at 914-273-2227. Our department will contact you to discuss further details and fees.

District/School: _____   Phone: _____

Address: _____

Contact Name: _____   Title: _____

E-mail: _____   Fax: _____

School Enrollment: _____   Number of Students Impacted: _____   Grade Level: _____

Have you purchased the following: ❏ Student Editions   ❏ Teacher Editions   ❏ Kits

Briefly explain how you plan to implement or how you are implementing the program in your school.

_____

_____

Teacher's Edition

Table of Contents

Investigating Earth Systems Team vi
Acknowledgements viii
The American Geological Institute and *Investigating Earth Systems* xi
Developing *Investigating Earth Systems* xii
Investigating Earth Systems Modules xiii
Investigating Earth Systems:
    Correlation to the National Science Education Standards xiv
Using *Investigating Earth Systems* Features in Your Classroom xvi
Using the *Investigating Earth Systems* Web Site xxx
Enhancing Teacher Content Knowledge xxxi
Managing Inquiry in Your *Investigating Earth Systems* Classroom xxxii
Assessing Student Learning in *Investigating Earth Systems* xxxv
Investigating Earth Systems Assessment Tools xxxviii
Reviewing and Reflecting upon Your Teaching xlii
Investigating Fossils: Introduction 1
Students Conceptions about Fossils 2
Investigating Fossils: Module Flow 4
Investigating Fossils: Module Objectives 5
National Science Education Content Standards 8
Key NSES Content Standards Addressed in *IES* Fossils 9
Key AAAS Benchmarks
    Addressed in *IES* Fossils 10
Materials and Equipment List for Investigating Fossils 13
Pre-assessment 17
Introducing the Earth System 23
Introducing Inquiry Processes 27
Introducing Fossils 29
Why are Fossils Important? 31
Investigation 1: The Properties of Fossils 33
Investigation 2: Sediment Size and Fossil Formation 63
Investigation 3: Conditions for Fossil Formation 105
Investigation 4: Fossils through Geologic Time 139
Investigation 5: Comparing Fossils over Time 181
Investigation 6: Adaptations to a Changing Environment 211
Investigation 7: Being a Paleontologist 239
Reflecting 267
Appendices: Alternative End-of-Module Assessment 270
                    Assessment Tools 274
                    Blackline Masters 284

Investigating Earth Systems Team

Project Staff

Michael J. Smith, Principal Investigator
    Director of Education, American Geological Institute
John B. Southard, Senior Writer
    Professor of Geology, Massachusetts Institute of Technology
Matthew Smith, Project Coordinator
    Programs Manager, American Geological Institute
William O. Jones, Contributing Writer
    American Geological Institute
Caitlin N. Callahan, Project Assistant
    American Geological Institute
William S. Houston, Field Test Coordinator
    American Geological Institute
Harvey Rosenbaum, Field Test Evaluator
    Montgomery County School District, Maryland
Fred Finley, Project Evaluator
    University of Minnesota
Lynn Lindow, Pilot Test Evaluator
    University of Minnesota

Original Project Personnel

Robert L. Heller, Principal Investigator
Charles Groat, United States Geological Survey
Colin Mably, LaPlata, Maryland
Robert Ridky, University of Maryland
Marilyn Suiter, American Geological Institute

National Advisory Board

Jane Crowder
   Middle School Teacher, WA
Kerry Davidson
   Louisiana Board of Regents, LA
Joseph D. Exline
   Educational Consultant, VA
Louis A. Fernandez
   California State University, CA
Frank Watt Ireton
   National Earth Science Teachers Association, DC
LeRoy Lee
   Wisconsin Academy of Sciences, Arts and Letters, WI
Donald W. Lewis
   Chevron Corporation, CA
James V. O'Connor (deceased)
   University of the District of Columbia, DC
Roger A. Pielke Sr.
   Colorado State University, CO
Dorothy Stout
   Cypress College, CA
Lois Veath
   Advisory Board Chairperson - Chadron State College, NE

National Science Foundation Program Officers

Gerhard Salinger
Patricia Morse

Acknowledgements

Principal Investigator

Michael Smith is Director of Education at the American Geological Institute in Alexandria, Virginia. Dr. Smith worked as an exploration geologist and hydrogeologist. He began his Earth Science teaching career with Shady Side Academy in Pittsburgh, PA in 1988 and most recently taught Earth Science at the Charter School of Wilmington, DE. He earned a doctorate from the University of Pittsburgh's Cognitive Studies in Education Program and joined the faculty of the University of Delaware School of Education in 1995. Dr. Smith received the Outstanding Earth Science Teacher Award for Pennsylvania from the National Association of Geoscience Teachers in 1991, served as Secretary of the National Earth Science Teachers Association, and is a reviewer for Science Education and The Journal of Research in Science Teaching. He worked on the Delaware Teacher Standards, Delaware Science Assessment, National Board of Teacher Certification, and AAAS Project 2061 Curriculum Evaluation programs.

Senior Writer

John Southard received his undergraduate degree from the Massachusetts Institute of Technology in 1960 and his doctorate in geology from Harvard University in 1966. After a National Science Foundation postdoctoral fellowship at the California Institute of Technology, he joined the faculty at the Massachusetts Institute of Technology, where he is currently Professor of Geology Emeritus. He was awarded the MIT School of Science teaching prize in 1989 and was one of the first cohorts of first MacVicar Fellows at MIT, in recognition of excellence in undergraduate teaching. He has taught numerous undergraduate courses in introductory geology, sedimentary geology, field geology, and environmental Earth Science both at MIT and in Harvard's adult education program. He was editor of the Journal of Sedimentary Petrology from 1992 to 1996, and he continues to do technical editing of scientific books and papers for SEPM, a professional society for sedimentary geology. Dr. Southard received the 2001 Neil Miner Award from the National Association of Geoscience Teachers.

Project Director/Curriculum Designer

Colin Mably has been a key curriculum developer for several NSF-supported national curriculum projects. As learning materials designer to the American Geological Institute, he has directed the design and development of the IES curriculum modules and also training workshops for pilot and field-test teachers.

Teacher's Edition

Project Team
Marcus Milling
Executive Director - AGI, VA
Michael Smith
Principal Investigator
Director of Education - AGI, VA
Colin Mably
Project Director/Curriculum Designer
Educational Visions, MD
Fred Finley
Project Evaluator
University of Minnesota, MN
Lynn Lindow
Pilot Test Evaluator
University of Minnesota, MN
Harvey Rosenbaum
Field Test Evaluator
Montgomery School District, MD
Ann Benbow
Project Advisor - American Chemical Society, DC
Robert Ridky
Original Project Director
University of Maryland, MD
Chip Groat
Original Principal Investigator
University of Texas - El Paso, TX
Marilyn Suiter
Original Co-principal Investigator
AGI, VA
William Houston
Project Manager
Eric Shih - Project Assistant

Original and Contributing Authors
Oceans
George Dawson
Florida State University, FL
Joseph F. Donoghue
Florida State University, FL
Ann Benbow
American Chemical Society
Michael Smith
American Geological Institute
Soil
Robert Ridky
University of Maryland, MD
Colin Mably - LaPlata, MD
John Southard
Massachusetts Institute of Technology, MA
Michael Smith
American Geological Institute
Fossils
Robert Gastaldo
Colby College, ME
Colin Mably - LaPlata, MD
Michael Smith
American Geological Institute
Climate and Weather
Mike Mogil
How the Weather Works, MD

Ann Benbow
American Chemical Society
Joe Moran
American Meteorological Society
Michael Smith
American Geological Institute
Energy Resources
Laurie Martin-Vermilyea
American Geological Institute
Michael Smith
American Geological Institute
Dynamic Planet
Michael Smith
American Geological Institute
Rocks and Landforms
Michael Smith
American Geological Institute
Water as a Resource
Ann Benbow
American Chemical Society
Michael Smith
American Geological Institute
Materials and Minerals
Mary Poulton
University of Arizona, AZ
Colin Mably - LaPlata, MD
Michael Smith
American Geological Institute

Content Reviewers
Louis Bartek
University of North Carolina
Gary Beck - BP Exploration
Steve Bergman
University of Texas-Dallas
Joseph Bishop
Johns Hopkins University/NOAA
Kathleen Carrado
Argonne National Laboratory
Sandip Chattopadhyay
R.S. Kerr Environmental Research Center
Bob Christman
Western Washington University
Donald Conte
California University of California
Norbert E. Cygan - AAPG
Tom Dignes
Mobil Technology Corporation
Neil M. Dubrovsky
United States Geological Survey
Robert J. Finley
Illinois State Geological Survey
Anke Friedrich
California Institute of Technology
Rick Fritz - AAPG
Frank Hall - University of New Orleans
David Hawkins - Denison University
Martha House
California Institute of Technology
Travis Hudson
American Geological Institute
Allan P. Juhas - SEG

Dennis Lamb - Penn State
Donald Lewis - Happy Valley, CA
Kate Madin
Woods Hole Oceanographic Institute
John Madsen - University of Delaware
Carol Mankiewicz - Beloit College
Clyde J. Northrup
Boise State University
Lois K. Ongley, PhD - Bates College
Bruce Pivetz
ManTech Environmental Research Services
Eleanora I. Robbins
United States Geological Survey
Rob Ross
Paleontological Research Institution
Audrey Rule - Boise State University
Lou Solebello - Macon, GA
Steve Stanley - Johns Hopkins University
Sarah Tebbens - University of South Florida
Bob Tilling
United States Geological Survey
Michael Velbel
Michigan State University
Don Woodrow
Hobart and William Smith Colleges

Pilot Test Teachers
Debbie Bambino - Philadelphia, PA
Barbara Barden - Rittman, OH
Louisa Bliss - Bethlehem, NH
Mike Bradshaw - Houston TX
Greta Branch - Reno, NV
Garnetta Chain - Piscataway, NJ
Roy Chambers - Portland, OR
Laurie Corbett - Sayre, PA
James Cole - New York, NY
Collette Craig - Reno, NV
Anne Douglas - Houston, TX
Jacqueline Dubin - Roslyn, PA
Jane Evans - Media, PA
Gail Gant - Houston, TX
Joan Gentry - Houston, TX
Pat Gram - Aurora, OH
Robert Haffner - Akron, OH
Joe Hampel - Swarthmore, PA
Wayne Hayes - West Green, GA
Mark Johnson - Reno, NV
Cheryl Joloza - Philadelphia, PA
Jeff Luckey - Houston, TX
Karen Luniewski
Reistertown, MD
Cassie Major - Plainfield, VT
Carol Miller - Houston, TX
Melissa Murray - Reno, NV
Mary-Lou Northrop

Investigating Earth Systems: Fossils

Tracey Oliver - Philadelphia, PA
Nicole Pfister - Londonderry, VT
Beth Price - Reno, NV
Joyce Ramig - Houston, TX
Julie Revilla - Woodbridge, VA
Steve Roberts - Meredith, NH
Cheryl Skipworth - Philadelphia, PA
Brent Stenson - Valdosta, GA
Elva Stout - Evans, GA
Regina Toscani - Philadelphia, PA
Bill Waterhouse - North Woodstock, NH
Leonard White - Philadelphia, PA
Paul Williams - Lowerford, VT
Bob Zafran - San Jose, CA
Missi Zender - Twinsburg, OH

Field Test Teachers
Eric Anderson - Carson City, NV
Katie Bauer - Rockport, ME
Kathleen Berdel - Philadelphia, PA
Wanda Blake - Macon, GA
Beverly Bowers - Mannington, WV
Rick Chiera - Monroe Falls, OH
Don Cole - Akron, OH
Patte Cotner - Bossier City, LA
Johnny DeFreese - Haughton, LA
Mary Devine - Astoria, NY
Cheryl Dodes - Queens, NY
Brenda Engstrom - Warwick, RI
Lisa Gioe-Cordi - Brooklyn, NY
Pat Gram - Aurora, OH
Mark Johnson - Reno, NV
Chicory Koren - Kent, OH
Marilyn Krupnick - Philadelphia, PA

Melissa Loftin - Bossier City, LA
Janet Lundy - Reno, NV
Vaughn Martin - Easton, ME
Anita Mathis - Fort Valley, GA
Laurie Newton - Truckee, NV
Debbie O'Gorman - Reno, NV
Joe Parlier - Barnesville, GA
Sunny Posey - Bossier City, LA
Beth Price - Reno, NV
Stan Robinson - Mannington, WV
Mandy Thorne - Mannington, WV
Marti Tomko - Westminster, MD
Jim Trogden - Rittman, OH
Torri Weed - Stonington, ME
Gene Winegart - Shreveport, LA
Dawn Wise - Peru, ME
Paula Wright - Gray, GA

IMPORTANT NOTICE

The *Investigating Earth Systems*™ series of modules is intended for use by students under the direct supervision of a qualified teacher. The experiments described in this book involve substances that may be harmful if they are misused or if the procedures described are not followed. Read cautions carefully and follow all directions. Do not use or combine any substances or materials not specifically called for in carrying out experiments. Other substances are mentioned for educational purposes only and should not be used by students unless the instructions specifically indicate.

The materials, safety information, and procedures contained in this book are believed to be reliable. This information and these procedures should serve only as a starting point for classroom or laboratory practices, and they do not purport to specify minimal legal standards or to represent the policy of the American Geological Institute. No warranty, guarantee, or representation is made by the American Geological Institute as to the accuracy or specificity of the information contained herein, and the American Geological Institute assumes no responsibility in connection therewith. The added safety information is intended to provide basic guidelines for safe practices. It cannot be assumed that all necessary warnings and precautionary measures are contained in the printed material and that other additional information and measures may not be required.

This work is based upon work supported by the National Science Foundation under Grant No. 9353035 with additional support from the Chevron Corporation. Any opinions, findings, and conclusions or recommendations expressed in this publication are those of the authors and do not necessarily reflect the views of the National Science Foundation or the Chevron Corporation. Any mention of trade names does not imply endorsement from the National Science Foundation or the Chevron Corporation.

Teacher's Edition

The American Geological Institute and Investigating Earth Systems

Imagine more than 500,000 Earth scientists worldwide sharing a common voice, and you've just imagined the mission of the American Geological Institute. Our mission is to raise public awareness of the Earth sciences and the role that they play in mankind's use of natural resources, mitigation of natural hazards, and stewardship of the environment. For more than 50 years, AGI has served the scientists and teachers of its Member Societies and hundreds of associated colleges, universities, and corporations by producing Earth science educational materials, *Geotimes*–a geoscience news magazine, GeoRef–a reference database, and government affairs and public awareness programs.

So many important decisions made every day that affect our lives depend upon an understanding of how our Earth works. That's why AGI created *Investigating Earth Systems*. In your *Investigating Earth Systems* classroom, you'll discover the wonder and importance of Earth science. As you investigate minerals, soil, or oceans — do field work in nearby beaches, parks, or streams, explore how fossils form, understand where your energy resources come from, or find out how to forecast weather — you'll gain a better understanding of Earth science and its importance in your life.

We would like to thank the National Science Foundation and the AGI Foundation Members that have been supportive in bringing Earth science to students. The Chevron Corporation provided the initial leadership grant, with additional contributions from the following AGI Foundation Members: Anadarko Petroleum Corp., The Anschutz Foundation, Baker Hughes Foundation, Barrett Resources Corp., BPAmoco Foundation, Burlington Resources Foundation, CGG Americas, Inc., Conoco Inc., Consolidated Natural Gas Foundation, Diamond Offshore Co., EEX Corp., ExxonMobil Foundation, Global Marine Drilling Co., Halliburton Foundation, Inc., Kerr McGee Foundation, Maxus Energy Corp., Noble Drilling Corp., Occidental Petroleum Charitable Foundation, Parker Drilling Co., Phillips Petroleum Co., Santa Fe Snyder Corp., Schlumberger Foundation, Shell Oil Company Foundation, Southwestern Energy Co., Texaco, Inc., Texas Crude Energy, Inc., Unocal Corp. USX Foundation (Marathon Oil Co.).

We at AGI wish you success in your exploration of the Earth System!

Michael J. Smith
Director of Education, AGI

Marcus E. Milling
Executive Director, AGI

Developing Investigating Earth Systems

Welcome to *Investigating Earth Systems (IES)! IES* was developed through funding from the National Science Foundation and the American Geological Institute Foundation. Classroom teachers, scientists, and thousands of students across America helped to create *IES*. In the 1997-98 school year, scientists and curriculum developers drafted nine *IES* modules. They were pilot tested by 43 teachers in 14 states from Washington to Georgia. Faculty from the University of Minnesota conducted an independent evaluation of the pilot test in 1998, which was used to revise the program for a nationwide field test during the 1999-2000 school year. A comprehensive evaluation of student learning by a professional field-test evaluator showed that *IES* modules led to significant gains in student understanding of fundamental Earth science concepts. Field-test feedback from 34 teachers and content reviews from 33 professional Earth scientists were used to produce the commercial edition you have selected for your classroom.

Inquiry and the interrelation of Earth's systems form the backbone of *IES*. Often taught as a linear sequence of events called "the scientific method," inquiry underlies all scientific processes and can take many different forms. It is very important that students develop an understanding of inquiry processes as they use them. Your students naturally use inquiry processes when they solve problems. Like scientists, students usually form a question to investigate after first looking at what is observable or known. They predict the most likely answer to a question. They base this prediction on what they already know to be true. Unlike professional scientists, your students may not devote much thought to these processes. In order to be objective, students must formally recognize these processes as they do them. To make sure that the way they test ideas is fair, scientists think very carefully about the design of their investigations. This is a skill your students will practice throughout each *IES* module.

All *Investigating Earth Systems* modules also encourage students to think about the Earth as a system. Upon completing each investigation they are asked to relate what they have learned to the Earth Systems (see the *Earth System Connection* sheet in the **Appendix**). Integrating the processes of the biosphere, geosphere, hydrosphere, and atmosphere will open up a new way of looking at the world for most students. Understanding that the Earth is dynamic and that it affects living things, often in unexpected ways, will engage them and make the topics more relevant.

We trust that you will find the Teacher's Edition that accompanies each student module to be useful. It provides **Background Information** on the concepts explored in the module, as well as strategies for incorporating inquiry and a systems-based approach into your classroom. Enjoy your investigation!

Investigating Earth Systems: Fossils

Investigating Earth Systems Modules

Climate and Weather

Energy Resources

Fossils

Materials and Minerals

Oceans

Our Dynamic Planet

Rocks and Landforms

Soil

Water as a Resource

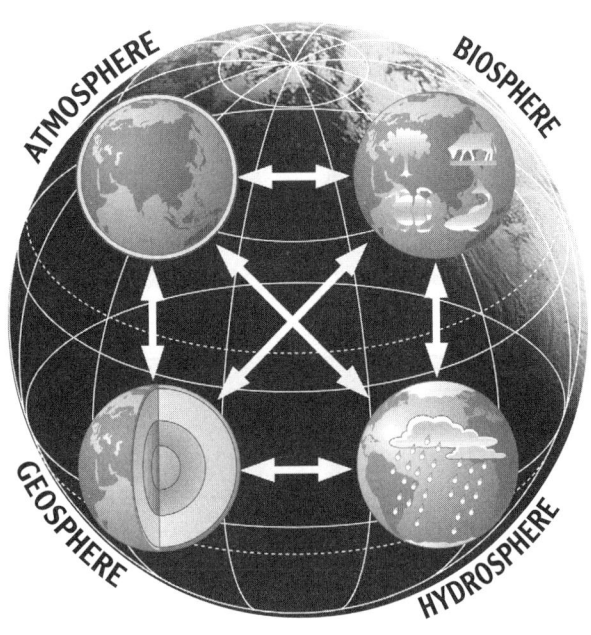

Investigating Earth Systems: Correlation to the National Science Education Standards

National Science Education Content Standards Grades 5 – 8

	Soil	Rocks and Landforms	Oceans	Climate and Weather	Our Dynamic Planet	Materials and Minerals	Energy Resources	Water as a Resource	Fossils
UNIFYING CONCEPTS AND PROCESSES									
System, order and organization	•	•	•	•	•	•	•	•	•
Evidence, models, and explanation	•	•	•	•	•	•	•	•	•
Constancy, change, and measurement	•	•	•	•	•	•	•	•	•
Evolution and equilibrium		•	•	•			•	•	
Form and function									•
SCIENCE AS INQUIRY									
Identify questions that can be answered through scientific investigations	•	•	•	•	•	•	•	•	•
Design and conduct scientific investigations	•	•	•	•	•	•	•	•	•
Use tools and techniques to gather, analyze, and interpret data	•	•	•	•	•	•	•	•	•
Develop descriptions, explanations, predictions and models based on evidence	•	•	•	•	•	•	•	•	•
Think critically and logically to make the relationships between evidence and explanation	•	•	•	•	•	•	•	•	•
Recognize and analyze alternative explanations and predictions	•	•	•	•	•	•	•	•	•
Communicate scientific procedures and explanations	•	•	•	•	•	•	•	•	•
Use mathematics in all aspects of scientific inquiry	•	•	•	•	•	•	•	•	•
Understand scientific inquiry	•	•	•	•	•	•	•	•	•
PHYSICAL SCIENCE									
Properties and Changes of Properties in Matter	•	•	•		•	•	•	•	
Motions and Forces	•		•						
Transfer of Energy		•	•	•	•	•	•		
LIFE SCIENCE									
Populations and Ecosystems			•				•	•	•
Diversity and Adaptation of Organisms			•		•				•

Teacher's Edition

Investigating Earth Systems: Correlation to the National Science Education Standards

National Science Education Content Standards Grades 5 – 8

	Soil	Rocks and Landforms	Oceans	Climate and Weather	Our Dynamic Planet	Materials and Minerals	Energy Resources	Water as a Resource	Fossils
EARTH AND SPACE SCIENCE									
Structure of the Earth system	•	•	•	•	•	•	•	•	•
Earth's History	•	•	•	•	•	•	•	•	•
Earth in the Solar System			•	•	•		•	•	
SCIENCE AND TECHNOLOGY									
Abilities of technological design	•	•	•	•	•	•	•	•	•
Understandings about science and technology		•	•			•	•	•	
SCIENCE IN PERSONAL AND SOCIAL PERSPECTIVES									
Personal health	•							•	
Populations, resources, and environment	•					•	•	•	
Natural Hazards		•		•	•	•			
Risks and benefits					•		•		
Science and technology in society	•	•	•	•	•	•	•	•	•
HISTORY AND NATURE OF SCIENCE									
Science as a human endeavor	•	•	•	•	•	•	•	•	•
Nature of science	•	•	•	•	•	•	•	•	•
History of science			•		•				•

© It's About Time, Inc.

Investigating Earth Systems: Fossils

Using Investigating Earth Systems Features in Your Classroom

1. Pre-assessment

Designed under the umbrella framework of "science for all students," meaning that all students should be able to engage in inquiry and learn core science concepts, *Investigating Earth Systems* helps you to tailor instruction to meet your students' needs. A crucial first step in this framework is to ascertain what knowledge, experience, and understanding your students bring to their study of a module. The pre-assessment consists of five questions geared to the major concepts and understandings targeted in the unit. Students write and draw what they know about the major topics and concepts. This information is recorded and shared in an informal discussion prior to engaging in hands-on inquiry. The discussion enables students to recognize how much there is to learn and appreciate, and that by exploring the unit together, the entire classroom can emerge from the experience with a better understanding of core concepts and themes. Students' responses provide crucial pre-assessment data for you. By examining their written work and probing for further detail during the classroom conversation, you can identify strengths and weaknesses in students' understandings, as well as their abilities to communicate that understanding to others. It is important that the pre-assessment not be viewed as a test, and that judgments about the accuracy of responses not be evaluated in writing or through your comments during the conversation. The goal is to ascertain and probe, not judge, and to create a safe classroom environment in which students feel comfortable sharing their ideas and knowledge. Students revisit these pre-assessment questions informally throughout the unit. At the end of the unit, students respond to the same four questions in the section called **Back to the Beginning**. The pre-assessment thus helps you and your students to make judgments about their growth in understanding and ability throughout the module.

Teacher's Edition

2. The Earth System

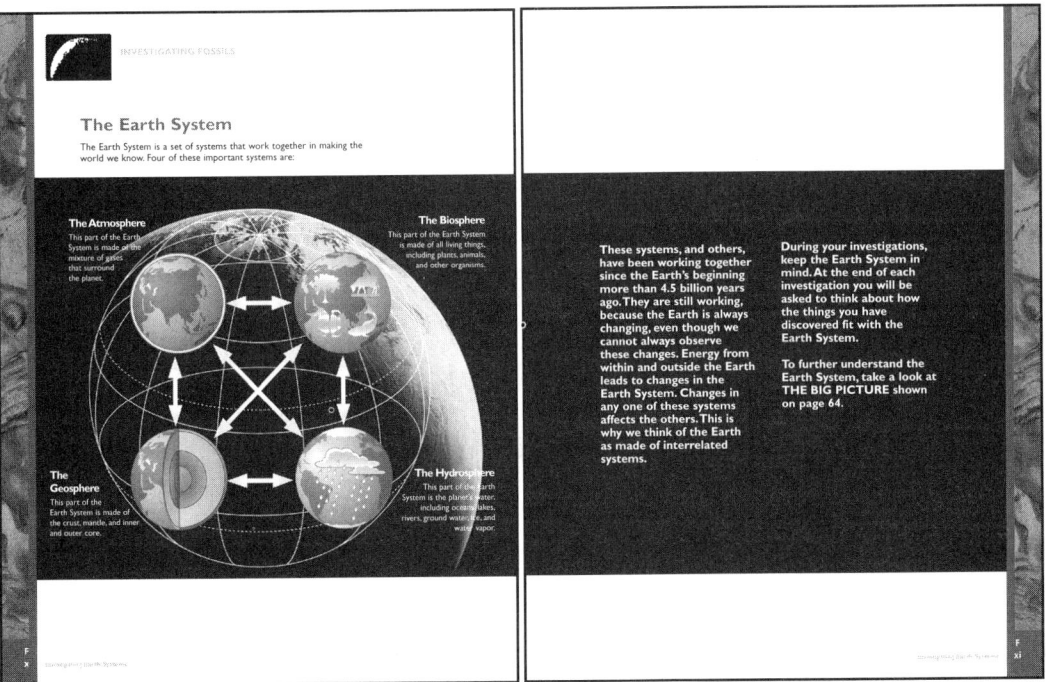

National Science Education Standards link...

"A major goal of science in the middle grades is for students to develop an understanding of Earth (and the solar system) as a set of closely coupled systems. The idea of systems provides a framework in which students can investigate the four major interacting components of the Earth System – geosphere (crust, mantle, and core), hydrosphere (water), atmosphere (air), and the biosphere (the realm of living things)."

NSES content standard D "Developing Student Understanding" (pages 158-159)

Understanding the Earth system is an overall goal of the *Investigating Earth Systems* series. It is a difficult and complex set of concepts to grasp, because it is inferred rather than observed directly. Yet even the smallest component of Earth science can be linked to the Earth system. As your students progress through each module, an increasing number of connections with the Earth system will arise. Your students may not, however, immediately see these connections. At the end of every investigation, they will be asked to link what they have discovered with ideas about the Earth system. They will also be asked to write about this in their journals. A **Blackline Master** (*Earth System Connection* sheet) is available in each Teacher's Edition. Students can use this to record connections that they make as they complete each investigation. At the very end of the module they will be asked to review everything they have learned in relation to the Earth system. The aim is for students to have a working understanding of the Earth System by the time they complete grade 8. They will need your help accomplishing this.

Investigating Earth Systems: Fossils

For example, in *Investigating Rocks and Landforms*, students work with models to simulate Earth processes, such as erosion of stream sediment and deposition of that sediment on floodplains and in deltas. Changes in inputs in one part of the system (say rainfall, from the atmosphere), affect other parts of the system (stream flows, erosion on river bends, amount of sediment carried by the stream, and deposition of sediment on floodplains or in deltas). These changes affect, in turn, other parts of the system (for example, floods that affect human populations, i.e., the biosphere). In the same module, students explore the rock record within their community and develop understandings about how interactions between the hydrosphere, atmosphere, geosphere, and biosphere change the landscape over time. These are just some of the many ways that *Investigating Earth Systems* modules foster and promote student thinking about the dynamic nature and interactions of Earth systems—biosphere, geosphere, atmosphere, and hydrosphere.

3. Introducing Inquiry Processes

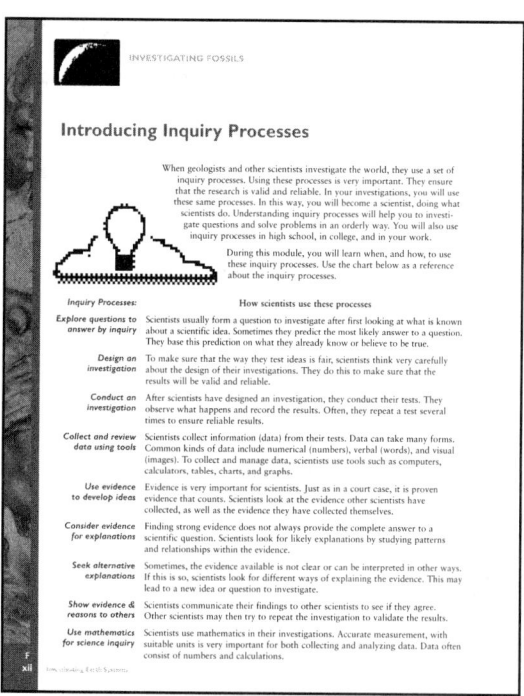

Inquiry is at the heart of *Investigating Earth Systems*. That is why each module title begins with the title "Investigating." In the National Science Education Standards, inquiry is the first Content Standard. NSES then lists a range of points about inquiry. These fundamental components of inquiry were written into the list shown at the beginning of each student module. It is very important that students be reminded of the steps in the inquiry process as they perform them. Inquiry depends on active student participation. Ideas on how to make inquiry successful in the classroom appear throughout the modules and in the "Managing Inquiry in Your *Investigating Earth Systems* Classroom" section of this Teacher's Edition.

It is very important that students develop an understanding of the inquiry processes as they use them. Stress the importance of inquiry processes as they occur in your investigations. Provoke students to think about why these processes are important. Collecting good data, using evidence, considering alternative explanations, showing evidence to others, and using mathematics are all essential to *IES*. Use examples to demonstrate these processes whenever possible. At the end of every investigation, students are asked to reflect on the scientific inquiry processes they used. Refer students to the list of inquiry processes on page x of the Student Book as they think about scientific inquiry and answer the questions.

4. Introducing the Module

Each *IES* module begins with photographs and questions. This is an introduction to the module for your students. It is designed to give them a brief overview of the content of the module and set their investigations into a relevant and meaningful context. Students will have had a variety of experiences with the content of the module. This is an opportunity for them to offer some of their own experiences in a general discussion, using these questions as prompts. This section of each *IES* module follows the pre-assessment, where students spend time thinking about what they already know about the content of the module. The photographs and questions can be used to focus the students' thinking.

The ideas students share in the introduction to the module provide you with additional pre-assessment data. The experiences they describe and the way in which they are discussed will alert you to their general level of understanding about these topics. To encourage sharing and to provide a record, teachers find it useful to quickly summarize the main points that emerge from discussion. You can do this on the chalkboard or flipchart for all to see. This can be displayed as students work through the module and added to with each new experience. For your own assessment purposes, it will be useful to keep a record of these early indicators of student understanding.

5. Key Question

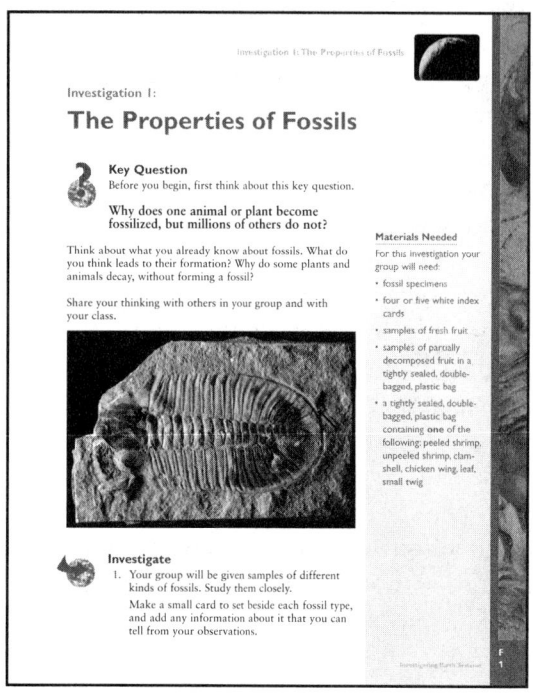

Each *Investigating Earth Systems* investigation begins with a **Key Question** – an open-ended question that gives teachers the opportunity to explore what their students know about the central concepts of the activity. Uncovering students' thinking (their prior knowledge) and exposing the diversity of ideas in the classroom are the first steps in the learning cycle. One of the most fundamental principles derived from many years of research on student learning is that:

"Students come to the classroom with preconceptions about how the world works. If their initial understanding is not engaged, they may fail to grasp the new concepts and information that are taught, or they may learn them for the purposes of a test but revert to their preconceptions outside the classroom." (*How People Learn: Bridging Research and Practice*, National Research Council, 1999, P. 10.)

This principle has been illustrated through the *Private Universe* series of videotapes that show Harvard graduates responding to basic science questions in much the same way that fourth grade students do. Although the videotapes revealed that the Harvard graduates used a more sophisticated vocabulary, the majority held onto the same naïve, incorrect conceptions of elementary school students. Research on learning suggests that the belief systems of students who are not confronted with what they believe and adequately shown why they should give up that belief system remain intact. Real learning requires confronting one's beliefs and testing them in light of competing explanations.

Drawing out and working with students' preconceptions is important for learners. In *Investigating Earth Systems*, the **Key Question** is used to ascertain students' prior knowledge about the key concept or Earth science processes or events explored in the activity. Students verbalize what they think about the age of the Earth, the causes of volcanoes, or the way that the landscape changes over time before they embark on an activity designed to challenge and test these beliefs. A brief discussion about the diversity of beliefs in the classroom makes students consider how their ideas compare to others and the evidence that supports their view of volcanoes, earthquakes, or seasons.

xx   Investigating Earth Systems: Fossils

Teacher's Edition

The **Key Question** is not a conclusion, but a lead into inquiry. It is not designed to instantly yield the "correct answer" or a debate about the features of the question, or to bring closure. The activity that follows will provide that discussion as students analyze and discuss the results of inquiry. Students are encouraged to record their ideas in words and/or drawings to ensure that they have considered their prior knowledge. After students discuss their ideas in pairs or in small groups, teachers activate a class discussion. A discussion with fellow students prior to class discussion may encourage students to exchange ideas without the fear of personally giving a "wrong answer." Teachers sometimes have students exchange papers and volunteer responses that they find interesting.

Some teachers prefer to have students record their responses to these questions. They then call for volunteers to offer ideas up for discussion. Other teachers prefer to start with discussion by asking students to volunteer their ideas. In either situation, it is important that teachers encourage the sharing of ideas by not judging responses as "right" or "wrong." It is also important that teachers keep a record of the variety of ideas, which can be displayed in the classroom (on a sheet of easel pad paper or on an overhead transparency) and referred to as students explore the concepts in the module. Teachers often find that they can group responses into a few categories and record the number of students who hold each idea. The photograph in each **Key Question** section was designed to stimulate student thinking and help students to make the specific kinds of connections emphasized in each activity.

6. Investigate

Investigating Earth Systems is a hands-on, minds-on curriculum. In designing *Investigating Earth Systems*, we were guided by the research on learning, which points out how important ***doing*** Earth Science is to ***learning*** Earth Science. Testing of *Investigating Earth Systems* activities by teachers across America provided critical testimonial and quantitative measures of the importance of the activities to student learning. In small groups and as a class, students take part in doing hands-on experiments, participating in field work, or searching for answers using the Internet and reference materials. **Blackline Masters** are included in the Teacher's Editions for any maps or illustrations that are essential for students to complete the activity.

Investigating Earth Systems: Fossils xxi

Each part of an *Investigating Earth Systems* investigation, as well as the sequence of activities within a module, moves from concrete to abstract. Hands-on activities provide the basis for exploring student beliefs about how the world works and to manipulate variables that affect the outcomes of experiments, models, or simulations. Later in each activity, formal labels are applied to concepts by introducing terminology used to describe the processes that students have explored through hands-on activity. This flow from concrete (hands-on) to abstract (formal explanations) is progressive – students begin to develop their own explanations for phenomena by responding to questions within the **Investigate** section.

Each activity has instructions for each part of the investigation. Materials kits are available for purchase, but you will also need to obtain some resources from outside suppliers, such as topographic and geologic maps of your community, state, or region. The *Investigating Earth Systems* web site will direct you to sources where you can gather such materials.

Most **Investigate** activities will require between one and two class periods. The variety of school schedules and student needs makes it difficult to predict exactly how much time your class will need. For example, if students need to construct a graph for part of an investigation, and the students have never been exposed to graphing, then this investigation may require additional time and could become part of a mathematics lesson.

The most challenging aspect of *Investigating Earth Systems* for teachers to "master" is that the **Investigate** section of each activity has been designed to be student-driven. Students learn more when they have to struggle to "figure things out" and work in collaborative groups to solve problems as a team. Teachers will have to resist the temptation to provide the answers to students when they get "stuck" or hung up on part of a problem. Eventually, students learn that while they can call upon their teacher for assistance, the teacher is not going to "show them the answer." Field testing of *Investigating Earth Systems* revealed that teachers who were most successful in getting their students to solve problems as a team were patient with this process and steadfast in their determination to act as facilitators of learning during the **Investigate** portion of activities. As one teacher noted, "My response to questions during the investigation was like a mantra, 'What do you think you need to do to solve this?' My students eventually realized that although I was there to provide guidance, they weren't going to get the solution out of me."

Another concern that many teachers have when examining *Investigating Earth Systems* for the first time is that their students do not have the background knowledge to do the investigations. They want to deliver a lecture about the phenomena before allowing students to do the investigation. Such an approach is common to many traditional programs and is inconsistent with the pedagogical theory used to design *Investigating Earth Systems*. The appropriate place for delivering a lecture or reading text in *Investigating Earth Systems* is following the investigation, not preceding it.

Teacher's Edition

For example, suppose a group of students has been asked to interpret a map. The traditional approach to science education is for the teacher to give a lecture or assign a reading, "How to Interpret Maps," then give students practice reading maps. *Investigating Earth Systems* teachers recognize that while students may lack some specific skills (reading latitude and longitude, for example), within a group of four students, it is not uncommon for at least one of the students to have a vital skill or piece of knowledge that is required to solve a problem. The one or two students who have been exposed to (or better yet, understood) latitude and longitude have the opportunity to shine within the group by contributing that vital piece of information or demonstrating a skill. That's how scientific research teams work – specialists bring expertise to the group, and by working together, the group achieves something that no one could achieve working alone. The **Investigate** section of *Investigating Earth Systems* is modeled in the spirit of the scientific research team.

7. Inquiry

Inquiry is the first content standard in the National Science Education Standards (NSES). The American Association for the Advancement of Science's (AAAS) Benchmarks for Science Literacy also places considerable emphasis on scientific inquiry (see excerpts on the following page). *IES* has been designed to remind students to reflect on inquiry processes as they carry out their investigations. The student journal is an important tool in helping students to develop these understandings. In using the journal, students are modeling what scientists do. Your students are young scientists as they investigate Earth science questions. Encourage your students to think of themselves in this way and to see their journals as records of their investigations.

Inquiry
Representing Information

Communicating findings to other scientists is very important in scientific inquiry. In this investigation it is important for you to find good ways of showing what you learned to others in your class. Be sure your maps and displays are clearly labeled and well organized.

An icon was developed to draw students' attention to brief descriptions of inquiry processes in the margins of the student module. The icon and explanations provide opportunities to direct students' attention to what they are doing, and thus serve as an important metacognitive tool to stimulate thinking about thinking.

Investigating Earth Systems: Fossils   **xxiii**

National Science Education Standards link...

Content Standard A
As a result of activities in grades 5-8, all students should develop:
- Abilities necessary to do scientific inquiry
- Understandings about scientific inquiry

Abilities Necessary to do Scientific Inquiry
- Identify questions that can be answered through scientific investigations
- Use appropriate tools and techniques to gather, analyze, and interpret data
- Develop descriptions, explanations, predictions, and models using evidence
- Think critically and logically to make the relationships between evidence and explanations
- Recognize and analyze alternative explanations and predictions
- Communicate scientific procedures and explanations
- Use mathematics in all aspects of scientific inquiry

(From National Science Education Standards, pages 145-148)

Benchmarks for Science Literacy link...

The Nature of Science Inquiry: Grades 6 through 8
- At this level, students need to become more systematic and sophisticated in conducting their investigations, some of which may last for several weeks. That means closing in on an understanding of what constitutes a good experiment. The concept of controlling variables is straightforward, but achieving it in practice is difficult. Students can make some headway, however, by participating in enough experimental investigations (not to the exclusion, of course, of other kinds of investigations) and explicitly discussing how explanation relates to experimental design.

- Student investigations ought to constitute a significant part—but only a part—of the total science experience. Systematic learning of science concepts must also have a place in the curriculum, for it is not possible for students to discover all the concepts they need to learn, or to observe all of the phenomena they need to encounter, solely through their own laboratory investigations. And even though the main purpose of student investigations is to help students learn how science works, it is important to back up such experience with selected readings. This level is a good time to introduce stories (true and fictional) of scientists making discoveries – not just world-famous scientists, but scientists of very different backgrounds, ages, cultures, places, and times.

(From Benchmarks for Science Literacy, page 12)

Teacher's Edition

8. Digging Deeper

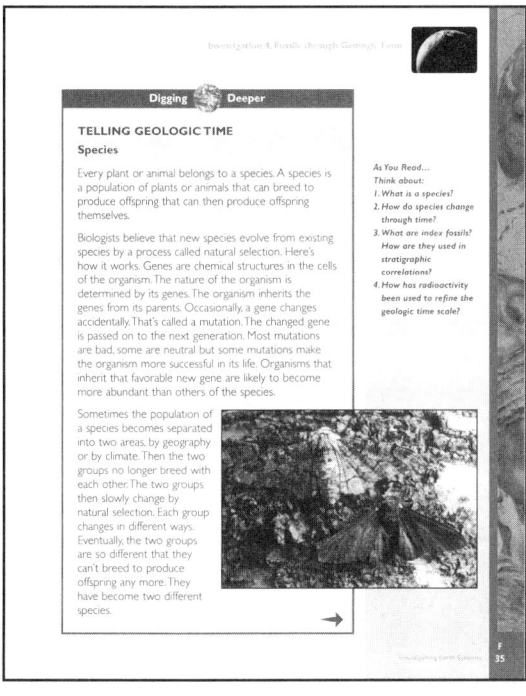

This section provides text, illustrations, data tables, and photographs that give students greater insight into the concepts explored in the activity. Teachers often assign **As You Read** questions as homework to guide students to think about the major ideas in the text. Teachers can also select questions to use as quizzes, rephrasing the questions into multiple choice or "true/false" formats. This provides assessment information about student understanding and serves as a motivational tool to ensure that students complete the reading assignment and comprehend the main ideas.

This is the stage of the activity that is most appropriate for teachers to explain concepts to students in whole-class lectures or discussions. References to **Blackline Masters** are available throughout the Teacher's Edition. They refer to illustrations from the textbook that teachers may photocopy and distribute to students or make overhead transparencies for lectures or presentations.

9. Review and Reflect

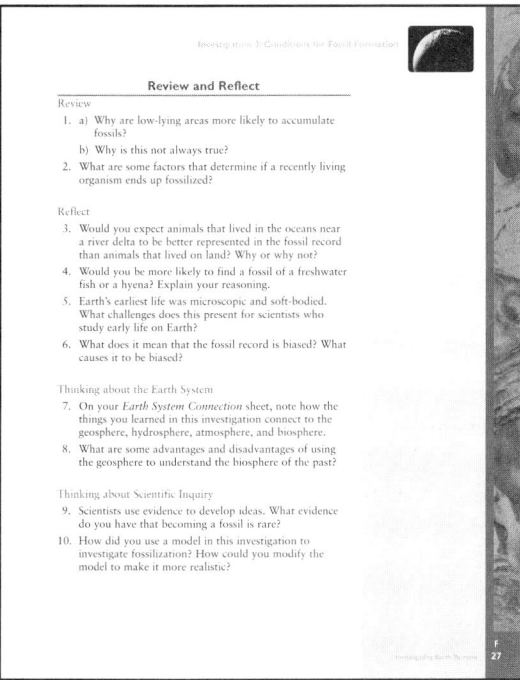

Questions in this feature ask students to use the key principles and concepts introduced in the activity. Students are sometimes presented with new situations in which they are asked to apply what they have learned. The questions in this section typically require higher-order thinking and reasoning skills than the **As You Read** questions. Teachers can assign these questions as homework, or have students complete them in groups during class. Assigning them as homework economizes time available in class, but has the drawback of making it difficult for students to collectively revisit the understanding that they developed as they worked through the concepts as a group

Investigating Earth Systems: Fossils   **XXV**

during the investigation. A third alternative is, of course, to assign the work individually in class. When students work through application problems in class, teachers have the opportunity to interact with students at a critical juncture in their learning – when they may be just on the verge of "getting it."

Review and Reflect prompts students to think about what they have learned, how their work connects with the Earth system, and what they know about scientific inquiry. Another one of the important principles of learning used to guide the selection of content in *Investigating Earth Systems* was that:

"To develop competence in an area of inquiry, students must (a) have a deep foundation of factual knowledge, (b) understand facts and ideas in the context of a conceptual framework, and (c) organize knowledge in ways that facilitate retrieval and application." (*How People Learn: Bridging Research and Practice* National Research Council, 1999, P. 12.)

Reflecting on one's learning and one's thinking is an important metacognitive tool that makes students examine what they have learned in the activity and then think critically about the usefulness of the results of their inquiry. It requires students to take stock of their learning and evaluate whether or not they really understand "how it fits into the Big Picture." It is important for teachers to guide students through this process with questions such as "What part of your work demonstrates that you know and can do scientific inquiry? How does what you learned help you to better understand the Earth system? How does your work contribute or relate to the concepts of the Big Picture at the end of the module?"

10. Final Investigation: Putting It All Together

In the final investigation in each *Investigating Earth Systems* module, your students will apply all the knowledge they have about the topics explored to solve a practical problem or situation. Requiring students to apply all they have gained toward a specific outcome should serve as the main assessment information for the module. A sample assessment rubric is provided in the back of this Teacher's Edition. Whatever rubric you employ, it is important that you share this with students at the outset of the final investigation so that they understand the criteria upon which their work will be judged.

Teacher's Edition

The instructions provided to students are purposely open-ended, but can be completed to various levels depending upon how much knowledge students apply. During the final investigation, your role is to be a participant observer, moving from group to group, noticing how students go about the investigation and how they are applying the experience and understanding they have gained from the module.

11. Reflecting

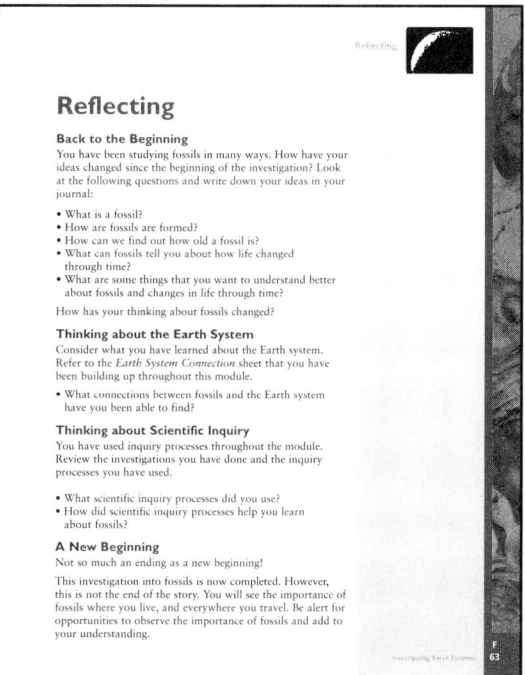

Now that students are at the end of the module, they are provided with questions that ask them to reflect upon all that they have learned about Earth science, inquiry, and the Earth system. The first set of questions (**Back to the Beginning**) are the same questions used in the pre-assessment. Teachers often ask students to revisit their initial responses and provide new answers to demonstrate how much they have learned.

Investigating Earth Systems: Fossils **xxvii**

12. The Big Picture

The five key concepts below underlie Earth science in general and *Investigating Earth Systems* in particular. Collectively, the nine modules in the *Investigating Earth Systems* series are designed to help students understand each of these concepts by the time they complete grade 8. Many of the concepts that underlie the Big Picture may be difficult for students to grasp easily. As students develop their ideas through inquiry-based investigations, you can help them to make connections with these key scientific concepts. As a reminder of the importance of the major understandings, the Student Book has a copy of the Big Picture in the back of the book near the **Glossary**.

Be on the lookout for chances to remind students that:
- Earth is a set of closely linked systems.
- Earth's processes are powered by two sources: the Sun and Earth's own inner heat.
- The geology of Earth is dynamic, and has evolved over 4.5 billion years.
- The geological evolution of Earth has left a record of its history that geoscientists interpret.
- We depend upon Earth's resources—both mined and grown.

13. Glossary

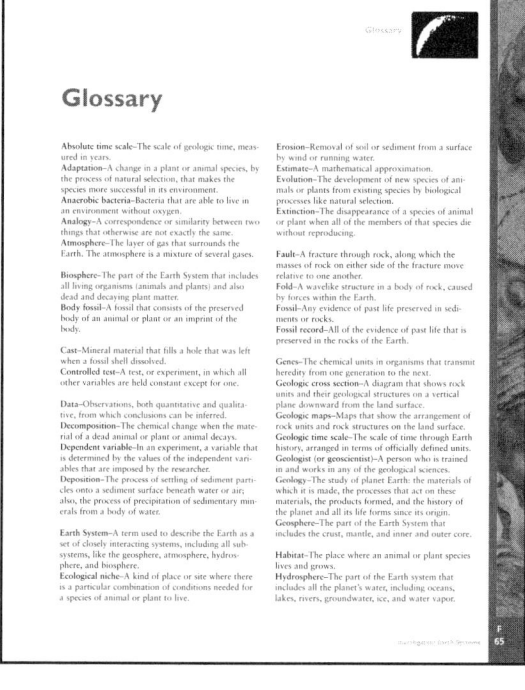

Words that may be new or unfamiliar to students are defined and explained in the **Glossary** of the Student Book. Teachers use their own judgment about selecting the terms that appear in the **Glossary** that are most important for their students to learn. Teachers typically use discretion and consider their state and local guidelines for science content understanding when assigning importance to particular vocabulary, which in most cases is very likely to be a small subset of all the scientific terms introduced in each module and defined in the **Glossary**.

References

How People Learn: Bridging Research and Practice (1999) Suzanne Donovan, John Bransford, and James Pellegrino, editors. National Academy Press, Washington, DC. 78 pages. The report is also available online at www.nap.edu.

Using the Investigating Earth Systems Web Site

www.agiweb.org/ies

The *Investigating Earth Systems* web site has been designed for teachers and students.
- Each *Investigating Earth Systems* module has its own web page that has been designed specifically for the content addressed within that module.
- Module web sites are broken down by investigation and also contain a section with links to relevant resources that are useful for the module.
- Each investigation is divided into materials and supplies needed, **Background Information,** and links to resources that will help you and your students to complete the investigation.

Enhancing Teacher Content Knowledge

Each *Investigating Earth Systems* module has a specific web page that will help teachers to gather further **Background Information** about the major topics covered in each activity.

Example from *Investigating Rocks and Landforms* – Investigation 1

Different Types of Rock

To learn more about different types of rocks, visit the following web sites:

- What are the basic types of rock?, Rogue Community College
This site lists the basic descriptions of sedimentary, metamorphic and igneous rocks. Detailed information on each type of rock is also available.
(http://www.jersey.uoregon.edu/~mstrick/AskGeoMan/geoQuerry13.html)

1. *Sedimentary Rocks:*
- Sedimentary Rocks, University of Houston
Detailed description of the composition, classification, and formation of sedimentary rocks.
(http://ucaswww.mcm.uc.edu/geology/maynard/INTERNETGUIDE/appendf.htm)
- Image Gallery for Geology, University of North Carolina
See more examples of sedimentary rocks.
(http://www.geosci.unc.edu/faculty/glazner/Images/SedRocks/SedRocks.html)
- Sedimentary Rocks Laboratory, Georgia Perimeter College
Read a thorough discussion of clastic, chemical, and organic sedimentary rocks. Illustrations accompany each description.
(http://www.gpc.peachnet.edu/~pgore/geology/historical_lab/sedrockslab.php)
- Textures and Structures of Sedimentary Rocks, Duke University
View a collection of slides of different sedimentary rocks as either outcrops or thin sections viewed through a microscope.
(http://www.geo.duke.edu/geo41/seds.htm)
- Sedimentary Rocks, Washington State University
Learn more about sedimentary processes, environments of deposition in relation to different sedimentary rocks. Topics covered include depositional environments, chemical or mechanical weathering, deposition and lithification, and classification.
(http://www.wsu.edu/~geology/geol101/sedimentary/seds.htm)

Obtaining Resources

The inquiry focus of *Investigating Earth Systems* will require teachers to obtain local or regional maps, rocks, and data. The *Investigating Earth Systems* web site helps teachers to find such materials. The web page for each *Investigating Earth Systems* module provides a list of relevant web sites, maps, videos, books, and magazines. Specific links to sources of these materials are often provided.

Managing Inquiry in Your Investigating Earth Systems Classroom

Materials

The proper management of materials can make the difference between a productive, positive investigation and a frustrating one. If your school has purchased the materials kit (available through It's About Time Publishing) most materials have been supplied. In many cases there will be additional items that you will need to supply as well. This can include photocopies or transparencies (**Blackline Masters** are available in the **Appendix**), or basic classroom supplies like an overhead projector or water source. On occasion, students will bring in materials. If you do not have the materials kit, a master list of materials for the entire module precedes the first investigation. Tips on using and managing materials accompany each investigation.

Safety

Each activity has icons noting safety concerns. In most cases, a well-managed classroom is the best preventive measure for avoiding danger and injury. Take time to explain your expectations before beginning the first investigation. Read through the investigations with your students and note any safety concerns. The activities were designed with safety in mind and have been tested in classrooms. Nevertheless, be alert and observant at all times. Often, the difference between an accident and a calamity is simple monitoring.

Time

This module can be completed in six weeks if you teach science in daily 45-minute class periods. However, there are many opportunities to extend the investigations, and perhaps to shorten others. The nature of the investigations allows for some flexibility.

An inquiry approach to science education requires the careful management of time for students to fully develop their investigative experience and skills. Most investigations will not easily fit into one 45-minute lesson. You may feel it necessary to extend them over two or more class periods. Some investigations include long-term studies. Where this is the case you may need to allow time for data collection each day, even after moving on to the next investigation.

Classroom Space

On days when students work as groups, arrange your classroom furniture into small group areas. You may want to have two desk arrangements—one for group work and one for direct instruction or quiet work time.

The Student Journal

The student journal is an important component of each *IES* module. (See the **Appendix** in this Teacher's Edition for a **Blackline Master** of the Journal cover sheet.) Your students are young scientists as they investigate Earth science questions. Encourage your students to think of themselves in this way and to see their journals as records of their investigations.

The journal serves other functions as well. It is a key component in performance assessment, both formative and summative. (Formative evaluation involves the ongoing evaluation of students' level of understanding and their development of skills and attitudes. Summative evaluation is designed to determine the extent to which instructional objectives have been achieved for a topic.) Encourage your students to record observations, data, and experimental results in their journals. Answers to **Review and Reflect** questions at the end of each investigation should also be recorded in the journal. It is very important that students have enough time to review, reflect, and update their journals at the end of each investigation.

Frequent feedback is essential if students are to maintain good journals. This is difficult but not impossible. For many teachers, the prospect of collecting and assessing anywhere from 20 to over 100 journals in a planning period, then returning them the next day, seems prohibitive. This does not need to be the case. If you use a simple rubric, and collect journals often, it is possible to assess 100 journals in an hour. It may not be necessary to write comments every time you collect journals; in some cases, it is equally effective to address trends in student work in front of the whole class. For example, students will inevitably turn in journals that contain no dates and/or headings. This leaves many questions unanswered and makes their work very hard to interpret. You might want to consider keeping your own teacher journal for this module. This makes a great template for evaluating student journals. In addition to documenting class activities, you might want to make notes on classroom management strategies, materials and supplies, and procedural modifications. Sample rubrics are included in the **Appendix**.

Student Collaboration

The National Science Education Standards and Benchmarks for Science Literacy emphasize the importance of student collaboration. Scientists and others frequently work in teams to investigate questions and solve problems. There are times, however, when it is important to work alone. You may have students who are more comfortable working this way. Traditionally, the competitive nature of school curricula has emphasized individual effort through grading, "honors" classes, and so on. Many parents will have been through this experience themselves as students and will be looking for comparisons between their children's performance and other students. Managing collaborative groups may therefore present some initial problems, especially if you have not organized your class in this way before.

Below are some key points to remember as you develop a group approach.

- Explain to students that they are going to work together. Explain *why* ("two heads are better than one" may be a cliché—but it is still relevant).
- Stress the responsibility each group member has to the others in the group.
- Choose student groups carefully to ensure each group has a balance of ability, special talents, gender and ethnicity.
- Make it clear that groups are not permanent and they may change occasionally.
- Help students see the benefits of learning with and from each other.
- Ensure that there are some opportunities for students to work alone (certain activities, writing for example, are more efficiently done in solitude).

Student Discussion

Encourage all students to participate in class discussions. Typically, several students dominate discussion while others hesitate to volunteer comments. Encourage active participation by explicitly stating that you value all students' comments. Reinforce this by not rejecting answers that appear wrong. Ask students to clarify contentious comments. If you ask for students' opinions, be prepared to accept them uncritically.

Teacher's Edition

Assessing Student Learning in Investigating Earth Systems

The completion of the final investigation serves as the primary source of summative assessment information. Traditional assessment strategies often give too much attention to the memorization of terms or the recall of information. As a result, they often fall short of providing information about students' ability to think and reason critically and apply information that they have learned. In *Investigating Earth Systems*, the solutions students provide to the final investigation in each module provide information used to assess thinking, reasoning, and problem-solving skills that are essential to life-long learning.

Assessment is one of the key areas that teachers need to be familiar with and understand when trying to envision implementing *Investigating Earth Systems*. In any curriculum model, the mode of instruction and the mode of assessment are connected. In the best scheme, instruction and assessment are aligned in both content and process. However, to the extent that one becomes an impediment to reform of the other, they can also be uncoupled. *Investigating Earth Systems* uses multiple assessment formats. Some are consistent with reform movements in science education that *Investigating Earth Systems* is designed to promote. **Project-based assessment,** for example, is built into every *Investigating Earth Systems* culminating investigation. At the same time, the developers acknowledge the need to support teachers whose classroom context does not allow them to depart completely from "traditional" assessment formats, such as paper and pencil tests.

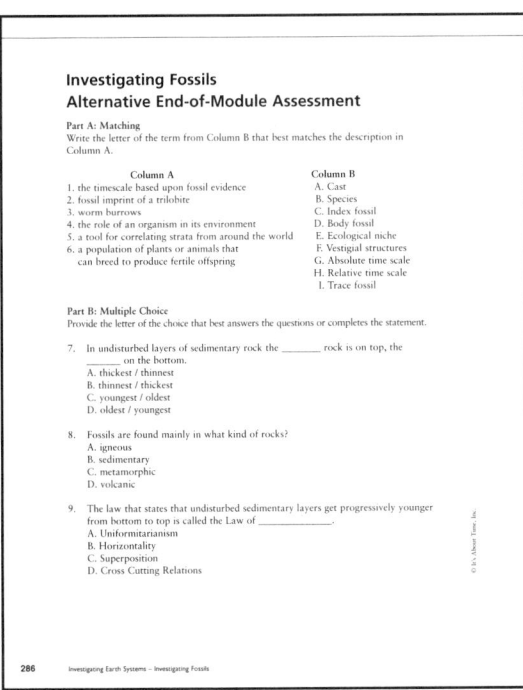

In keeping with the discussion of assessment outlined in the National Science Education Standards (NSES), teachers must be careful while developing the specific expectations for each module. Four issues are of particular importance in that they may present somewhat new considerations for teachers and students. These four issues are dealt with on the next two pages.

Investigating Earth Systems: Fossils **XXXV**

1. Integrative Thinking

The National Science Education Standards (NSES) state: "Assessments must be consistent with the decisions they are designed to inform." This means that as a prerequisite to establishing expectations, teachers should consider the use of assessment information. In *Investigating Earth Systems*, students often must be able to articulate the connection between Earth science concepts and their own community. This means that they have to integrate traditional Earth science content with knowledge of their surroundings. It is likely that this kind of integration will be new to students, and that they will require some practice at accomplishing it. Assessment in one module can inform how the next module is approached so that the ability to apply Earth science concepts to local situations is enhanced on an ongoing basis.

2. Importance

An explicit focus of NSES is to promote a shift to deeper instruction on a smaller set of core science concepts and principles. Assessment can support or undermine that intent. It can support it by raising the priority of in-depth treatment of concepts, such as students evaluating the relevance of core concepts to their communities. Assessment can undermine a deep treatment of concepts by encouraging students to parrot back large bodies of knowledge-level facts that are not related to any specific context in particular. In short, by focusing on a few concepts and principles, deemed to be of particularly fundamental importance, assessment can help to overcome a bias toward superficial learning. For example, assessment of terminology that emphasizes deeper understanding of science is that which focuses on the use of terminology as a tool for communicating important ideas. Knowledge of terminology is not an end in itself. Teachers must be watchful that the focus remains on terminology in use, rather than on rote recall of definitions. This is an area that some students will find unusual if their prior science instruction has led them to rely largely on memorization skills for success.

3. Flexibility

Students differ in many ways. Assessment that calls on students to give thoughtful responses must allow for those differences. Some students will find the open-ended character of the *Investigating Earth Systems* module reports disquieting. They may ask many questions to try to find out exactly what the finished product should look like. Teachers will have to give a consistent and repeated message to those students, expressed in many different ways, that the ambiguity inherent in the open-ended character of the assessments is an opportunity for students to show what they know in a way that makes sense to them. This also allows for the assessments to be adapted to students with differing abilities and proficiencies.

4. Consistency

While the module reports are intended to be flexible, they are also intended to be consistent with the manner in which instruction happens, and the kinds of inferences that are going to be made about students' learning on the basis of them. The *Investigating Earth Systems* design is such that students have the opportunity to learn new material in a way that places it in context. Consistent with that, the module reports also call for the new material to be expressed in context. Traditional tests are less likely to allow this kind of expression, and are more likely to be inconsistent with the manner of teaching that *Investigating Earth Systems* is designed to promote. Likewise, in that *Investigating Earth Systems* is meant to help students relate Earth Science to their community, teachers will be using the module reports as the basis for inferences regarding the students' abilities to do that. The design of the module reports is intended to facilitate such inferences.

An assessment instrument can imply but not determine its own best use. This means that *Investigating Earth Systems* teachers can inadvertently assess module reports in ways that work against integrative thinking, a focus on important ideas, flexibility in approach, and consistency between assessment and the inferences made from that assessment.

All expectations should be communicated to students. Discussing the grading criteria and creating a general rubric are critical to student success. Better still, teachers can engage students in modifying and/or creating the criteria that will be used to assess their performance. Start by sharing the sample rubric with students and holding a class discussion. Questions that can be used to focus the discussion include: Why are these criteria included? Which activities will help you to meet these expectations? How much is required? What does an "A" presentation or report look like? The criteria should be revisited throughout the completion of the module, but for now students will have a clearer understanding of the challenge and the expectations they should set for themselves.

Investigating Earth Systems Assessment Tools

Investigating Earth Systems provides you with a variety of tools that you can use to assess student progress in concept development and inquiry skills. The series of evaluation sheets and scoring rubrics provided in the back of this Teacher's Edition should be modified to suit your needs. Once you have settled on the performance levels and criteria and modified them to suit your particular needs, make the evaluation sheets available to students, preferably before they begin their first investigation. Consider photocopying a set of the sheets for each student to include in his or her journal. You can also encourage your students to develop their own rubrics. The final investigation is well-suited for such, since students will have gained valuable experience with criteria by the time they get to this point in the module. Distributing and discussing the evaluation sheets will help students to become familiar with and know the criteria and expectations for their work. If students have a complete set of the evaluation sheets, you can refer to the relevant evaluation sheet at the appropriate point within an *IES* lesson.

1. Pre-Assessment

The pre-assessment activity culminates with students putting their journals together and adding their first journal entry. It is important that this not be graded for content. Credit should be given to all students who make a reasonable attempt to complete the activity. The purpose of this pre-assessment is to provide a benchmark for comparison with later work. At the end of the module, the central questions of the pre-assessment are repeated in the section called **Back to the Beginning**.

2. Assessing the Student Journal

As students complete each investigation, reinforce the need for all observations and data to be organized well and added to the journals. Stress the need for clarity, accurate labeling, dating, and inclusion of all pertinent information. It is important that you assess journals regularly. Students will be more likely to take their journals seriously if you respond to their work. This does not have to be particularly time-consuming. Five types of evaluation instruments for assessing journal entries are available at the back of this Teacher's Edition to help you provide prompt and effective feedback. Each one is explained in turn below.

Journal-Entry Evaluation Sheet

This sheet provides you with general guidelines for assessing student journals. Adapt this sheet so that it is appropriate for your classroom. The journal entry evaluation sheet should be given to students early in the module, discussed with students, and used to provide clear and prompt feedback.

Journal-Entry Checklist

This checklist provides you and your students with a guide for quickly checking the quality and completeness of journal entries. You can assign a value to each criterion, or assign a "+" or "-" for each category, which you can translate into points later. However you choose to do this, the point is to make it easy to respond to students' work quickly and efficiently. Lengthy comments may not be necessary. Depending on time constraints, you may not have time to write comments each time you evaluate journals. The important thing is that students get feedback—they will do better work if they see that you are monitoring their progress.

Key-Question Evaluation Sheet

This sheet will help students to learn the basic expectations for the warm-up activity. The **Key Question** is intended to reveal students' conceptions about the phenomena or processes explored in the activity. It is not intended to produce closure, so your assessment of student responses should not be driven by a concern for correctness. Instead, the evaluation sheet emphasizes that you want to see evidence of prior knowledge and that students should communicate their thinking clearly. It is unlikely that you will have time to apply this assessment every time students complete a warm-up activity, yet in order to ensure that students value committing their initial conceptions to paper and taking the warm-up seriously, you should always remind students of the criteria. When time permits, use this evaluation sheet as a spot check on the quality of their work.

Investigation Journal-Entry Evaluation Sheet

This sheet will help students to learn the basic expectations for journal entries that feature the write-up of investigations. *IES* investigations are intended to help students to develop content understanding and inquiry abilities. This evaluation sheet provides a variety of criteria that students can use to ensure that their work meets the highest possible standards and expectations. When assessing student investigations, keep in mind that the **Investigate** section of an *IES* lesson corresponds to the explore phase of the learning cycle (engage, explore, apply, evaluate) in which students explore their conceptions of phenomena through hands-on activity. Using and discussing the evaluation sheet will help your students to internalize the criteria for their performance. You can further encourage students to internalize the criteria by making the criteria part of your "assessment conversations" with them as you circulate around the classroom and discuss student work. For example, while students are working, you can ask them criteria-driven questions such as: "Is your work thorough and complete? Are all of you participating in the activity? Do you each have a role to play in solving the problem?" and so on.

Review and Reflect Journal-Entry Evaluation Sheet

Reviewing and reflecting upon one's work is an important part of scientific inquiry and is also important to learning science. Depending upon whether you have students complete the work individually or within a group, the **Review and Reflect** portion of each investigation can be used to provide information about individual or collective understandings about the concepts and inquiry processes explored in the investigation. Whatever choice you make, this evaluation sheet provides you with a few general criteria for assessing content and thoroughness of student work. Adapt and modify the sheet to meet your needs. Consider involving students in selecting and modifying the criteria for evaluating their end of investigation reflections.

3. Assessing Group Participation

One of the challenges to assessing students who work in collaborative teams is assessing group participation. Students need to know that each group member must pull his or her weight. As a component of a complete assessment system, especially in a collaborative learning environment, it is often helpful to engage students in a self-assessment of their participation in a group. Knowing that their contributions to the group will be evaluated provides an additional motivational tool to keep students constructively engaged. These evaluation forms (**Group-Participation Evaluation Sheets I and II**) provide students with an opportunity to assess group participation. In no case should the results of this evaluation be used as the sole source of assessment data. Rather, it is better to assign a weight to the results of this evaluation and factor it in with other sources of assessment data. If you have not done this before, you may be surprised to find how honestly students will critique their own work, often more intensely than you might do.

4. Assessing the Final Investigation

Students' work throughout the module culminates with the final investigation. To complete it, students need a working knowledge of previous activities. Because it refers back to the previous steps, the last investigation is a good review and a chance to demonstrate proficiency. For an idea on how to use the last investigation as a performance-based exam, see the section in the **Appendix**.

5. Assessing Inquiry Processes

There is an obvious difficulty in assessing individual student proficiency when the students work within a collaborative group. One way to do this is to have a group present its results followed by a question-and-answer session. You can direct questions to individual students as a way of checking proficiency. Another is to have every student write a report on his or her role in the investigation, after first making it clear what this report should contain. Individual interviews are clearly the best option but may not be feasible given the time constraints of most classes.

6. Traditional Assessment Options

A traditional paper-and pencil-exam is included in the **Appendices**. While performance-based assessments may offer teachers more insight into student skill levels, computer-generated tests are also useful—especially so in states with state-sponsored exams. Additionally, some students are strong in one area and not as strong in another. Using a variety of methods for assessing and grading students' progress offers a more complete picture of the success of the student—and the teacher.

Reviewing and Reflecting upon Your Teaching

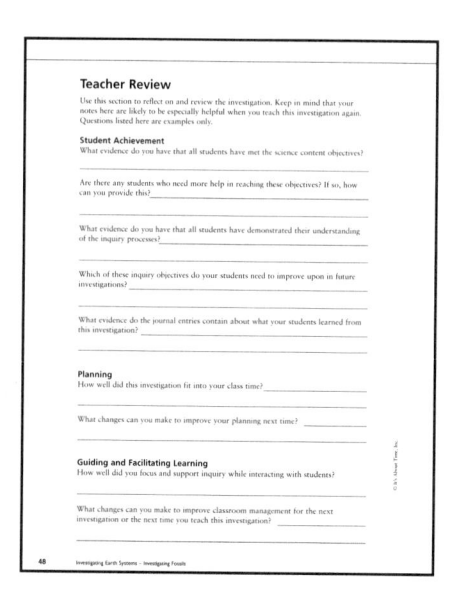

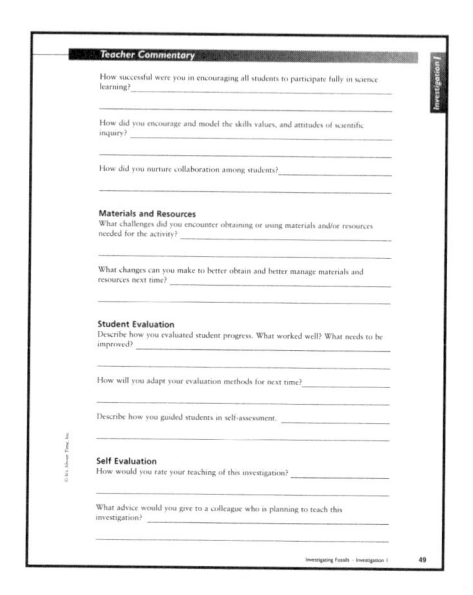

Reviewing and Reflecting upon Your Teaching provides an important opportunity for professional growth. A two-page Teacher Review form is included at the end of each investigation. The purpose of these reviews is to help you to reflect on your teaching of each investigation. We suggest that you try to answer each question at the completion of each investigation, then go back to the relevant section of this Teacher's Edition and write specific comments in the margins. Use the comments the next time you teach the investigation. For example, if you found that you were able to make substitutions to the list of materials needed, write a note about those changes in the margin of that page of this Teacher's Edition.

Investigating Earth Systems: Fossils

Investigating Fossils: Introduction

The Earth has been inhabited by living things since very early in its four-and-a-half-billion-year history. For most of that time, however, up until about six hundred million years ago, organisms were very primitive, as are their direct descendants, the bacteria and cyanobacteria that still survive and thrive today. With the development of more modern eukaryotic cells (cells that have a true nuclear membrane) around that time, the pace of evolution picked up greatly, and by 500 million years ago all of the major phyla of marine invertebrates (mollusks, brachiopods, bryozoans, echinoderms, etc.) had made their appearance. The fossil record of early life, before the appearance of invertebrates with hard skeletal material, is very scanty. Specialists need to know just where to look, how to collect, and how to prepare specimens using microscopic techniques. Large fossils (often called macrofossils) become much easier to find, in the right kinds of sedimentary rocks, after the great, explosive development of shelled invertebrates at the beginning of the Cambrian Period, about 540 million years ago. Eventually, both plants and animals invaded the land, which is an environment much more hostile to life than the oceans. Life both on land and in the sea has had its ups and downs in the past half billion years, however: there have been several major episodes during which large percentages of all life forms on Earth became extinct. The cause (or causes) of these episodes, called mass extinctions, is not yet entirely clear. After each, however, the surviving forms underwent explosive evolutionary development to fill the niches vacated by the great extinctions.

A fossil is any evidence of past plant or animal life contained in sediment or a sedimentary rock. For most organisms, fossilization is a very unusual event. Decay of organic matter in the surface environment of the Earth is the rule rather than the exception. Most surface environments, whether under the atmosphere or underwater, are well oxygenated, and the presence of oxygen, along with water, leads to decay, whereby the organic matter that constitutes the tissues of the dead organism is converted back largely to carbon dioxide and water. Only when an organism is rapidly buried by an influx of sediment and is sealed off from the surface environment can it escape decay and become fossilized as the sediment is slowly transformed into sedimentary rock. The picture is better, of course, with animals with hard skeletal materials, although they are susceptible to dissolution by water percolating through the sediments. For this reason, it is much less common to see the actual preserved shell than the negative imprint of the shell where the shell material itself has been dissolved away and perhaps replaced with other solid material.

More Information...on the Web

Go to the *Investigating Earth Systems* web site www.agiweb.org/ies/ for links to a variety of other web sites that will help you deepen your understanding of content and prepare you to teach this module, *Investigating Fossils*.

Students Conceptions about Fossils

Most of your students will have seen fossils in museums, classrooms, or on television, yet many middle-school students have not developed a formal scientific conception of what a fossil is or how it forms. For example, some students do not think of trace fossils or impressions as fossils. They are more likely to equate fossils with bones (vertebrates) than with impressions or spores (plants) or with burrows, tracks, molds, and casts of invertebrates. Most students understand that fossils reveal evidence of earlier life (students commonly refer to this as "prehistoric life") and of extinct animals and plants, yet they do not understand that fossils can be studied to understand how life has *changed* through time. Students also have a variety of nonscientific ideas about how fossils form. They generally know that decay is involved and may equate fossilization with "hardening" of the organism, yet many do not understand how deposition (burial) and sediment size affect fossilization.

Field tests of the program revealed that middle-school students have a variety of ideas about fossils. Not all students have the same ideas, but the following sampling of responses will give you a general sense of what you might expect middle-school students, as they come into the module, to know about several aspects of fossils. A more extensive sampling of responses is presented in the pre-assessment section of this Teacher's Edition.

Ideas about what a fossil is:
- A fossil is an old object that was buried under the Earth a long time ago and rocks have formed around it, so it is preserved.
- A fossil can be a footprint that was preserved by rock forming around it.
- Fossils are the remains or imprint of an object.

Ideas about how fossils form:
- Fossils might have formed in muddy places where an animal got trapped in the mud and hardened.
- Fossils might be formed when oceans or lakes dry up and fish or shells get left on or in the ground.

Introduction

- When fossils start out to become fossils, they form mud around them and it keeps building up and starts drying out to form rock.

Ideas about what fossils can tell us about changing life:
- Fossils can show different extinct organisms.
- Fossils can tell us something about why they are gone [extinct].
- Fossils can tell us that Earth contained life long ago and that it is very old.

Questions about fossils or changes in life through time:
- How do you tell how old a fossil is?
- Where is the best place for a fossil to form?
- Where do fossils form?
- How long does it take for a fossil to form?

It is crucial that you find out what informal ideas your students already have about fossils before beginning this module. The pre-assessment activity will tell you much of what you need to know in addressing your students' unique needs.

Investigating Fossils: Module Flow

Activity Summaries	Emphasis
Pre-Assessment Students describe their understanding of key concepts explored in the module.	Recording initial content knowledge and understanding.
Introducing Fossils Students discuss their ideas and experiences related to the topics they will be investigating.	Putting the investigations into a meaningful context.
Investigation 1: The Properties of Fossils Students first examine a collection of fossils (animal and plant). They then examine a collection of decomposing organic materials and make predictions about the potential for fossilization.	Observing and noting properties, making inferences and predictions, and using analogies.
Investigation 2: Sediment Size and Fossil Formation Using sports balls as an analogy, students examine and measure sediments of different sizes and explore different grain sizes. They test the relationship between sediment size and the quality of "fossil" impressions.	Making comparisons, measuring, averaging data, building analogies, developing and testing hypotheses, and sharing results with others.
Investigation 3: Conditions for Fossil Formation Students search the school grounds for evidence of living organisms, death, and decay, and then model the burial of organic material through erosion and deposition. Students play a simple game to examine factors that control fossilization.	Observing, detecting, gathering evidence, modeling, and relating models to the real-world situations.
Investigation 4: Fossils through Geologic Time Students are introduced to the magnitude of geologic time. They develop analogies using linear measurement and movie-making to help them understand the time scales over which evolution occurs. Finally, students correlate rock layers to explore relative age dating.	Measuring and averaging data, using mathematics to build models, interpreting evidence, and exploring relative and absolute age dating and scientific laws.
Investigation 5: Comparing Fossils over Time Students make a comparative study between fossil clams and shells of recent clams. They use this to study evidence of how species evolve over time.	Observing, describing, recording, making comparisons, researching, and sharing results.
Investigation 6: Adaptations to a Changing Environment Students explore evolutionary adaptation through a simulated design of animals that are adapted to particular environments. Students explore recent evolution of horses as an example of adaptation.	Relating form to function, investigating adaptation, developing hypotheses, making inferences, and sharing results.
Investigation 7: Being a Paleontologist Students are given an "unknown" fossil and are asked to use all the knowledge they have gained, as well as additional information, to create a profile of the fossil.	Synthesizing results, applying results of prior experiments, and communicating findings.
Reflecting Students review the science content and inquiry processes they used throughout the module.	Assessing student learning.

Introduction

Investigating Fossils: Module Objectives

Investigation	Science Content	Inquiry Process Skills
Investigation 1: The Properties of Fossils Students observe fossils and objects that have the potential to become fossils	Students will collect evidence that: 1. Living things can become fossils. 2. Most fossils resemble modern life forms. 3. Some parts of organisms are more likely to become fossils than others. 4. Decomposers break down dead organic matter. 5. Fossil formation is connected to the biosphere, the hydrosphere, the atmosphere, and the geosphere.	Students will: 1. Make observations using the senses. 2. Record observations in a variety of ways. 3. Use tools (such as magnifiers) to make observations. 4. Seek connections between sets of observations. 5. Collate observations. 6. Devise questions to investigate. 7. Communicate observations and findings to others.
Investigation 2: Sediment Size and Fossil Formation Students investigate the effect that particle size has on fossil definition.	Students will collect evidence that: 1. Sediment particles come in different sizes. 2. The size of sediment particles affects how well the features of fossils are preserved. 3. Particle size can be measured and compared. 4. Fossil formation is connected to the biosphere, the hydrosphere, the atmosphere, and the geosphere.	Students will: 1. Make observations using the senses. 2. Record observations in a variety of ways. 3. Devise a method of measurement. 4. Conduct an investigation into particle size and fossil formation. 5. Predict possible outcomes of the investigation. 6. Communicate observations and findings to others.
Investigation 3: Conditions for Fossil Formation Students examine and model fossil-forming conditions.	Students will collect evidence that: 1. Fossils form only under certain conditions. 2. Conditions that retard decomposition contribute to fossil formation. 3. Fossil formation is a comparatively rare occurrence. 4. Fossil formation is connected to the biosphere, the hydrosphere, the atmosphere, and the geosphere.	Students will: 1. Make observations about potential fossil-forming conditions around the school. 2. Generate questions about fossil formation. 3. Use models to investigate fossil-forming conditions. 4. Predict possible outcomes from the fossil-forming model. 5. Record observations from the model. 6. Make connections between the model and real-world conditions. 7. Communicate data and conclusions to others.

Investigating Fossils: Module Objectives

Investigation	Science Content	Inquiry Process Skills
Investigation 4: Fossils through Geologic Time Students model geologic time and the formation of the fossil record.	Students will collect evidence that: 1. The fossil record provides evidence of past life. 2. Fossil age is connected to the rock layers in which fossils are found. 3. In undisturbed rock, the oldest layers are deepest. 4. Fossil formation is connected to the biosphere, the hydrosphere, the atmosphere, and the geosphere.	Students will: 1. Use mathematics to make a model to scale. 2. Use a model of rock layers to investigate how the fossil record is formed. 3. Collect and analyze data. 4. Compare model-produced data with other representations of the same data set. 5. Draw conclusions about life and geologic time from several models. 6. Communicate data and conclusions to others.
Investigation 5: Comparing Fossils over Time Students investigate how organisms have changed over time.	Students will collect evidence that: 1. Living things have changed over time. 2. Fossils are a record of how living things have changed over time. 3. There are similarities and differences between fossil and modern organisms. 4. Fossil formation is connected to the biosphere, the hydrosphere, the atmosphere, and the geosphere.	Students will: 1. Observe and describe fossils. 2. Use measurements to describe fossils. 3. Make accurate representations of fossils. 4. Interpret data. 5. Compare and contrast fossils with modern organisms. 6. Use multiple resources to research fossils. 7. Share information about fossils. 8. Communicate data and conclusions to others.
Investigation 6: Adaptations to a Changing Environment Students design a new animal to reflect adaptations to a changing environment.	Students will collect evidence that: 1. Characteristics and behaviors of organisms enable them to survive and reproduce in their habitat. 2. Organisms evolve and adapt to a changing environment through natural selection. 3. An ecological niche is the overall role of a species in its environment.	Students will: 1. Consider questions for inquiry. 2. Relate characteristics of organisms to the role each plays in its survival. 3. Develop a hypothesis. 4. Propose an experiment or study to test a hypothesis. 5. Apply their knowledge and understanding to design an organism that reflects successful adaptation to environmental change. 6. Communicate findings and ideas to others.

Introduction

Investigating Fossils: Module Objectives

Investigation	Science Content	Inquiry Process Skills
Investigation 7: Being a Paleontologist Students make a fossil profile, applying their knowledge of fossils and how they form.	Students will collect evidence that: 1. Information about fossil formation can be deduced from a fossil itself. 2. Fossils can be traced to particular geographic areas. 3. Fossil formation is connected to the biosphere, the hydrosphere, the atmosphere, and the geosphere.	Students will: 1. Deduce information from a fossil. 2. Use maps and other tools to research a fossil. 3. Use a number of resources to research a fossil. 4. Collate information about a fossil. 5. Create a display communicating information about a fossil.

National Science Education Content Standards

Investigating Earth Systems is a Standards-driven curriculum. That is, the scope and sequence of the series is derived from, and driven by, the National Science Education Standards (NSES) and the American Association for the Advancement of Science (AAAS) Benchmarks for Science Literacy (BSL). Both specify content standards that students should know by the completion of eighth grade.

Unifying Concepts and Processes
- Systems, order, and organization
- Evidence, models, and explanation
- Constancy, change, and measurement
- Evolution and equilibrium

Science as Inquiry
- Identify questions that can be answered through scientific investigations
- Design and conduct a scientific investigation
- Use tools and techniques to gather, analyze, and interpret data
- Develop descriptions, explanations, predictions, and models based upon evidence
- Think critically and logically to make the relationships between evidence and explanation
- Recognize and analyze alternative explanations and predictions
- Communicate scientific procedures and explanations
- Use mathematics in all aspects of scientific inquiry
- Understand scientific inquiry

Life Science
- Populations and ecosystems
- Diversity and adaptation of organisms

Earth and Space Science
- Structure of the Earth system
- Earth's history
- Earth in the Solar System

History and Nature of Science
- Science as a human endeavor
- Nature of science
- History of science

Introduction

Key NSES Content Standards Addressed in *IES Fossils*

1. Fossils provide important evidence of how life and environmental conditions have changed.

2. Living organisms have played many roles in the Earth system, including affecting the composition of the atmosphere, producing some types of rocks, and contributing to the weathering of rocks.

3. Biological evolution accounts for the diversity of species developed through gradual processes over many generations. Species acquire many of their unique characteristics through biological adaptation, which involves the selection of naturally occurring variations in populations. Biological adaptations include changes in structures, behaviors, or physiology that enhance survival and reproductive success in a particular environment.

4. Millions of species of animals, plants, and microorganisms are alive today. Although different species might look dissimilar, the unity among organisms becomes apparent from an analysis of internal structures, the similarity of their chemical processes, and the evidence of common ancestry.

5. Populations of organisms can be categorized by the function they serve in an ecosystem. Plants and some microorganisms are producers—they make their own food. All animals, including humans, are consumers, and obtain food by eating other organisms. Decomposers, primarily bacteria and fungi, are consumers that use waste materials and dead organisms for food.

6. Extinction of a species occurs when the environment changes and the adaptive characteristics of a species are insufficient to allow its survival. Fossils indicate that many organisms that lived long ago are extinct. Extinction of species is common; most of the species that have lived on the Earth no longer exist.

7. Evolution is a series of changes, sometimes gradual, sometimes sporadic, that accounts for the present form and function of objects, organisms, and natural and designed systems. The general idea of evolution is that the present arises from materials and forms of the past.

8. Form and function are complimentary aspects of objects, organisms, and systems in the natural and designed world. The form or shape of an object is frequently related to use, operation, or function.

9. The Earth processes we see today, including erosion, movement of the lithospheric plates, and changes in atmospheric composition, are similar to those that occurred in the past. Earth history is also influenced by occasional catastrophes, such as the impact of an asteroid or comet.

10. Some changes in the solid Earth can be described as the "rock cycle." Old rocks at the Earth's surface weather, forming sediments that are buried, then compacted, heated, and often recrystallized into new rock. Eventually, those new rocks may be brought to the surface by the forces that drive plate motions, and the rock cycle continues.

11. Landforms are the result of a combination of constructive and destructive forces. Constructive forces include crustal deformation, volcanic eruption, and deposition of sediment, while destructive forces include weathering and erosion.

12. Lithospheric plates on the scales of continents and oceans constantly move at rates of centimeters per year in response to movements in the mantle. Major geological events, such as earthquakes, volcanic eruptions, and mountain building, result from these plate movements.

13. Soil consists of weathered rocks and decomposed organic material from dead plants, animals, and bacteria. Soils are often found in layers, with each having a different chemical composition and texture.

14. Scientists formulate and test their explanation of nature using observations, experiments, and theoretical and mathematical models. Although all scientific ideas are tentative and subject to change and improvements in principle, for most major ideas in science, there is much experimental and observational confirmation.

15. Models are tentative schemes or structures that correspond to real objects, events, or classes of events, and that have explanatory power. Models help scientists and engineers understand how things work.

Key AAAS Benchmarks Addressed in *IES Fossils*

The Living Environment, Section A: Diversity of Life

1. A great variety of living things can be sorted into groups in many ways, using various features to decide which things belong to which group.

2. In classifying organisms, biologists consider details of internal and external structures to be more important than behavior or general appearance.

3. For sexually reproducing organisms, a species comprises all organisms that can mate with one another to produce fertile offspring.

The Living Environment, Section D: Interdependence of Life

1. Changes in an organism's habitat are sometimes beneficial and sometimes harmful.

2. In all environments—freshwater, marine, forest, desert, grassland, mountain, and others—organisms with similar needs may compete with one another for resources, including food, space, water, air, and shelter. In any particular environment, the growth and survival of organisms depends upon the physical conditions.

3. Two types of organisms may interact with one another in several ways: They may be involved in a producer/consumer, predator/prey, or parasite/host relationship.

The Living Environment, Section E: Flow of Matter and Energy

Over the whole Earth, organisms are growing, dying and decaying, and new organisms are being produced by the old ones.

Introduction

The Living Environment, Section F: Evolution of Life

1. Individuals of the same kind differ in their characteristics, and sometimes differences give individuals an advantage in surviving and reproducing.
2. Fossils can be compared to one another and to living organisms according to their similarities and differences. Some organisms that lived long ago are similar to existing organisms, but some are quite different.
3. Small differences between parents and offspring can accumulate (through selective breeding) in successive generations so that descendants are very different from their ancestors.
4. Individuals with certain traits are more likely than others to survive and have offspring. Changes in environmental conditions can affect the survival of individual organisms and entire species.
5. Many thousands of layers of sedimentary rock provide evidence for the long history of the Earth and for the long history of changing life forms whose remains are found in the rocks. More recently deposited rock layers are more likely to contain fossils resembling existing species.

The Human Organism, Section A: Human Identity

1. Fossil evidence is consistent with the idea that human beings evolved from earlier species.

The Designed World, Section C: Energy Sources and Use

1. The Sun is the main source of energy for people and they use it in various ways. The energy in fossil fuels such as oil and coal comes indirectly from the Sun, because the fuels come from plants that grew long ago.

The Physical Setting, Section B: The Earth

1. Climates have sometimes changed abruptly in the past as a result of changes in the Earth's crust, such as volcanic eruptions or impacts of huge rocks from space. Even relatively small changes in atmospheric or oceanic content can have widespread effects on climate if the change lasts long enough.
2. The cycling of water in and out of the atmosphere plays an important role in determining climatic patterns. Water evaporates from the surface of the Earth, rises and cools, condenses into rain or snow, and falls again to the surface. The water falling on land collects in rivers and lakes, soil, and porous layers of rock, and much of it flows back into the ocean.
3. Human activities, such as reducing the amount of forest cover, increasing the amount and variety of chemicals released into the atmosphere, and intensive farming, have changed the Earth's land, oceans, and atmosphere. Some of these changes have decreased the capacity of the environment to support some life forms.

Common Themes, Section B: Models

1. Models are often used to think about processes that happen too slowly, too quickly, or on too small a scale to be observed directly, or that are too vast to be changed deliberately, or that are potentially dangerous.

Common Themes, Section C: Constancy and Change

1. Physical and biological systems tend to change until they become stable and remain that way unless their surroundings change.

Introduction

Materials and Equipment List for *Investigating Fossils*

Pre-Assessment

Each group of students will need:
- poster board, poster paper, or butcher paper
- Student Journal cover sheet, one for each student (**Blackline Master** *Fossils* P.2)

Teachers will need:
- overhead projector, chalkboard, or flip-chart paper
- transparency of **Blackline Master** *Fossils* P.1, **Questions about Fossils**

Materials Needed for Each Group per Investigation

Investigation 1
- fossil specimens
- four or five white index cards
- samples of fresh fruit
- samples of partially decomposed fruit in a tightly sealed, double-bagged, plastic bag
- a tightly sealed, double-bagged, plastic bag containing one of the following: peeled shrimp, unpeeled shrimp, clamshell, chicken wing, leaf, small twig

Investigation 2

Part A
- small amount of each sediment type for observation: clay, fine sand, and coarse sand
- magnifier
- microscope (optional)
- sheet of white paper and black paper
- different-sized spherical objects (i.e., marbles, table-tennis balls, tennis balls, softballs, volleyballs, soccer balls, and basketballs—about three per group)
- metric measuring tape
- calculator (optional)

Part B
- newspapers to cover desk
- petroleum jelly
- small container

- sample of **one** of the following: clay, fine sand, or coarse sand (enough to fill a small container to a depth of about 1 cm)
- plaster (molding plaster or plaster of Paris)
- water supply
- plastic spoon
- leaf, clamshell, and piece of dried fruit

Investigation 3

Part A

- stream table, or similar setup
- wooden block (or books) to tilt stream table
- dry sand (as fine as possible)
- watering can
- water source
- 2 tree leaves, pre-soaked in water overnight
- 2 clamshells
- topographic map of your local area, or physical map of your region *

Part B

- photocopy of the *Wheel of Fossilization* on page F23 of the student text to use as a cutout, **Blackline Master** *Fossils* 3.1, **Wheel of Fossilization**.
- cardboard
- scissors
- sharpened pencil or dowel

Investigation 4

Part A

- metric measuring tape (as long as possible)
- chalk

Part B

- photocopy of chart showing dates when various kinds of animals first appeared in the fossil record (**Blackline Master** *Fossils* 4.2, **Life through Time Chart**)
- chart paper
- calculator

---

* The *Investigating Earth Systems* web site www.agiweb.org/ies/ provides suggestions for obtaining these resources.

Introduction

Part C
- photocopy of **Blackline Master** *Fossils* **4.3, Stratigraphic Section**)
- photocopy of diagram on page F32 of the Student Book (**Blackline Master** *Fossils* **4.4, Stratigraphic Cross Section**)

Investigation 5
- fossil clamshell
- hand lens
- eight index cards
- metric ruler, or tape measure
- pencil and other drawing implements
- paper clip or a stapler
- fresh clamshells (with clam removed)

Investigation 6
- gaming die
- poster board
- colored pencils or markers

Investigation 7
- unknown fossil
- metric ruler and measuring tape
- fossil record charts
- set of known fossil samples
- state or regional geologic map*
- access to research material**
- materials to create a display

General Supplies
Although the investigations can be done with the specific materials listed, it is always a good idea to build up a supply of general materials.

- 2 or 3 large clear plastic storage bins about 30 cm x 45 cm x 30 cm deep, with lids (these can be used for storage and also make good water containers)

---

* The *Investigating Earth Systems* web site www.agiweb.org/ies/ provides suggestions for obtaining these resources.
** The *Investigating Earth Systems* web site www.agiweb.org/ies/ provides topical Internet sites and a list of resources that will aid student research.

- 2 or 3 plastic buckets and one large water container (camping type with a faucet)
- rolls of masking tape, duct tape, and clear adhesive tape
- rolls of plastic wrap and aluminum foil
- clear, self-locking plastic bags (various sizes)
- ball of string and spools of sewing thread
- pieces of wire (can be pieces of wire coat hangers)
- stapler, staples, paper clips, and binder fasteners
- safety scissors and one sharp knife
- cotton balls, tongue depressors
- plastic and paper cups of various sizes
- empty coffee and soup cans, empty boxes and egg cartons
- several clear plastic soda bottles (various sizes)
- poster board, overhead transparencies, tracing paper, and graph paper
- balances and/or scales, weights, spring scales
- graduated cylinders, hot plates, microscopes
- safety goggles
- disposable latex gloves
- lab aprons or old shirts
- first aid kit

Introduction

Pre-assessment

Overview

During the pre-assessment phase, the students complete an open-ended survey of their knowledge and understanding of key concepts explored in the *Investigating Fossils* module. Students are given five questions to consider and their responses become the first entry in their journal.

Preparation and Materials Needed

Preparation:
This pre-assessment activity does not appear in the Student Book. However, to find out what your students already know about fossils, it is crucial that you conduct this pre-assessment before introducing the module and distributing the Student Books. Make sure that your students clearly understand that the pre-assessment is not a test. Explain to them that, by reviewing the pre-assessment at the end of the module, they can compare how their ideas and knowledge about the materials in the *Investigating Fossils* module have changed as a result of their investigations. Tell them that the pre-assessment will also help you gauge how successful the investigations have been for everyone.

After the pre-assessment but before distributing the Student Books, take some time to reflect on the ideas your students have. This is the starting point. You need to ensure that what follows fits with your students' prior knowledge.

Materials:
- poster board, poster paper, or butcher paper
- overhead projector, chalkboard, or flip-chart paper
- overhead transparency of questions (**Blackline Master** *Fossils* P.1)
- Student Journal cover sheet, one for each student (**Blackline Master** *Fossils* P.2)

Suggested Teaching Procedure

1. Let students know that what they write in this exercise will become their first entry in a scientific journal that they will keep throughout the module. Explain that each person is going to write down all the ideas that they have about the answers to questions dealing with fossils and evolution of life. The reason for this is to provide them, and you, with a starting point for their investigations. Tell students that when they have finished the module, they will answer these same questions again. This will allow them, and you, to compare how their knowledge about fossils and evolution has changed as a result of their investigations.

2. Display the pre-assessment questions on an overhead projector, or provide each student with a copy of the questions (**Blackline Master** *Fossils* P.1). Have students write responses to these questions in their journals.

Allow a reasonable period of time for all students to respond. Circulate around the classroom, prompting students to provide as much detail as possible.

> - What is a fossil?
> - How are fossils formed?
> - How can we find out how old a fossil is?
> - What can fossils tell you about how life has changed through time?
> - What are some things that you want to understand better about fossils and changes in life through time?

Sample Student Responses

Ideas about what a fossil is:

A fossil is a piece of an animal or plant that hardens into rock over a long period of time.

A fossil is an imprint or remainder of prehistoric life.

A fossil is an old object that was buried under the Earth a long time ago and rocks have formed around it, so it is preserved.

A fossil can be a footprint that was preserved by rock forming around it.

Most fossils are of living objects.

Fossils are the remains or imprint of an object.

Ideas about how fossils form:

Fossils might have formed in muddy places where an animal got trapped in the mud and hardened.

Fossils might be formed when oceans or lakes dry up and fish or shells get left on or in the ground.

Fossils are made when the bones of animal do not decay after death and are preserved in the soil.

If a shell or organism dies in the ocean and is not disturbed, the imprint in the mud may stay for many years until the water recedes.

When fossils start out to become fossils, they form mud around them and it keeps building up and starts drying out to form rock.

Fossils are made by an object that has been buried under layers of rock and soil.

Introduction

> **Ideas about what fossils can tell us about changing life:**
> Fossils can tell us how old the planet is.
> Fossils can tell us what may happen in the future.
> Fossils can show different extinct organisms.
> Fossils can tell us something about why they are gone [extinct].
> They can tell us about different trees that we may have once had on Earth because of a fossil leaf.
> Fossils can tell us that Earth contained life long ago and that it is very old.
>
> **Questions about fossils or changes in life through time:**
> How do you tell how old a fossil is?
> Where is the best place for a fossil to form?
> What was the largest fossil ever found?
> How can you tell which animal or plant a fossil came from?
> How do you tell what a fossil is?
> How old can fossils be?
> Wouldn't leaves rot in mud before they could dry up and become a fossil?
> How far down do fossils go?
> Are fossils only of living objects?
> Where do fossils form?
> How long does it take for a fossil to form?

3. Give each student a copy of the journal cover sheet (**Blackline Master** *Fossils* P. 2). Direct students to insert the journal cover sheet and their pre-assessment into their journal. Explain that they now have one of the most important tools for this investigation into fossils: their own scientific journal.

Teaching Tip

What form will journals take? Using loose-leaf notebook paper in a thin three-ring binder enables students to add or remove pages easily. On the downside, loose-leaf pages are more easily lost and students must maintain a regular supply of paper. If you prefer to have students keep journals in composition notebooks or laboratory notebooks, have them trim the journal cover sheet to the appropriate size and paste it onto the first page of their notebooks.

4. Divide students into groups. Instruct the groups to discuss the following:
   - ideas we have about fossils and changing life
   - questions we have about fossils and changing life

One member of the group should record his/her group's ideas and questions on a sheet of poster board, poster paper, or butcher paper.

5. Discuss student responses by having each group, in turn, report on its ideas. As groups are responding, build up two important lists (ideas and questions) for everyone to see (on a chalkboard, flip-chart paper, poster board, or an overhead transparency).

6. Direct students to add these "ideas" and "questions" to their journals.

7. This completes the pre-assessment phase. Distribute copies of *Investigating Fossils*.

Assessment Opportunity

The ideas about fossils and fossilization that your students offer here will provide you with pre-assessment data. The experiences they describe, and the way in which they are discussed, will alert you to their general level of understanding about these topics. To encourage this, and to provide a record, it may be useful to quickly summarize the main points about fossils and changing life on Earth that emerge from discussion. You could do this on a chalkboard or flip chart for all to see. This can be displayed as students work through the module, and added to with each new experience. For your own assessment purposes, it will be useful to keep a record of these early indicators of student understanding.

Introduction

NOTES

INVESTIGATING FOSSILS

The Earth System

The Earth System is a set of systems that work together in making the world we know. Four of these important systems are:

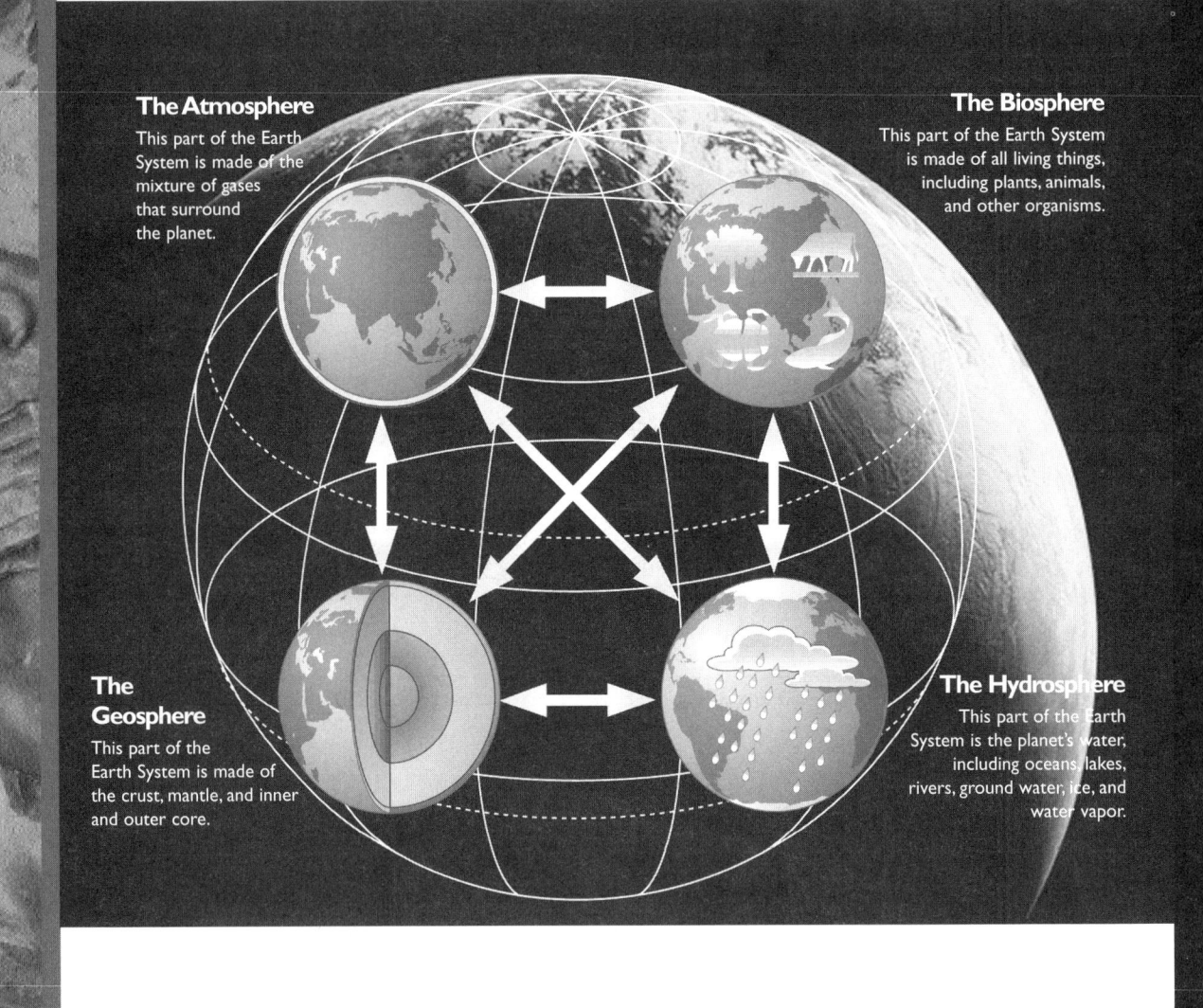

The Atmosphere
This part of the Earth System is made of the mixture of gases that surround the planet.

The Biosphere
This part of the Earth System is made of all living things, including plants, animals, and other organisms.

The Geosphere
This part of the Earth System is made of the crust, mantle, and inner and outer core.

The Hydrosphere
This part of the Earth System is the planet's water, including oceans, lakes, rivers, ground water, ice, and water vapor.

Introduction

Introducing the Earth System

Understanding the Earth System is an overall goal of the *Investigating Earth Systems* series. The fact that the Earth functions as a whole, and that all its parts operate together in meaningful ways to make the planet work as a single unit, underlies each module. Each module guides the students in considering this fundamental principle.

At the end of every investigation, students are asked to link what they have discovered with ideas about the Earth System. Questions are provided to guide their thinking, and they are asked to write their responses in their journals. They are also reminded on occasion to record the information on an *Earth System Connection* sheet. This sheet will provide a cumulative record of the connections that the students find as they work through the investigations in the module.

Not all the connections between the things they have been investigating and the Earth System will be immediately apparent to your students. They will probably need your help to understand how some of the things they have been investigating connect to the Earth System. However, by the time they complete the *Investigating Earth Systems* modules to the end of eighth grade, they should have a working knowledge of how they and their environment function as a system within a system, within a system...of the Earth System.

This module will help your students to understand that fossils and the rock record provide important evidence that help scientists to understand not only the evolution of life on Earth, but also the evolution of the Earth system. Fossils, now part of the geosphere, were once part of the biosphere, and the organisms they represent interacted with the atmosphere, the hydrosphere, and with other living organisms in the biosphere. Fossils are key indicators of past environmental conditions (warm versus cold climate, terrestrial versus marine environment, and so on). *Investigating Fossils* will help students to develop an appreciation for and understanding of these important Earth systems connections.

Distribute copies of the *Earth System Connection* sheet (**Blackline Master** *Fossils* I.1) available at the back of this Teacher's Edition. Have the students place the sheets in their journals. The two sheets may also be copied onto 11 × 17 paper.

Explain to the students that at the end of each investigation they will be asked to reflect on how the questions and outcomes of their investigation relate to the Earth System. Tell them that they should enter any new connections that they discover on the *Earth System Connection* sheet. Encourage them to also include connections that they have made on their own. That is, they should not limit their entries to just those suggested in the **Thinking about the Earth System** questions in **Review and Reflect**. Use the **Review and Reflect** time to direct students' attention to how local issues relate to the questions they have been investigating. By the end of the module, students should have as complete an *Earth System Connection* sheet to *Investigating Fossils* as possible.

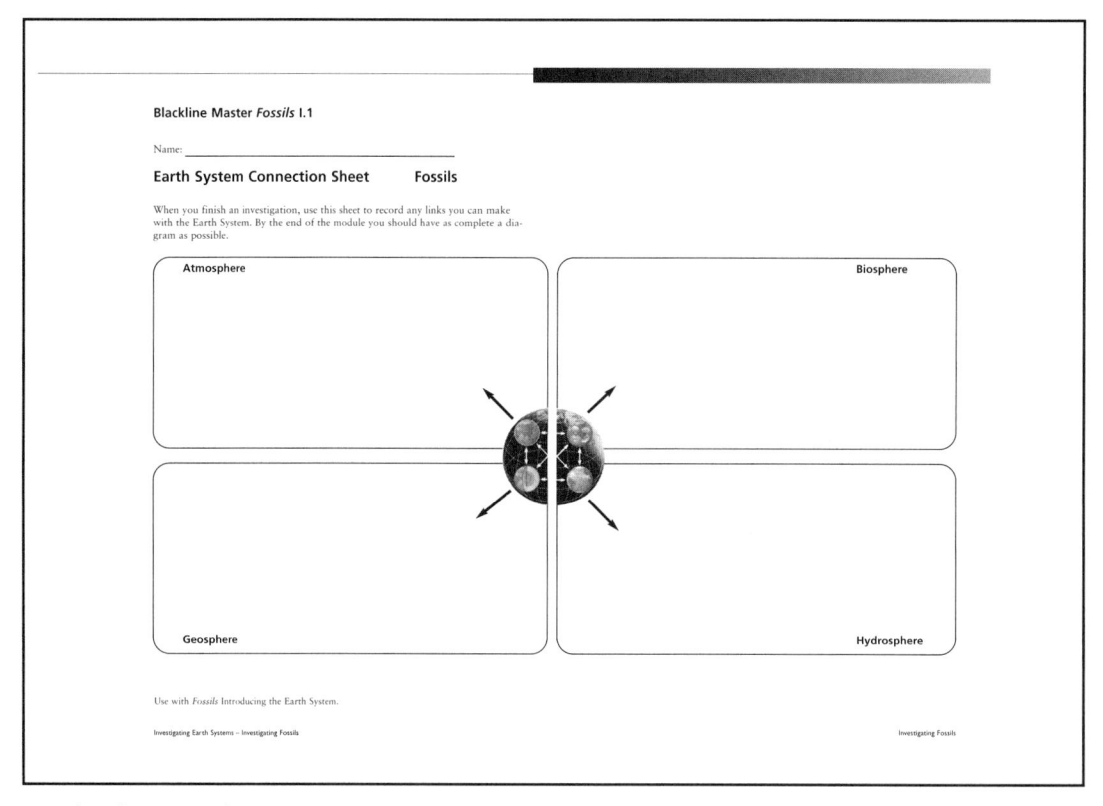

(can be photocopied onto 11x17 paper)

Introduction

Illustration By Dennis Falcon

Investigating Fossils – Introduction 25

INVESTIGATING FOSSILS

Introducing Inquiry Processes

When geologists and other scientists investigate the world, they use a set of inquiry processes. Using these processes is very important. They ensure that the research is valid and reliable. In your investigations, you will use these same processes. In this way, you will become a scientist, doing what scientists do. Understanding inquiry processes will help you to investigate questions and solve problems in an orderly way. You will also use inquiry processes in high school, in college, and in your work.

During this module, you will learn when, and how, to use these inquiry processes. Use the chart below as a reference about the inquiry processes.

Inquiry Processes:	How scientists use these processes
Explore questions to answer by inquiry	Scientists usually form a question to investigate after first looking at what is known about a scientific idea. Sometimes they predict the most likely answer to a question. They base this prediction on what they already know or believe to be true.
Design an investigation	To make sure that the way they test ideas is fair, scientists think very carefully about the design of their investigations. They do this to make sure that the results will be valid and reliable.
Conduct an investigation	After scientists have designed an investigation, they conduct their tests. They observe what happens and record the results. Often, they repeat a test several times to ensure reliable results.
Collect and review data using tools	Scientists collect information (data) from their tests. Data can take many forms. Common kinds of data include numerical (numbers), verbal (words), and visual (images). To collect and manage data, scientists use tools such as computers, calculators, tables, charts, and graphs.
Use evidence to develop ideas	Evidence is very important for scientists. Just as in a court case, it is proven evidence that counts. Scientists look at the evidence other scientists have collected, as well as the evidence they have collected themselves.
Consider evidence for explanations	Finding strong evidence does not always provide the complete answer to a scientific question. Scientists look for likely explanations by studying patterns and relationships within the evidence.
Seek alternative explanations	Sometimes, the evidence available is not clear or can be interpreted in other ways. If this is so, scientists look for different ways of explaining the evidence. This may lead to a new idea or question to investigate.
Show evidence & reasons to others	Scientists communicate their findings to other scientists to see if they agree. Other scientists may then try to repeat the investigation to validate the results.
Use mathematics for science inquiry	Scientists use mathematics in their investigations. Accurate measurement, with suitable units is very important for both collecting and analyzing data. Data often consist of numbers and calculations.

Investigating Earth Systems

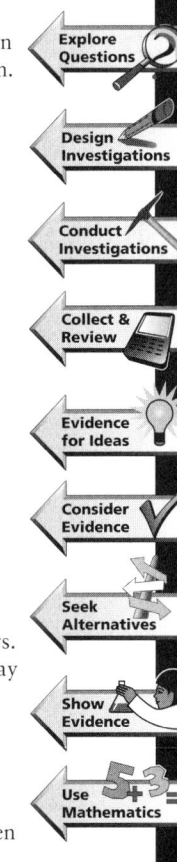

Introduction

Introducing Inquiry Processes

Inquiry is at the heart of *Investigating Earth Systems*. That is why each module title begins with the word *Investigating*. In the National Science Education Standards, inquiry is the first content standard. (See **Inquiry** on page xxiii of this Teacher's Edition.)

Inquiry depends upon active student participation. It is very important to remind students of the steps in the **Inquiry Process** as they perform them. Icons that correspond to the nine major components of inquiry appear in the margins of this Teacher's Edition. They point out opportunities to teach and assess inquiry understandings and abilities. Stress the importance of inquiry processes as they occur in your investigations. Provoke students to think about *why* these processes are important. Collecting good data, using evidence, considering alternative explanations, showing evidence to others, and using mathematics are all essential to *IES*. Use examples to demonstrate these processes whenever possible.

At the end of every investigation, students are asked to reflect upon their thinking about scientific inquiry. Refer students to the list of inquiry processes as they answer these questions.

Teaching Tip

If the reading level of the descriptions of inquiry processes is too advanced for some students, you could provide them with illustrations or examples of each of the processes. You may wish to provide students with a copy of the inquiry processes to include in their journals (**Blackline Master** *Fossils* I.2).

Introducing Fossils

Have you ever realized that algae can become fossilized?

Have you ever seen the remains of organisms in rocks?

Have you ever noticed how some rocks are arranged in layers?

Have you ever seen silt that has been washed from the land?

Introduction

Introducing Fossils

Use this introduction to the module to set your students' investigations into a meaningful context.

This is an opportunity for students to offer some of their own experiences with fossils in a general discussion, using the questions below the photos as prompts. Some students may be able to cite additional experiences to those asked for here. Encourage a wide-ranging discussion.

Because your students have just spent time in the pre-assessment phase of this module thinking about and discussing what they already know about fossils, it probably is not necessary to have them complete another journal entry. They will be anxious to get to work on their investigations.

You may want to quickly summarize the main points that emerge from the discussion. You could do this on a chalkboard, an easel pad, or an overhead transparency. For your own assessment purposes, it will be useful to keep a record of these early indicators of student understanding.

About the Photos

The upper left photograph shows the sticky mats of photosynthetic cyanobacteria known as stromatolites forming in shallow marine waters. As sediment is washed over and deposited on the mat, a new mat of bacteria grows. Repeated cycles of growth and deposition produce a finely layered structure now recognized in fossils dating back 3.5 billion years. Photosynthetic bacteria played an important role in the evolution of Earth's atmosphere. Some scientists have argued that the proliferation of cyanobacteria until about 1 billion years ago may reflect the absence of predators, implying that "slime" ruled the Earth for more than 2.5 billion years.

The upper right photograph reveals casts and molds of invertebrates. Most fossils form when hard parts of organisms are buried in sediment, where they decompose slowly enough for the rock to preserve their shape as the sediment becomes lithified (turned into rock). Fossils, like these marine clams, provide important information about past environmental conditions. The study of ancient organisms and their relationship to their environment is known as paleoecology.

The photograph in the lower left of the Grand Canyon, Arizona, reveals millions of years of Earth history recorded in the layers of sedimentary rocks. Simple geological laws of interpreting the rock record are explored in this module and will help students to better understand how geologists explore how our Earth system and its life forms change over time.

The lower right photograph reveals how polygons form in drying mud (silt and clay). On occasion, new sediment washed into these desiccation cracks and the polygonal structure is preserved in layers of rock. Finding ancient mud cracks and other sedimentary structures can tell geologists about environmental conditions in the region at the time in which they formed.

Investigating Fossils

INVESTIGATING FOSSILS

Why Are Fossils Important?

The word fossil comes from the Latin word *fossilis*, meaning "dug up." Today, the word generally refers to any evidence of past life, from insects preserved in amber to imprints of a dinosaur's foot.

To hold a fossil is to hold millions of years of history in the palm of your hand. The ridges, bumps, and curves of a fossilized clam are the same ridges, bumps, and curves that existed as it filtered water from the sea long ago. Studying fossils provides clues about the Earth's past, its climate, natural disasters, changing landforms, and changing oceans. Fossils tell about history and, like all good history, they help you to understand both the present and the future.

What Will You Investigate?

You and your group will be acting as detectives, trying to figure out how fossils form, where they form, and where they might be found today. In this way, you will be doing the work of a paleontologist, a geoscientist who studies life in prehistoric times by using fossil evidence.

Here are some of the things that you will investigate:

- why some things become fossils, but others do not;
- how the environment affects how fossils form;
- how fossils show the age of the Earth;
- how life has changed over time;
- what paleontologists do.

Introduction

Why Are Fossils Important?

About the Photo
In this photograph instructors and students are examining a geologic exposure for fossil remains. Fossils in this exposure are abundant and can be seen weathering out of the rock.

What Will You Investigate?

It is important for students to get a sense of where they are headed in the module. They need your help to connect what seem like unrelated investigations into a cohesive network of ideas. Reviewing this section of the introduction is the first step toward constructing a conceptual framework of "the Big Picture" as it is explored in *Investigating Fossils* (see page F64 of the Student Edition). This framework includes five main concepts:
- why some things become fossils, but others do not;
- how the environment affects how fossils form;
- what fossils reveal about Earth's history;
- how life has changed over time; and
- what paleontologists do.

This would be a good time to review with students the titles of the investigations in the Table of Contents. Ask students to explain how the titles of the investigations relate to the descriptions in **What Will You Investigate?**

Discussing the final investigation will help students to understand the overall goal of the module. In **Investigation 7**, students research a fossil and create a fossil "portrait" that depicts what the organisms was like, where and when it lived, how it became fossilized, the rock it was in, and other factors. Consider introducing students to evaluation rubrics so that they can see how their work will be assessed. Sample rubrics are included in the back of this Teacher's Edition.

NOTES

Teacher Commentary

INVESTIGATION 1: THE PROPERTIES OF FOSSILS

Background Information

Fossils

A fossil is any evidence of past plant or animal life contained in a sediment or a sedimentary rock. There are two kinds of fossils: body fossils and trace fossils. Body fossils are the actual organism or some part of it, or the imprint of the organism or some part of it. Even more abundant than body fossils, however, are trace fossils, which are physical evidence of the life activities of now-vanished organisms. Tracks, trails, burrows, feeding marks, and resting marks are all trace fossils. Trace fossils are useful for geologists and paleontologists because certain kinds of organisms, which live in specific environmental conditions, make distinctive traces. When your students hear the word "fossil," they probably think of shells or dinosaur bones. These are indeed good examples of body fossils, but there are many other kinds of fossils, including both body fossils and trace fossils.

In relatively young sediments and rocks, the actual body parts of organisms are often preserved. In older rocks, however, the body parts are usually dissolved away, or recrystallized, or replaced by another kind of mineral. Even so, the imprints of the organisms are still preserved, and they can be studied if the rock splits apart in the right place and with the right orientation to reveal the imprint. Paleontologists usually collect large numbers of rock pieces and then split them in the laboratory with special mechanical splitting devices to try to find at least a few fossils.

Fossilization

For the body of an organism to become preserved as a fossil, it must escape destruction, at least in part, both before and after it is buried with sediments. Destruction before burial might result from chemical and/or biological decomposition, or from mechanical effects like abrasion and/or breakage during transport by wind or water currents, or a combination of both. There is a very high probability that any organism on Earth will be either consumed by another organism or decomposed by microorganisms following death. For an organism or body part to become a fossil, it must either live within or be moved to a place where it can be buried and isolated from decay. The more rapid the burial, the less decay and the better the chance of preservation. Burial alone, however, does not guarantee that fossilization will occur, because conditions conducive to decomposition or dissolution often persist to great depths of burial.

Most subaerial environments (those exposed to the open air rather than being underwater) are fully oxygenated, so the soft tissues of dead organisms, whether plants or animals, are susceptible to decay. Microorganisms like bacteria are especially important in facilitating such decomposition. Many if not most subaqueous (underwater) environments are also oxygenated, owing to the ability of water to dissolve the oxygen of the atmosphere. For organisms to escape decay, burial must be extremely rapid, or the depositional environment must be anoxic (without the presence of oxygen). Some of the best-preserved soft body fossils have been found in deposits that are interpreted to have formed in marine basins in which there is little or no vertical exchange of water, so that the bottom waters are stagnant, but at the same time there is a rain of organic matter from the near-surface waters, the result being anoxic bottom waters. Free-floating

Investigating Fossils – Investigation 1

organisms that fall to the bottom in such a water body have an excellent chance of preservation. Probably the best modern example of such an environment is the Black Sea.

Hard skeletal materials, like bones and shells, have a far higher probability of preservation than soft tissues. For a bone or shell to be preserved, it must only survive breakage and abrasion before burial and chemical dissolution of its constituent mineral material before and after deposition. Even if the object is dissolved after deposition, it is likely to be represented by a cavity, which serves the paleontologist almost as well as the entire preserved object. Except in the youngest sedimentary rocks, imprints of the shells of marine invertebrates are just as common as the shells themselves, and usually even more so.

Fossiliferous Rocks
A rock that contains fossils is said to be fossiliferous (in contrast to unfossiliferous). Almost all fossils are contained in sedimentary rocks. They are virtually nonexistent in igneous rocks, and they are extremely uncommon in metamorphic rocks, although certain robust body fossils can survive a certain degree of metamorphism. Finding a fossil in a metamorphic rock is a significant and exciting event for a geologist, because it is extremely difficult otherwise to date the time of deposition of the sedimentary precursors of now-metamorphosed rocks. Not all sedimentary rocks, however, contain fossils. If they parachuted you out of an airplane to land on a random outcrop of sedimentary rock, the chance of your finding a fossil would be rather small—nowhere close to one hundred percent.

Some kinds of sedimentary rocks tend to be more fossiliferous than others. Limestones are the generally the most fossiliferous of sedimentary rocks. That should not be surprising, because most limestones consist in part, or even entirely, of the body parts of shelly marine organisms. Most coarse-grained limestones, and many fine-grained limestones as well, consist mostly of whole shells or fragments of shells. Such fragments, although recognizably derived from whole organisms, are not usually the subject of special study by paleontologists, because they are not sufficiently intact to carry detailed information about the nature of the organisms from which they were derived (although technically they are still classified as fossils).

Many shales, which are derived from freshly deposited mud, are fossiliferous as well, because certain organisms like to live on muddy sea floors. Shales are often rich in trace fossils, but less so in body fossils except when the chemical conditions during deposition were conducive to preservation rather than decomposition. The best representatives of soft-bodied organisms are from shales, although, frustratingly for paleontologists, instances of such preservation are very uncommon. Many sandstones are fossiliferous as well, although the body fossils in sandstones are usually relatively robust shelly materials, which are not highly susceptible to chemical decomposition. Conglomerates are the least fossiliferous of sedimentary rocks.

More Information…on the Web
Visit the *Investigating Earth Systems* web site www.agiweb.org/ies/ for links to a variety of other web sites that will help you deepen your understanding of content and prepare you to teach this module

Teacher Commentary

Investigation Overview

Students will explore their ideas about the properties of fossils. Students begin by describing a collection of fossils and considering what was fossilized and what seems to be missing. Students then explore decomposition by examining fresh fruit versus decomposing fruit, and by making predictions about the parts of various plants and animals that are likely to become fossilized if left to decay.

The **Digging Deeper** reading section elaborates upon the definition of fossils and the processes of decomposition and fossilization. This overview helps students begin to think about the reasons why it is very unlikely for a dead organism to become part of the fossil record. This understanding will be incomplete (related explorations into other aspects of fossilization will follow), but this investigation will be an important first step in beginning to understand the nature of the fossil record.

Goals and Objectives

As a result of this investigation, students will develop a better understanding of the role of decomposition and the presence of hard parts to fossilization and will begin to develop a conceptual understanding of what a fossil is. Students will improve their ability to make and record observations and information in a clear and systematic way.

Science Content Objectives

Students will collect evidence that:

1. Living things can become fossils.
2. Fossils resemble modern life forms.
3. Some parts of organisms are more likely to become fossils than others.
4. Decomposers break down dead matter.
5. Fossil formation is connected to the biosphere, the hydrosphere, the atmosphere, and the geosphere.

Inquiry Process Skills

Students will:

1. Make observations using the senses.
2. Record observations in a variety of ways.
3. Use tools (such as magnifiers) to make observations.
4. Seek connections between sets of observations.
5. Collate observations.
6. Devise questions to investigate.
7. Communicate observations and findings to others.

Connections to Standards and Benchmarks

In this investigation, your students will be investigating the process of decomposition and the properties of fossils. These observations will start them on the road to understanding the National Science Education Standards and AAAS Benchmarks shown below.

NSES Links

- Fossils provide important evidence of how life and environmental conditions have changed.

- Living organisms have played many roles in the Earth system, including: producing some types of rocks, and contributing to the weathering of rocks.

- Millions of species of animals, plants, and microorganisms are alive today. Although different species might look dissimilar, the unity among organisms becomes apparent from an analysis of internal structures, the similarity of their chemical processes, and the evidence of common ancestry.

AAAS Links

- A great variety of living things can be sorted into groups in many ways using various features to decide which things belong to which group.

- Fossils can be compared to one another and to living organisms according to their similarities and differences. Some organisms that lived long ago are similar to existing organisms, but some are quite different.

- Over the whole Earth, organisms are growing, dying, and decaying, and new organisms are being produced by the old ones.

Teacher Commentary

Preparation and Materials Needed

Preparation
This investigation requires about three 40-minute class periods to complete, depending on the depth of investigation and inquiry you have students pursue.

- **Day One:** Have students address the **Key Question**, observe and describe the collection of fossils, and discuss their observations and questions with others (**Steps 1–3**).

- **Day Two:** Students can observe the fresh versus decomposing fruit, the various samples of organic material, and participate in a class discussion about the conditions for fossilization (**Steps 4–6**). Assign the **Digging Deeper** reading section and the **As You Read** questions for homework.

- **Day Three:** Review the main ideas of the reading and have students work through the **Review and Reflect** questions.

Before beginning this activity, you will need to obtain index cards and a variety of fossil samples for **Steps 1–3** of the investigation. It is strongly recommended that your students have actual fossil samples, not plastic replicas. Such replicas, while looking quite authentic, do not give students the thrill of handling something from long ago. They do not feel like fossils, nor do they have the appropriate weight. There is also a risk that some students may be led to misconceptions about fossils. If fossils have not been supplied in kit form, if your school does not possess a fossil collection, or if you do not have a personal fossil collection, you will need to find a source of fossils. It is always worth asking the students themselves if anyone has a collection. If your school is in a fossil-rich area, you may be able to use a field trip to collect them. However, it is important that the collection be as varied in age and type as possible. You will need fossils of both animals and plants.

Museums or geology departments at universities may have collections that you can borrow for classroom study. The *Investigating Earth Systems* web site www.agiweb.org/ies/ provides suggestions for locating such resources.

Steps 4 and **5** of the investigation require advance preparation. For **Step 4**, you will need to allow a piece of fruit (peach, apricot) to decompose for a period of ten days before this activity. Double-bag the fruit and leave it in a warm area to maximize decomposition. Bring to class (or ask that a student bring) a fresh sample of the same fruit for comparison on the day of the investigation. Keep the material on ice or in the refrigerator between classes.

Step 5 requires a collection of materials (double-bagged as a safety precaution). These include a whole shrimp (uncooked with shell and head if possible), a peeled shrimp (flesh), a chicken wing (skin, flesh, and bone), a leaf (non-leathery), and a twig or small piece of wood. These specimens correspond to the variety of organisms found in the fossil record: clamshell and shrimp = invertebrates; wing = vertebrate; green leaf = non-woody plant material; small twig = petrified wood. You need only enough samples so that each group has a sample to observe at the start of the investigation. Allowing students to share the material between groups will enable you to reduce expenses (i.e., purchase one or two chicken wings and shrimp, then double up on the leaf, twig, and clamshell).

Because of the health risk associated with salmonella in uncooked chicken, and the risk of bacteria with perishable items, it is crucial that you prepare these bags ahead of time and keep them refrigerated until they are used. If frozen, they must be fully thawed out for use. Bags should be the high-quality "locking" type. Tape the lock with masking or duct tape for extra security. Keep the material on ice or in the refrigerator between classes.

Working in Groups

If your students are not used to working in small collaborative groups, spend some time helping them understand how to do this. Keep in mind that some students might find this difficult (some prefer to work alone). Help them see that collaborating means working together as a team, with each group member sharing and contributing. Each person in the group will be depending on each other member. Sometimes the work may be shared, with different group members doing different parts. Sample rubrics for evaluating group participation are provided in this Teacher's Edition (see **Group-Participation Evaluation Sheets I and II**). Discuss the criteria with your students to help to reinforce the importance of individual accountability and cooperation.

Materials
- fossil specimens *
- four or five white index cards
- samples of fresh fruit
- samples of partially decomposed fruit in a tightly sealed, double-bagged, plastic bag
- a tightly sealed, double-bagged, plastic bag containing **one** of the following: peeled shrimp, unpeeled shrimp, clamshell, chicken wing, leaf, small twig

* The *Investigating Earth Systems* web site www.agiweb.org/ies/ provides suggestions for obtaining these resources.

Teacher Commentary

NOTES

Investigating Fossils

Investigation 1: The Properties of Fossils

Investigation 1:
The Properties of Fossils

Explore Questions

Key Question
Before you begin, first think about this key question.

Why does one animal or plant become fossilized, but millions of others do not?

Show Evidence

Think about what you already know about fossils. What do you think leads to their formation? Why do some plants and animals decay, without forming a fossil?

Share your thinking with others in your group and with your class.

Materials Needed

For this investigation your group will need:
- fossil specimens
- four or five white index cards
- samples of fresh fruit
- samples of partially decomposed fruit in a tightly sealed, double-bagged, plastic bag
- a tightly sealed, double-bagged, plastic bag containing **one** of the following: peeled shrimp, unpeeled shrimp, clam-shell, chicken wing, leaf, small twig

Conduct Investigations

Investigate
1. Your group will be given samples of different kinds of fossils. Study them closely.

   Make a small card to set beside each fossil type, and add any information about it that you can tell from your observations.

Teacher Commentary

Key Question

Use the **Key Question** as a brief warm-up activity (5 to 10 minutes) designed to elicit students' ideas about the topic explored in the investigation. Emphasize thinking and sharing of ideas. Avoid seeking closure (i.e., the "right answer"). Closure will come through inquiry, reading the text (**Digging Deeper**), discussing the ideas (lecture), and reflecting on what was learned at the end of the investigation. Make students feel comfortable sharing their ideas by avoiding commentary on the correctness of responses.

Write the **Key Question** on the chalkboard or on an overhead transparency. Have the students record their answers in their journals. Tell them to think about and answer the question individually. Tell them to write as much as they know, providing as much detail as possible. Emphasize that the current date and the prompt (the question, a meaningful heading, etc.) should be included in journal entries.

Discuss students' ideas. Ask for a volunteer to record responses on the chalkboard or overhead projector. This allows you to circulate among the students, encouraging them to copy the notes in an organized way. The result of your discussion should reveal a variety of ideas about how the use of materials has changed over time.

Student Conceptions about Why a Plant or Animal Becomes Fossilized

The pre-assessment will have given you a sense of what your students already know about fossils and what they do not know. Many might have definite ideas about fossils, perhaps recognizing them as organisms that have "turned to stone." Some students might have visited museums and other centers where fossils are on display. Others may connect fossils with ideas from television or the movies. Students' ideas about life through time, however, might be much more confused than those about fossils. Some might think that dinosaurs and humans coexisted. As with many adults, the concept of time passing over millions of years is very hard to imagine. Your students are likely to need a good deal of help in appreciating the scale of geologic time.

Answer for the Teacher Only

For the body of an organism to become preserved as a fossil, it must escape mechanical destruction and decomposition, at least in part, both before and after it is buried with sediments. There is a very high probability that any organism on Earth will be either consumed by another organism or decomposed by microorganisms following death.

> **Assessment Tool**
>
> Key-Question Evaluation Sheet
> Use this evaluation sheet to help students understand and internalize basic expectations for the warm-up activity. The **Key-Question Evaluation Sheet** emphasizes that you want to see evidence of prior knowledge and that students should communicate their thinking clearly. You will not likely have time to apply this assessment every time students complete a warm-up activity; yet, in order to ensure that students value committing their initial conceptions to paper and are taking the warm-up seriously, you should always remind them of the criteria. When time permits, use this evaluation sheet as a spot check on the quality of their work.

> **About the Photo**
>
> The photograph shows a trilobite from the Middle Cambrian found in the Burgess Shale Member of the Stephen Formation, near Field, British Columbia, Canada. It was collected by a famous paleontologist—Charles D. Walcott. Trilobites flourished in the Paleozoic Era.

Investigate

Teaching Suggestions and Sample Answers

Let students know that the goal of this investigation is for them to examine fossils and recently living things to explore the **Key Question**—why does one animal or plant become fossilized, but millions of others do not? They will make observations of fossils and recently living things and discuss their observations. Discussion questions will help them to better understand what happens to an organism after death that might affect the chances that any part of it will become a fossil.

1. Distribute fossil specimens and index cards to student groups.

Teacher Commentary

NOTES

Investigating Fossils

INVESTIGATING FOSSILS

Inquiry

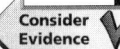

Observations and Inferences

An observation is what you can see, smell, hear, touch, or in some way measure. An inference is what you believe to be true on the basis of your observations. An inference can lead to a prediction, especially if it can be proved or disproved.

⚠️ Do not open any of the sealed bags. Do not eat any food in the lab.

a) What kinds of animals are represented (mammals, birds, reptiles, insects, shellfish)? What kinds of plants, if any, are represented?

2. Compare your fossils with those of other students.

    a) What do they all have in common?

    b) How are they different?

3. Discuss the following questions in your group. Record your answers in your journal.

    a) What kinds of things became fossilized (bones, skin, muscle, leaves, flowers, bark)?

    b) What kinds of living things seem to be missing from this collection?

    c) Do you think all living things can become fossils? Why or why not?

    d) List some questions of your own about the fossils.

4. Observe samples of fresh fruit and fruit that has been decomposing for several days. The decomposing fruit is contained in a sealed, double-bagged plastic bag. Handle the samples carefully, and do not open the bag.

    a) Describe the changes that seem to be happening to the decomposing fruit.

    b) What do you think caused these changes?

Teacher Commentary

a) Answers will vary depending upon the collection of specimens that you assemble for the investigation. The categories that your students use to describe the fossils will depend upon their background knowledge. Ask students to note the distinguishing features that support their conclusions about the kinds of animals and plants represented.

2. This step allows students to compare different examples of the same kinds of fossils (different fossil clams, for example).

   a) Answers will vary. Students might note that all seem to have the same general shape or structure.

   b) Answers will vary. Students might note that although the shape and structure are similar, there are slight differences in the size between different samples of the same kind of fossil, or that some fossils seem to be better preserved or show more detail than others even though they are the same kind of fossil.

3. Your students might never have considered these questions before. The idea that some parts of organisms are more, or less, likely to become fossils may be a new idea for them. Give these students the opportunity to discuss their ideas fully. Give students the opportunity to discuss these questions in their groups. Circulate to check and comment upon their work.

   a) Answers will vary, but in general, students are likely to find that the hard parts of organisms became fossilized.

   b) Students will note that soft parts (skin, hair, muscles, internal organs, etc.) of animals are missing from the collection of fossils.

   c) Answers will vary. Some students might suggest that given the right conditions, any living thing has the potential to become a fossil.

   d) Answers will vary. As you circulate, check student journals to ensure that they have written down at least one question related to the collection of fossils.

4. At this point, distribute the bagged collection of fresh and decomposing fruit to each group. Remind students that safety precautions (lower left corner of the page) must be followed.

   a) Observations might include noting that the decomposing fruit has a different color and a less firm texture, and perhaps that mold has begun to grow.

   b) Students might simply state that decomposition caused the fruit to change over time. Some students may note that warmth (lack of refrigeration) aided this process.

Investigating Fossils

Investigation 1: The Properties of Fossils

Evidence for Ideas

c) What do you think is the likelihood of the fruit becoming a fossil, either wholly or in part? Be sure to explain your answer.

d) When would the fruit be more likely to become a fossil — if it decomposed quickly, decomposed slowly, or did not decompose at all? Explain your answer.

Conduct Investigations

5. Examine one of the following items contained in a tightly sealed, double-bagged plastic bag: peeled shrimp, unpeeled shrimp, chicken wing, clamshell, green leaf, small twig.

Evidence for Ideas

a) As you examine your item, carefully record your observations in a data table like the one shown.

b) Think about its chance of becoming a fossil, either wholly or in part. From what you can infer from your observations, record a prediction in the table.

c) Record a reason for your prediction.

Meat items should be fresh and kept refrigerated when not in use. Notify your teacher immediately of any leaking fluid, because it may carry disease. Wipe off desks and tables when you are done.

Fossil Formation of Dead Organisms

Item	Observations	Prediction (Can it become a fossil?)	Reason (Use an analogy if possible.)
unpeeled shrimp			
chicken wing			
clamshell			
green leaf			
small twig			

Show Evidence

6. As a class, discuss the following questions. Take notes during the class discussion, completing the chart and recording your answers. Be sure to ask for clarification if you are unsure of another group's observations, predictions, or reasons.

Consider Evidence

a) In the right conditions, which of the items might become a fossil? Why is that?

b) Which of the items might have only some of their parts become a fossil, and which parts?

c) Which of the items would be very unlikely to have any of their parts become a fossil? Why is that?

d) How do you think decomposition affects fossilization? Why do you think so?

Inquiry

Predictions

Keep in mind that predictions that you made do not need to be correct. Scientists often make many incorrect predictions or hypotheses before finding one that stands up to repeated testing.

Using Analogies

Predictions are often based on common experiences. You can compare your observations with previous experiences and base your prediction on what you are already familiar with. For example, in this investigation you might base your prediction on the fact that an unpeeled shrimp has a coating that looks like, and feels like, plastic.

Investigating Earth Systems

Teacher Commentary

    c) Students are likely to believe that the "harder" part of the fruit (pit or seeds) are more likely to become fossilized and to claim that harder material does not decompose as quickly as softer material (or that it does not decompose at all). Many students have had the experience of finding a very old peach pit and can relate this experience to the investigation.

    d) Students are likely to respond that the less the fruit decomposes, the more likely it is to become fossilized. The poor, rotten condition of the decomposing fruit should help students to understand that decomposition decreases the likelihood of something being preserved as a fossil.

5. Distribute the bagged collection of materials to each group. These include a whole shrimp (uncooked with shell and head if possible), a peeled shrimp (flesh), a chicken wing (skin, flesh, and bone), a leaf (non-leathery), and twig or small piece of wood. These specimens correspond to the variety of organisms found in the fossil record: clamshell and unpeeled shrimp = invertebrates; chicken wing = vertebrate; green leaf = non-woody plant material; twig = petrified wood.

Teaching Tip
Because of the health risk associated with salmonella in uncooked chicken, and the risk of bacteria with perishable items, it is crucial that you prepare these bags ahead of time and keep them refrigerated until they are used. If frozen, they must be fully thawed out for use. Bags should be the high-quality "locking" type. Tape the lock with masking or duct tape for extra security. Tell students why they are not to open or pierce the bags. They should not handle the bags too roughly. You might want to demonstrate how to observe texture without applying great pressure.

    a)–c) Answers will vary. Check data tables for completeness. Students are most likely to claim that the bone of the chicken, the clamshell, and the small twig can become a fossil because they have hard parts. They are likely to claim that the soft parts of the shrimp, the chicken, and the leaf will decompose and not become a fossil. They may claim that the protective slightly harder cover of the shrimp (the exoskeleton) can become a fossil and that the other soft part will decompose.

6. Be sure to make time for this discussion so that students can share their ideas with others.

    a) Students are most likely to claim that chicken bone, the clamshell, and the small twig can become a fossil. In reality, any of the items can become a fossil, given the right conditions.

    b) Students will probably note that the bones of the chicken wing might become a fossil because the flesh and muscle will decompose. Middle-school students commonly associate fossils with bones and may cite this experience.

c) Students are likely to claim that the leaf and the unpeeled shrimp will be very unlikely to become a fossil because the soft part of the shrimp will decompose and the leaf will dry up and disintegrate.

d) Students will note that decomposition decreases the likelihood of fossilization because the material that decomposes "goes away."

Assessment Tools

Investigation Journal-Entry Evaluation Sheet
Use this sheet as a general guideline for assessing student journals, adapting it to your classroom if desired. You should give the **Journal-Entry Evaluation Sheet** to students early in the module, discuss it with them, and use it to provide clear and prompt feedback.

Investigation Journal-Entry Checklist
Use this checklist as a guide for quickly checking the quality and completeness of journal entries.

Teacher Commentary

NOTES

INVESTIGATING FOSSILS

Digging Deeper

FOSSILIZATION

What is a Fossil?

A fossil is any evidence of past life. Fossils formed from animal bodies or their imprints are called body fossils. When people think about fossils, they usually think about body fossils. Trace fossils are another kind of fossil. A trace fossil is any evidence of the life activity of an animal that lived in the past. Burrows, tracks, trails, feeding marks, and resting marks are all examples of trace fossils. It is usually hard to figure out exactly which kind of animal made a particular trace fossil. Trace fossils are useful to paleontologists (scientists who study fossils), however, because they tell something about the environment where the animal lived and the animal's behavior.

As You Read...
Think about:
1. What is a fossil?
2. Give two examples of a body fossil.
3. Can a plant yield a trace fossil? Why or why not?
4. What are organic compounds made up of?
5. Under what conditions is decomposition the fastest? Under what conditions is it the slowest?
6. What are some ways that animals become fossilized?

Evidence for Ideas

Teacher Commentary

Digging Deeper

This section provides text and photographs that give students greater insight into the factors that control decomposition and the likelihood of fossilization. You may wish to assign the **As You Read** questions as homework to guide students to think about the major ideas in the text.

As You Read...
Think about:
1. A fossil is any evidence of past life, including body fossils and trace fossils.

2. Two examples of body fossils include a fossil clamshell and a fossil bone.

3. No, a plant cannot yield a trace fossil because a trace fossil is evidence of the life activity of an animal that has lived in the past (the movement of an animal).

4. Organic compounds are made up mostly of carbon, oxygen, and hydrogen.

5. Decomposition is fastest when organisms are in water that contains dissolved oxygen. Decomposition and decay slow down when an organism is buried in fine mud because the mud cuts off the supply of water with oxygen.

6. One way that organisms become fossilized is when shells or bones are buried and not dissolved before the rock becomes solid. Another way is when an insect is trapped in resin, which hardens to a material called amber.

Assessment Opportunity
You may wish to rephrase selected questions from the **As You Read** section into multiple choice or true/false format to use as a quiz. Use this quiz to assess student understanding and as a motivational tool to ensure that students complete the reading assignment and comprehend the main ideas.

About the Photo
The photo shows fossil dinosaur bones exposed in the rock of the Jurassic Morrison Formation at Dinosaur National Monument, Utah.

Making Connections...*with the Local Area*
Encourage your students to brainstorm ideas about where they might find fossils. Examples might include private collections, rock shops, and science centers. They may find fossils exposed in such building materials as limestone or marble. They can also collect photographs from books and the Internet.

Investigation 1: The Properties of Fossils

Decomposition

Organisms are made up of chemical compounds, most of which are organic compounds. Organic compounds consist mainly of carbon, oxygen, and hydrogen. After a plant or animal dies, it decomposes. As organisms decompose, their organic compounds change into simpler compounds, mainly carbon dioxide and water. Decomposition is fastest when the organisms are in water that contains dissolved oxygen. Organisms can also decompose even without oxygen. Some kinds of bacteria feed on plant and animal tissues even though there is no oxygen. These are called anaerobic ("no air") bacteria. Sooner or later, almost all organic matter from plants and animals decays. Decay slows down only when the organic matter is buried in very fine mud. That seals the organic matter off from water with oxygen.

The soft parts of an organism decompose the fastest. You know how little time it takes for food to spoil and rot in warm weather when it is not in the refrigerator. Bones and shells decompose much more slowly. Over

Teacher Commentary

About the Photo

The photo shows burrows and other trace fossils in limestone. The penny toward the right side of the photo is used for scale purposes. Ask the students why they think these kinds of trace fossils are important to geologists. Lead them to appreciate that trace fossils provide important fossil evidence of many soft-bodied organisms, of which there are precious few body fossils preserved in the rock record.

INVESTIGATING FOSSILS

long times their mineral materials dissolve. That can happen rapidly when the shells and bones lie on the ground surface or on the sea bottom. If the shell or bone is buried in sediment, it dissolves more slowly. Sometimes the shells are not dissolved before the rock becomes solid, so they are preserved. The woody parts of plants that consist mostly of cellulose and lignin decompose much more slowly than the softer parts.

Fossilization

Most animals become fossilized by being buried in sediment. For them to be fossilized, they have to be buried and leave an imprint before they decompose. Animals without skeletons are seldom fossilized, because they decompose so fast. Animals with hard skeletons are much easier to fossilize. The most common fossils are shells of marine animals like clams, snails, or corals. Insects, with thin outside skeletons of chitin, are not as easy to fossilize. Sometimes an insect is trapped in sticky material, called resin, that comes out of some kinds of trees. Then the resin hardens to a material called amber. The insect fossil is preserved in the amber, often perfectly.

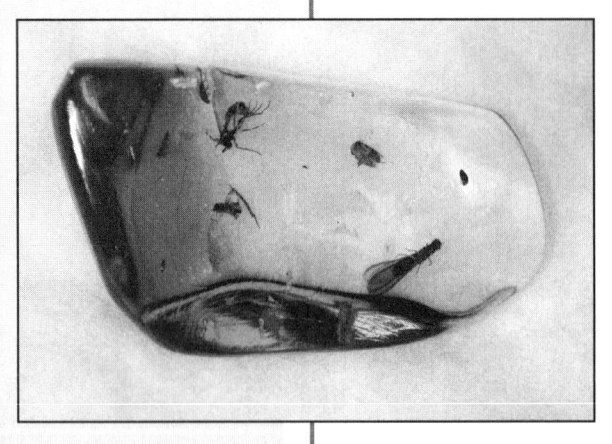

Sometimes the actual shell or bone is preserved. Usually, however, you see only its imprint. If the shell or bone resists being dissolved for a long enough time, the sediment around it turns into rock. Then, even though the shell or bone dissolves, the imprint is preserved. When a hammer splits the rock open, the fracture might pass through the imprint, and you see a fossil.

Teacher Commentary

About the Photo

The photograph shows insects in amber. Students may be familiar with the fact that insects can be fossilized and preserved in amber. This topic was sensationalized in the popular movie *Jurassic Park*, in which insects were the source of dinosaur DNA. In many works of fiction there is an element of truth. Although the process of insect fossilization was reasonably described in the movie, dinosaur DNA has not been recovered from such fossilized insects.

Investigation 1: The Properties of Fossils

Review and Reflect

Review

1. What kinds of plant and animal materials decompose most quickly?
2. What kinds of plant and animal materials take the longest to decompose?
3. What is the difference between a body fossil and a trace fossil?

Reflect

4. What kinds of materials from organisms have the best chance of becoming a fossil? Explain.
5. Which of the following natural processes did you model in the investigation? Explain your reasoning.
   - decomposition at the Earth's surface
   - scattering of organic matter by scavengers
   - decomposition after an organism is buried by sediments
6. Sediments can often accumulate very quickly in places where rivers flow into the open ocean. Would this be a likely or unlikely place for fossils to form? Explain your answer.

Thinking about the Earth System

7. From what you learned in this investigation, what connections can you make between the geosphere and the biosphere? Note any connections between these two spheres on your *Earth System Connection* sheet.
8. How are the atmosphere and hydrosphere involved in decomposition?
9. On your *Earth System Connection* sheet, note any roles that the atmosphere plays in the preservation of fossils.

Thinking about Scientific Inquiry

10. How is an observation different from an inference? Give an example of each from this investigation.
11. What is an analogy and why is it useful in scientific inquiry? Give an example.

Teacher Commentary

Review and Reflect

Review

Give your students ample time to review what they have learned. Help them see that while investigations provide some answers to scientific questions, they often raise additional questions. Spend some time having students talk about these possible questions.

1. The soft parts of plants and animals decompose the most quickly.

2. The hard parts (bones and shells) of animals and the hard, woody parts and seeds of plants take the longest to decompose.

3. Body fossils form from animal bodies or their imprints. Trace fossils are evidence of the life activity of an animal, including footprints, feeding marks, tracks, trails, and burrows. For example, a dinosaur bone would be a body fossil, but a dinosaur footprint would be a trace fossil.

Reflect

It is very important that your students be given adequate time to review and reflect on what they have done and understood in this investigation. Ensure that all students think about and discuss the questions listed here. Be on the lookout for any misunderstandings and, where necessary, help students to clarify their ideas.

4. The hard parts of organisms (shells, bones, teeth) have the best chance of becoming a fossil because they take a longer time to dissolve than the soft parts take to decompose.

5. With the exception of being placed within a plastic bag (to minimize odors), the ten-day-old fruit was a model of the process of decomposition at the Earth's surface. The other processes were not modeled to any significant degree in the investigation.

6. Places where sediment accumulates (e.g., at the mouths of rivers) are likely places for fossils to form because rapid burial of an organism by fine mud slows the process of decomposition.

Thinking about the Earth System

It is very important that students begin to relate what they are studying to the wider idea of the Earth System. This is a complex and largely inferred set of concepts that students cannot easily understand from direct observation. Remember, the goal is that students will have a working understanding of the Earth System by the time they complete eighth grade. Although it can be taught as a piece of information, true understanding is largely dependent upon comprehending how numerous specific Earth science concepts connect with the idea of the Earth as a system. Be sure to spend some time helping students to make what connections they can between the focus of their investigations and this wider aspect.

7. Students may note that when an organism (plant or animal, which is part of the biosphere) dies and is preserved as a fossil in rock, it "becomes" part of the geosphere. Thus, the geosphere holds the evidence to past life in the biosphere.

8. Decomposition occurs fastest in the presence of water (hydrosphere) and oxygen (atmosphere).

9. In general, students should note that the atmosphere (the oxygen in it) works to prevent the preservation of fossils. Students might note that insects that are trapped in resin are more likely to become part of the fossil record because the resin cuts off any bacteria from a supply of oxygen. This prevents decomposition. Taking a broader view, the atmosphere is one of the critical systems that helps to create sediments that bury organisms and preserve fossil remains. In that sense, and in others as well, the atmosphere is essential to fossil preservation.

Thinking about Scientific Inquiry

Science as inquiry is a theme that runs through all investigations. Students will need many investigative experiences to grasp the many processes and skills involved with scientific inquiry. This can be taught as a piece of information, but for a solid understanding, students need considerable firsthand experience.

Students are given many opportunities to think about the connections between their investigations and inquiry processes. At this level, students need to become more systematic and sophisticated in conducting their investigations, some of which may last for weeks or more. That means closing in on an understanding of what constitutes a good experiment. The concept of controlling variables is straightforward, but achieving it in practice is difficult. Students can make some headway, however, by participating frequently in experimental investigations (not to the exclusion, of course, of other kinds of investigations) and explicitly discussing how explanation relates to experimental design.

Teacher Commentary

10. An observation is based upon what you see, hear, feel, touch, or in some way measure. Inferences are what you believe to be true. Inferences are based on observations, but observations are not based upon inferences.

11. An analogy is a way of comparing one thing to another. An analogy might help you to make a prediction. For example, if you think that a clamshell is analogous to bone, and you know that bones can become fossils, then you might use this analogy to predict that a shell can become a fossil.

Assessment Tool
Review and Reflect Journal-Entry Evaluation Sheet
Depending on whether you have students complete the work individually or within a group, use the **Review and Reflect** part of the investigation to assess individual or collective understandings about the concepts and inquiry processes explored. Whatever choice you make, this evaluation sheet provides you with a few general criteria for assessing content and thoroughness of student work. Adapt and modify the sheet to meet your needs. Consider involving students in selecting and modifying the assessment criteria.

Teacher Review

Use this section to reflect on and review the investigation. Keep in mind that your notes here are likely to be especially helpful when you teach this investigation again. Questions listed here are examples only.

Student Achievement

What evidence do you have that all students have met the science content objectives?

Are there any students who need more help in reaching these objectives? If so, how can you provide this?

What evidence do you have that all students have demonstrated their understanding of the inquiry processes?

Which of these inquiry objectives do your students need to improve upon in future investigations?

What evidence do the journal entries contain about what your students learned from this investigation?

Planning

How well did this investigation fit into your class time?

What changes can you make to improve your planning next time?

Guiding and Facilitating Learning

How well did you focus and support inquiry while interacting with students?

What changes can you make to improve classroom management for the next investigation or the next time you teach this investigation?

Teacher Commentary

How successful were you in encouraging all students to participate fully in science learning? _____

_____

How did you encourage and model the skills values, and attitudes of scientific inquiry? _____

_____

How did you nurture collaboration among students? _____

_____

Materials and Resources

What challenges did you encounter obtaining or using materials and/or resources needed for the activity? _____

_____

What changes can you make to better obtain and better manage materials and resources next time? _____

_____

Student Evaluation

Describe how you evaluated student progress. What worked well? What needs to be improved? _____

_____

How will you adapt your evaluation methods for next time? _____

_____

Describe how you guided students in self-assessment. _____

_____

Self Evaluation

How would you rate your teaching of this investigation? _____

_____

What advice would you give to a colleague who is planning to teach this investigation? _____

_____

NOTES

Teacher Commentary

INVESTIGATION 2: SEDIMENT SIZE AND FOSSIL FORMATION

Background Information

Sediments and Sedimentary Rocks
Sediments
Sediments are natural Earth materials, in both particulate and dissolved form, that are produced by weathering of preexisting rock and then transported, by water, wind, or moving ice, to sites of deposition. Sediments come in a very wide range of sizes and compositions. There are two major realms of sediments and sedimentary rocks: siliciclastic and chemical. The origins of these two kinds are very different, and they need separate consideration. Siliciclastic sediments are those that consist of particles of minerals or rock that were derived from weathering of preexisting bedrock on the continents. The word "siliciclastic" implies two things: *silici-* stands for silicate minerals, the dominant kind of mineral in most rocks, and *-clastic* stands for breakage of rock into sedimentary particles. Chemical sediments are those that are precipitated from solution in natural surface waters, mainly lakes and oceans, from dissolved constituents derived from weathering of rocks exposed on the continents.

Siliciclastic Sediments
Bedrock exposed on land is subjected to weathering. Weathering is usually viewed as involving two different kinds of processes: mechanical, involving the physical disintegration of the rock; and chemical, involving the chemical decomposition of the constituent minerals of the rock. Some weathering processes are strictly mechanical. A good example is frost wedging, whereby the expansion of water when it freezes in cracks in the rock causes the rock to become more highly fractured. Chemical weathering occurs because most rocks consist partly or entirely of minerals that were formed deep in the Earth, at temperatures and pressures much higher than at the surface. Most such minerals are unstable under Earth-surface conditions, meaning that they tend to be converted by a variety of chemical reactions to other minerals, which are stable under Earth-surface conditions.

Commonly, however, the two kinds of weathering processes, physical and chemical, act together to convert exposed bedrock into individual particles of minerals and rock along with dissolved materials. Rock and mineral particles formed by weathering are transported over the Earth's surface by streams, by the wind, and by glaciers. In general, rivers are the most important agents of sediment transport. Most clastic sediment is ultimately deposited in the ocean, although much is deposited in large lakes and in closed basins on the continents.

Siliciclastic sediment is highly varied, in both composition and texture. (Texture is the word geologists use for rock geometry on the scale of individual grains: size, shape, and grain-to-grain arrangement.) Particle size ranges from enormous boulders down to very fine clay particles that are fractions of a micrometer (μm; 10^{-6} m) in size. Sedimentary material coarser than 2 mm is called gravel; material between 1/16 mm and 2 mm is called sand; and material finer than 1/16 mm is called mud. Mud is further subdivided into clay, finer than about 4 μm, and silt, coarser than about 4 μm. Most gravel consists of either rock fragments or coarse quartz; most sand consists of quartz, potassium feldspar, or sand-size rock fragments; most silt consists of fine quartz or potassic feldspar grains; and most clay consists of particles of clay minerals, a group of sheet silicates formed by weathering of aluminosilicate minerals.

Chemically Precipitated Sediments
Minerals in rocks that formed deep in the Earth tend to be chemically unstable under the conditions of the Earth's surface, and are transformed chemically into dissolved material and particles of new minerals that are stable under Earth-surface conditions. Some minerals, like halite, gypsum, calcite, or dolomite, simply dissolve, to produce ions in solution. Some silicate minerals, like olivine, are also dissolved in this way. Most of the important rock-forming silicate minerals that contain aluminum, however, weather in a different way: they are converted into dissolved ions together with fine particles of new aluminum-bearing minerals, mainly clay minerals. The ions that are released during chemical weathering are carried away in solution by running water, and are ultimately added to the content of dissolved materials in the oceans (although some accumulates in lakes and closed basins on the continents and sometimes remains there for geologically long times). On average, the oceans seem not to have become any saltier during the latter part of geologic time, so new minerals must be precipitated in the oceans all the time to balance the addition of dissolved constituents.

Some chemical sediments are inorganically precipitated directly out of seawater; halite and gypsum are good examples. The situation with dissolved silica, derived from weathering of silicate minerals, is somewhat different: certain kinds of free-floating unicellular marine organisms (diatoms, which are single-celled plants, and radiolarians, which are single-celled animals) secrete amorphous, noncrystalline silica to make their skeletons, so silica is removed from seawater almost entirely by biological rather than chemical processes.

Carbonate sediments are the most abundant chemically precipitated sediments. Ca^{2+} and Mg^{2+} ions are continuously added to the oceans from weathering of rocks containing calcium and magnesium. These ions combine with carbonate ions, CO_3^{2-}, to form the calcium carbonate minerals calcite and aragonite, $CaCO_3$, and dolomite, $CaMg(CO_3)_2$. The ultimate source of the carbonate ion is carbon dioxide, CO_2, supplied from the atmosphere and dissolved in the oceans. Some calcium carbonate is precipitated inorganically, but most is precipitated by marine organisms to build skeletons. Many kinds of organisms, mainly marine invertebrate animals like mollusks and corals, precipitate calcium carbonate. Some of these organisms precipitate calcite and some precipitate aragonite.

Diagenesis: The Conversion of Sediments to Sedimentary Rocks
Newly deposited sediments become buried more and more deeply as later sediments are deposited on top of them. As the sediment becomes more deeply buried, the temperature and the pressure increase. Diagenesis is the general term for all of the changes that sediments undergo as they are buried. As the forces between adjacent sediment particles increase, the particles are squeezed together and their packing becomes closer, and some of the water in the pore spaces is forced upward, out of the sediment. This process, called compaction, results in a decrease in the volume of the sediment. The thickness of a succession of sedimentary layers can decrease by as much as fifty percent by compaction. Sands, gravels, and coarse carbonate sediments undergo the least compaction,

Teacher Commentary

whereas muds and fine carbonate sediments undergo the greatest compaction. The sediment gradually becomes lithified (converted to solid rock), by welding of sediment particles together and by precipitation of new mineral material, called cement, in the pore spaces between the particles.

Sedimentary Environments
The Earth-surface environments where sediments accumulate are highly varied. Sediments accumulate in lakes, in rivers, and in the ocean, both shallow and deep. You might suppose that because rivers are the principal means of erosion of the continents, they would not accumulate thick successions of sediments. In the lower courses of many river systems, however, the Earth's crust is undergoing slow subsidence (a process by which local areas of the Earth's crust can be slowly lowered), making way for continued deposition of sediment by the river. In some cases, thousands of meters of sediment can accumulate in this way.

The greatest proportion of sediment is deposited in the oceans. Beaches, deltas, and broad continental shelves are important shallow depositional environments in the oceans. In the deep ocean, far from land, mostly fine sediment is deposited. Some is simply the very finest part of land-derived sediment, which settles very slowly to the bottom to form what is called abyssal clay. Rates of deposition are extremely slow: millimeters per thousand years. In areas where free-floating unicellular plants and animals are abundant in the surface waters of the ocean, tiny shells rain down to the ocean bottom to form deposits called organic ooze. Some of this (calcareous ooze) consists of calcium carbonate, and some (siliceous ooze) consists of amorphous silica.

More Information...on the Web
Visit the *Investigating Earth Systems* web site www.agiweb.org/ies/ for links to a variety of other web sites that will help you deepen your understanding of content and prepare you to teach this module

Investigation Overview

In this investigation, students look for the relationships between the quality of fossil impressions and the size of particles used to make the impressions. So that your students understand how to compare particle sizes (which are very small), they first model this with sports balls. The concept of "greater than/lesser than," and ways of expressing this mathematically are important in this part of the investigation. Students also explore Earth systems connections, because the weathering of rock is an ideal example of the interaction between the geosphere (rock), the hydrosphere (water), and atmosphere (air movement – wind).

Goals and Objectives

As a result of this investigation, students will develop a better understanding of the role of sediment size in fossil formation, the kinds of sedimentary rocks most likely to contain fossils, and how some of the more common invertebrate fossils form.

Science Content Objectives

Students will collect evidence that:

1. Sediment particles come in different sizes.
2. The size of sediment particles affects fossil definition.
3. Particle size can be measured and compared.
4. Fossil formation is connected to the biosphere, the hydrosphere, the atmosphere, and the geosphere.

Inquiry Process Skills

Students will:

1. Make observations using the senses.
2. Record observations in a variety of ways.
3. Devise a method of measurement.
4. Conduct an investigation into particle size and fossil formation.
5. Predict possible outcomes of the investigation.
6. Communicate observations and findings to others.

Teacher Commentary

Connections to Standards and Benchmarks

In this investigation, your students will be investigating the process of decomposition and the properties of fossils. These observations will start them on the road to understanding the National Science Education Standards and AAAS Benchmarks shown below.

NSES Links

- Fossils provide important evidence of how life and environmental conditions have changed.
- Living organisms have played many roles in the Earth system, including affecting the composition of the atmosphere, producing some types of rocks, and contributing to the weathering of rocks.
- Some changes in the solid Earth can be described as the "rock cycle." Old rocks at the Earth's surface weather, forming sediments that are buried, then compacted, heated, and often recrystallized into new rock. Eventually, those new rocks may be brought to the surface by the forces that drive plate motions, and the rock cycle continues.
- Models are tentative schemes or structures that correspond to real objects, events, or classes of events, and that have explanatory power. Models help scientists and engineers understand how things work.
- Scientists formulate and test their explanation of nature using observations, experiments, and theoretical and mathematical models. Although all scientific ideas are tentative and subject to change and improvements in principle, for most major ideas in science, there is much experimental and observational confirmation.

AAAS Link

- Many thousands of layers of sedimentary rock provide evidence for the long history of the Earth, and for the long history of changing life forms whose remains are found in the rocks. More recently deposited rock layers are more likely to contain fossils resembling existing species.

Preparation and Materials Needed

Preparation
This investigation will require about five 40-minute class periods to complete. To save a class period, prepare the fossil impressions yourself (**Step 2** of **Part B**) ahead of time.

- **Day One:** Work through the **Key Question** and have students complete **Steps 1** and **2** of **Part A** on sediment size.

- **Day Two:** Have students complete **Steps 3–6** of **Part A** on sediment size. Have students read **Part B** and think about **Question 1** for homework so that they come to class prepared to discuss their ideas about sediment grain size and fossil formation.

- **Day Three:** Have students complete **Steps 1** and **2** of **Part B**. Plaster models of fossil impressions will need to harden overnight.

- **Day Four:** Have students complete **Steps 3–6** of **Part B**, including the presentation of displays. Assign the **Digging Deeper** reading section (and the **As You Read** questions) for homework.

- **Day Five:** Review the main ideas in the reading and have students work through the questions in **Review and Reflect** to synthesize the main ideas of their investigations.

For **Part A** of this investigation, you will need to provide your students with small samples of clay, fine sand, and course sand. You can obtain clay and silt by collecting a soil sample, drying it out, and running it through a screen sieve. If you test the sieved material by rolling it between your finger and thumb — clay will feel powdery and silt will feel "gritty." You might also wish to procure a binocular microscope so that students can observe the finer-grained sediments more closely. Ask students or your school's physical education teacher to provide samples of sports balls for **Steps 3–6**. The items used in the activity do not need to exactly correspond to those listed in the table on page F10 — just use what is available and get a range of sizes.

For **Part B** of this investigation, you will need to provide your students with sand, silt, and clay so that students can compare the quality of fossil impressions formed in sediments of different sizes. You will also need as many small plastic containers as you have student groups. Each group will make three impressions (clamshell, leaf, slice of dried orange) in one of the three sizes of sediment. You ought to have at least two sets of impressions per sediment size in the event of breakage and to enable students to compare results across groups (i.e., evaluate reliability). You will need water, petroleum jelly, and a sufficient quantity of plaster of Paris to make the impressions (these need not be very thick). If you want to reduce the time needed for this activity, prepare the impressions yourself ahead of time and have students study the impressions.

Teacher Commentary

Materials
Part A
- small amount of each sediment type for observation: clay, fine sand, and coarse sand
- magnifier
- microscope (optional)
- sheet of white paper and black paper
- different-sized spherical objects (i.e., marbles, table-tennis balls, tennis balls, softballs, volleyballs, soccer balls, and basketballs—about three per group)
- metric measuring tape
- calculator (optional)

Part B
- newspapers to cover desk
- petroleum jelly
- small container
- sample of **one** of the following: clay, fine sand, or coarse sand (enough to fill a small container to a depth of about 1 cm)
- plaster (molding plaster or plaster of Paris)
- water supply
- plastic spoon
- leaf, clamshell, and piece of dried fruit

Investigating Water as a Resource

INVESTIGATING FOSSILS

Materials Needed

For this investigation your group will need:
- small amount of each sediment type: clay, fine sand, and coarse sand
- magnifier
- microscope (optional)
- sheet of white paper and black paper
- different-sized spherical objects (i.e., marbles, table-tennis balls, tennis balls, softballs, volleyballs, soccer balls, and basketballs—about three per group)
- metric measuring tape
- calculator (optional)
- newspapers to cover desk
- petroleum jelly
- small container
- plaster (molding plaster or plaster of Paris)
- water supply
- plastic spoon
- leaf, clamshell, and piece of dried fruit

Investigation 2:

Sediment Size and Fossil Formation

Key Question

Before you begin, first think about this key question.

Does sediment size affect how fossils form?

Think about what you know about how a fossil forms. If an animal dies and is buried by gravel, is it as likely to become a body fossil as when it is buried by mud? How might the size of grains of sediment affect whether or not a trace fossil can be formed?

Share your thinking with others in your group and with your class.

Investigate

Part A: Ranking Sediment According to Size

1. In your group, take a close look at samples of three different materials: clay, fine sand, and coarse sand.

Investigating Earth Systems

Teacher Commentary

Key Question

Use the **Key Question** as a brief warm-up activity to elicit students' ideas about the importance of sediment size on fossil formation. Emphasize thinking and sharing of ideas. Make students feel comfortable sharing their ideas by avoiding commentary on the accuracy of responses.

Have students read and record their answer to the **Key Question** in their journals. Ask for a volunteer to record responses on the chalkboard or overhead projector. This allows you to circulate among the students, encouraging them to copy the notes in an organized way. Discuss students' ideas about whether or not sediment size affects how fossils form.

Student Conceptions about Sediment Size and Fossil Formation

Some students may have had experience with sediment, and they may have some intuitive or experienced-based ideas about how the size of sediment might affect the quality of a fossil impression. Most will have played with sand and probably clay. However, they are unlikely to have considered these materials in terms of particle size. They may think of sand as being made up of grains, but they may not know that sand comes in different grain sizes (fine sand, coarse sand). Students may think of clay as being more like a thick paste, or like PlayDoh™, and not realize that it, too, is made of tiny particles. Clay particles are so small that they are difficult or impossible to see with the naked eye. Much of their knowledge about sediment depends on where students live. Those who live near slow-moving rivers, river plains, deltas, or large lakes may see sediment often. They may not, however, think of it as sediment. If students live near or have visited the coast, they will be more familiar with particles of sand.

About the Photo

The photograph shows La Brea Tar Pits, Los Angeles. The figures seen in the photo are models of mammoths that lived during the Pleistocene. Tar pits form when crude oil seeps to the surface through fissures in the Earth's crust; the light fraction of the oil evaporates, leaving behind the heavy tar, or asphalt, in sticky pools. The La Brea tar pits hold one of the richest, best preserved, and best studied assemblages of Pleistocene vertebrates, including at least 59 species of mammal and over 135 species of bird. The tar-pit fossils provide a record of life in southern California from 40,000 to 8000 years ago, including 660 species of vertebrates, plants, mollusks, and insects. Initially, people thought that the bones found in the tar were unfortunate cattle. It was not until 1901 that scientists began excavating the pits. (University of California Museum of Paleontology)

Answer for the Teacher Only
The finer the sediment, the greater the level of detail preserved in a fossil. Finer sediment also reduces the flow of water with oxygen to an organism that has died and become buried. As students learned in **Investigation 1**, burial in fine sediment slows the rate of decomposition.

> **Assessment Tool**
> Key-Question Evaluation Sheet
> Use this evaluation sheet to help students to understand and internalize basic expectations for the warm-up activity.

Investigate
Teaching Suggestions and Sample Answers

Students begin **Part A** of the investigation by comparing sediment of different sizes. Because it is difficult to comprehend the size differences between fine-grained sediment, students use spheres (sports balls) as an analogy for comparing the sizes. The investigation gives students an opportunity to use mathematics in their exploration of science concepts.

Part A: Ranking Sediment According to Size
1. Distribute materials to students. Tell students that the first few steps of the investigation will help them become familiar with different sizes of sediment. They will have to make careful observations and look closely for subtle differences at a small scale.

Teacher Commentary

NOTES

Investigating Fossils – Investigation 2

Investigating Fossils

Investigation 2: Sediment Size and Fossil Formation

Conduct Investigations

Place a small amount of each of these particles on white paper and also on black paper.

Look at them first with the unaided eye, then with a magnifier, and, if possible, through a microscope. Compare the sizes of grains of sediment for the three samples.

a) Which grains are largest, which are medium-sized, and which are smallest?

Evidence for Ideas

b) If you were to compare the sizes of the grains quantitatively (using numbers rather than just ranking them), how many times larger do you think the largest grain is, compared to the medium grain? How many times larger do you think the medium grain is, compared to the smallest grain?

Collect & Review

c) If you have access to a microscope with a scale, measure the size of the grains. You may have to measure several grains of each sediment and average the values. Record your results in your journal.

2. Sediment can range in size from large boulders to microscopic flakes of clay. Using a simple analogy, you can get a better idea of how the particle sizes compare with one another.

Obtain at least three different-sized spherical objects. Examples of some objects you can use are given on the following page.

Design Investigations

Discuss how you could measure them.

Share your method with other groups and agree on a single method of measurement for the whole class. It is also important to use the same unit of measurement—metric units are highly recommended.

a) Record your method and the units you chose to use in your journal.

Inquiry
Using Measurements

Measurements are important when collecting data. In this investigation your group will need to agree on the measurement units you will use. Consider the United States system of measurement (inches) or metric measurement (millimeters, centimeters). Be sure to have good reasons for what you decide.

Teacher Commentary

1. a) Of the samples students are given to examine, clay particles are the smallest, silt is medium-sized, and sand is the coarsest.

   b) Answers will vary. Students might guess that the largest grains are 10 to 50 times larger than the smallest grains.

   c) Coarse sand (approximately 2.0 mm in diameter) is 500 times larger than the largest clay particle (0.004 mm). A student can make this calculation using the data provided in the table on page F11.

   ## Teaching Tips
   If your students are using a binocular microscope to compare particle sizes, have them put a transparent metric ruler (with black markings) on the stage of the microscope to give them a sense of scale.

   It is very important that students do not get the impression that the only form of sediment is that which has formed from physical weathering (clastic sediment). This is the sediment type that they will be observing because it is the most readily available. A large part of the sedimentary record originates from the chemical precipitation of minerals, and it can be argued that these sediments preserve a larger part of the fossil record than those from clastic sedimentary settings. Make sure your students understand the distinction between clastic and chemical rocks, that both can preserve fossils, but that, in this investigation, they are focusing only on the fossilization process in clastic sediments.

2. Knowing that coarse sand is 500 times as large as coarse clay will not mean as much to students as a physical comparison of common objects. The sport ball activity is a model for using rank ordering in comparing sizes of objects. Once your students have established the idea that rank ordering is a legitimate method of comparing sizes, it will be easier for them to do the particle size comparison.

   a) Students might find some creative ways to measure the sports balls. Some will simply hold up a straight ruler and try to gauge the radius or diameter. Others may use string or a tape measure to wrap around a ball. Encourage different approaches to begin with. Ultimately, though, all students will need to agree upon a standard method and unit so that they can compare their data. What is important here is not so much the actual unit of measurement but the method of comparing sizes. In the end, you want students to understand that grain sizes of different sedimentary rocks can be compared to each other by using rank ordering and ratios.

Teaching Tips

This is a good opportunity to consult with the students' mathematics and geography teachers because scale is important for map reading. If you are short on time, you may want to have your students agree on their overall method of measurement in advance. This would reduce the time needed to reach a consensus, but will also limit the experience your students have with measuring and comparing.

Links with the rock cycle: Although this investigation focuses primarily on how sedimentary rock particles affect the likelihood of fossilization, an understanding of the rock cycle will better help students to appreciate this whole process. Their greatest difficulty will be to comprehend the time element involved in the rock cycle. However, if students have already completed the *Investigating Soil* module, they will have had some experience with rock abrasion and weathering processes (physical, chemical, and biological). In any event, what students do in this investigation will help them to become more knowledgeable about the rock cycle.

Teacher Commentary

NOTES

Investigating Fossils – Investigation 2

INVESTIGATING FOSSILS

3. When your group has measured the spheres, share the results. Devise a good way to display the whole class's results, perhaps on a chalkboard, dry-erase board, or overhead transparency sheet.

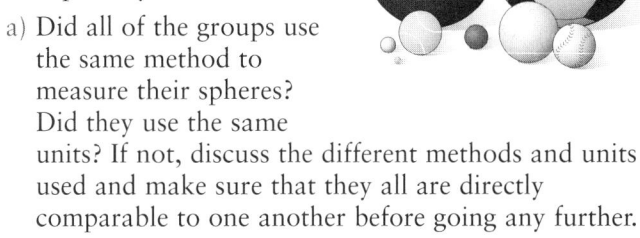

   a) Did all of the groups use the same method to measure their spheres? Did they use the same units? If not, discuss the different methods and units used and make sure that they all are directly comparable to one another before going any further.

   b) When all groups have contributed their data, create a chart in your journal. Design it like the one shown below (for convenience later on, list the spherical objects in descending order of size). Calculate and record the class's average measurement for each item.

Class Results from Measurements for Sizes of Spheres		
Object	Class's Average Measurement (include units)	Comparison
basketball		
soccer ball		
volleyball		
softball		
tennis ball		
table-tennis ball		
marble		
other		

4. Choose a way of comparing the sizes (ratio, percent, or other method) and record this in your journal. For example, is a soccer ball 100 times larger than a tennis ball? Five times? Is a table-tennis ball twice the size of a marble? How can you calculate this?

Teacher Commentary

> **Teaching Tip**
> To help your students become more adept in working with metric units, you might want to give them a weekend task of observing and recording as many uses of metric units as they can. Make a whole-class chart of their findings. Places where they are likely to find them include:
> - food packages (including beverage cans)
> - clothing patterns
> - international sports broadcasts
> - measuring cups and spoons
> - medicine droppers
> - rulers and measuring tapes
> - speedometers
> - cookbooks

3. Lead a class discussion of students' results.

   a) Answers will vary. It is important to discuss methods of measurement because variations in methods, as well as accuracy of measurements, need to be accounted for when comparing and averaging data. Help students to appreciate this important aspect of scientific inquiry.

   b) You can make an overhead transparency of **Blackline Master** *Fossils* 2.1: **Data Table for Class Results from Measurements for Sizes of Spheres** and use this to record results (averages) in a class discussion. An example of a comparison of sediment sizes is provided on the following page.

> **Teaching Tip**
> You may wish to use the following **Blackline Masters** to make overheads to use when discussing students' results:
> - *Fossils* 2.1, Data Table for Class Results from Measurements for Sizes of Spheres
> - *Fossils* 2.2, Data Table for Size of Different Sediment Types

> **Making Connections...with Mathematics**
> You might find it useful to coordinate this activity with the students' mathematics teacher so that methods of measuring spheres and ratios can be included as topics in other classes.

4. This is an opportunity for you to introduce the idea of a ratio, or comparisons between two numbers. Remind students that a comparison of numbers can be written as a ratio in different ways. For example, the ratio of the number of teachers to the number of students can be written as

   $$1 \text{ to } 25 \text{ ;} \qquad 1:25 \text{ ;} \qquad \text{or } \frac{1}{25}$$

   The order of the terms in a ratio is important, and the terms of the ratio must be in the same units of measurement.

Investigating Fossils – Investigation 2

Investigation 2: Sediment Size and Fossil Formation

Discuss the comparison method as a class.

a) When all groups are in agreement, record your comparison for each item. Include all calculations in your journal. If you use a calculator, include the setup for your calculations.

5. Copy the chart shown below into your journal:

Size of Different Sediment Types

Sediment Type	Size Range (particle diameter)	Comparison
Very Coarse Sand	1.0–2.0 mm	
Coarse Sand	0.5–1.0 mm	
Medium Sand	0.25–0.50 mm	
Fine Sand	0.125–0.250 mm	
Very Fine Sand	0.0625–0.1250 mm	
Silt	0.0040–0.0625 mm	
Clay	< 0.004 mm	

Using the same comparison method, compare the sediment types in the chart. Because the values are given as a *range*, not an average, you may want to use the largest (or smallest) value in the range to compare.

a) Record your size comparisons in your journal.

b) Which four spherical objects best represent the relative sizes of the four sediment grains?

6. Discuss your group's results with the rest of the class.

a) Explain your comparisons mathematically. How did you arrive at your numbers?

b) Did your group do anything different, compared to other groups? Explain.

Part B: Sediment Grain Size and Fossilization

1. Suppose a group of marine snails is buried in sediment after dying. By chance, one snail gets buried by coarse sand, another by fine sand, and a third by clay. In your group, discuss the questions on the following page.

Inquiry

Using Mathematics

Using mathematics as a tool helps scientists to be more precise about the observations they make. Data often consists of numbers and calculations. In this investigation you used calculations to make size comparisons.

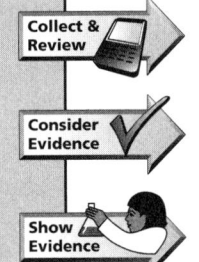

Teacher Commentary

a) Answers will vary. Students should provide calculations as evidence to support their claims about comparisons between objects.

5. The main point of comparing the range of sports-ball sizes to sediment grain size is that sports balls are visible, are easily measured, and have about the same size range as grains, from large to small. In these two data tables, the baseball is the rough equivalent of a coarse sand grain in terms of the size ratios.

   a) Students will find that clay is too fine to use as a comparator because it is has a diameter 1/500th that of very coarse sand. That would produce a comparison greater than the range of sizes of sports balls (a basketball is only about 40 times larger in diameter than a small marble). Using the coarsest silt (0.0625 mm) as a comparator provides the following comparisons. (Note: these are only examples to use as a guide rather than a scoring key. Each sediment comparison is from the coarsest silt to the coarsest grain size of each respective category. Your results may vary due to a variety of factors, most notably the air pressure in the inflatable sports balls.):

Sample Data Table: Sizes and Comparisons of Different types of Sediments and Spheres

Sediment Type	Size Range (particle diameter in mm)	Comparison coarsest to silt	Sphere	Diameter (in cm)	Comparison to small marble*
Very Coarse Sand	1.0-2.0	32	Basketball	35.0	36
Coarse Sand	0.5-1.0	16	Volleyball	20.6	24
Medium Sand	0.25-0.50	8	Baseball	7.25	8
Fine Sand	0.125-0.250	4	Table-tennis ball	3.72	4
Very Fine Sand	0.0625-0.1250	2	Marble	1.45	2
Silt	0.004-0.0625	1	Small marble	0.95	1
Clay	< 0.004				

*(rounded to nearest whole number)

   b) Answers will vary depending upon how students make comparisons. Seven sizes of sediment grains are listed in the table on page F11. A sample comparison chart for six kinds of spheres (using a small marble as a comparator) is shown in the chart above. This comparison produces a fair match to comparisons between sediment sizes. Students can conclude from this comparison that very coarse sand is about as many times larger than coarse silt as a basketball is larger than a small marble.

6. Students might need reminding that the metric system uses base 10. This means that all metric measures (linear, mass, volume, and others) are founded on units of 10. They may not easily recognize or appreciate that the English units are much more varied (four quarts in a gallon, three feet in one yard, and so on). The metric system is therefore easier to use. To convert one metric linear measure to another,

(for example, centimeters to millimeters) you just move the decimal point to the right or the left (millimeters to centimeters). It may help to have students think of money as a familiar base 10 number system.

- a) Answers will vary. Students should note what they based their comparisons upon. Chances are that they will compare various sediment types to silt or very fine sand and compare various kinds of spheres to a marble.

- b) Almost certainly each group will come up with its own methods of comparison. This is acceptable, so long as comparisons are valid and the measurement and mathematics are sound.

Part B: Sediment Grain Size and Fossilization

This part of the investigation builds upon the understanding of differences in sediment sizes developed in **Part A**, and is a direct exploration of the **Key Question**: Does sediment size affect how fossils form? In **Investigate, Part B**, students will examine the practical effects of sediment sizes on fossilization by building and testing models of fossil impressions. They begin by making predictions (which sediment size will leave the best impression, and why?), then they test their predictions using a clamshell, a leaf, and a slice of dried fruit.

1. Encourage students to discuss these questions carefully. They need to pool their experience and observations to figure out which grain size is more, or less, likely to produce a better impression, and why.

Teacher Commentary

NOTES

Investigating Fossils

INVESTIGATING FOSSILS

Inquiry
Hypotheses

A hypothesis is a testable statement or idea about how something works. It is based on what you think that you know or already understand. A hypothesis is never a guess. A hypothesis forms the basis for making a prediction and is used to design an experiment or observation. Guesses can be useful in science, but they are not hypotheses.

- Which sediment size do you think is likely to leave the most detailed impression of each of these items, and why?
- Which would make the least accurate impression, and why?
- Suppose that the snails were moving across the three kinds of sediment before their death. In which sediment is a trace fossil most likely to form? Why?

a) Record the results of your discussion in your journal. These are your predictions. Now you are going to have a chance to test them.

2. Your group will make an impression of a clamshell, a leaf, and a piece of dried fruit, using one of three sediments: coarse sand, fine sand, or clay. Then you will make an impression "fossil."

To share the work, each group will be responsible for one sediment sample. However, each group will test the same items and follow the same procedure.

Teacher Commentary

a) Answers will vary. Accept all reasonable answers supported by reasons (the "and why?" part of each question). Students are likely to predict that finer sediment will leave a more detailed impression. They may draw upon prior experience (the detail in footprints left in fine, dry soil compared to less detail preserved in footprints left in sand). Students may say that fine sediment will leave a better impression or trace than coarse sediment because fine sediment "sticks together better" than coarse sediment, which is a reasonable argument.

2. At a minimum, the class should make six containers of fossil impressions (two sets of three impressions in each of three different sizes of sediment). Depending upon the availability of materials, you may want nine or 12 sets of impressions (12 groups). Keep in mind that the fewer impressions you make, the less reliable the results because variability in how impressions are made has the potential to outweigh the effects of sediment size (e.g., pressing the leaf more firmly in the silt than in the clay). Take advantage of the opportunity to discuss reliability in experimentation with students.

Investigation 2: Sediment Size and Fossil Formation

Conduct Investigations

Here is the procedure for making impressions:
- Protect the surface of your desk by covering it with newspaper.
- Label a small container with the name of your group.
- Lubricate the insides of the container with petroleum jelly. (The container should be just big enough so that the leaf, the clamshell, and the fruit fit, with minimal extra space.)
- Add 1 cm of sediment (clay, fine sand, or coarse sand) to the container.
- Place each item on the bed of sediment.
- Gently push each item into the sediment. Hold it there for a moment, then carefully remove it and set it aside.
- Mix water with molding plaster or plaster of Paris. Stir and continue adding water until it has the consistency of thin pancake batter.
- Carefully spread an even layer of plaster on top of the imprint.
- Gently tap the sides of your container for one or two minutes. You should see tiny air bubbles come to the surface.
- Let the plaster harden overnight.

3. Carefully remove the plaster from the container, disposing of the sediment as directed by your teacher. Gently rinse and dry the plaster.

Collect & Review

Using a magnifying glass, observe the objects that were used to make the imprint.

Evidence for Ideas

a) Can you see their features in the plaster?

b) Is there any variation between the objects used to make the impression, and the quality of the impression? Explain.

Show Evidence

4. Prepare a display of your impression fossils, labeling the type of sediment used.

5. Observe other groups' impression fossils.

Evidence for Ideas

a) Which sediment type made the most detailed impression?

Investigating Earth Systems

F 13

Teacher Commentary

> **Teaching Tip**
> If you teach this module to several classes a day, or if you wish to save time, consider making the models in one class (or making them yourself ahead of time) and allowing students to study the finished models.

3. Advise students not to touch the surfaces of the impressions. Abrasion through handling can degrade or destroy the quality of the impression. You can point out to students that this is why paleontologists are often seen cleaning fossils with fine paintbrushes.

    a) Students should be able to see general features in the clay and silt and may even be able to see some basic features of the fossils in sand.

    b) In sand and silt, clamshells with deep growth ridges (see the illustration on page F44 of the Student Book) typically will make better fossil impressions than dried fruit or leaves. Exceptionally fine detail of leaf impressions can be preserved in clay on occasion.

4. This is an opportunity for you to draw students' attention to the value of finding clear, organized, and accurate ways of showing their findings to others. Encourage groups to be creative in the way they do this and to make sure that results are clear to others. Clear labels and good organization are both part of this. Remind students that all groups will be looking at each other's work.

5. a) Clay generally yields the most detailed impressions.

INVESTIGATING FOSSILS

b) Which sediment type made the least detailed impression?

c) Give evidence to explain your answers.

d) Do you accept your original prediction or do you reject it?

6. Discuss the results with the rest of the class.

a) What generalization can you make about sediment size and its relationship to imprint fossils? Is there agreement among your classmates about this generalization?

b) What are other kinds of fossils that you know about?

Do you think that the same relationship between sediment type and fossilization would be seen with other kinds of fossils as well? Explain your answer.

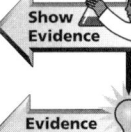

As You Read...
Think about:
1. *How are silt, clay, and mud related in terms of sediment size?*
2. *What are two ways that sediment is formed?*
3. *In what kind of sedimentary rock are fossils most common? Why?*
4. *Compare and contrast the formation of a mold fossil and a cast fossil.*

Digging Deeper

FOSSILIZATION AND SEDIMENT SIZE

Sediments

Sediment ranges in size from large boulders to very fine mud. Sediments coarser than 2 mm (millimeters) are called gravel. Sand is defined as sediment with sizes between one-sixteenth of a millimeter and 2 mm. All sediment finer than sand is called mud. The coarser part of the mud is called silt, and the finer part is called clay.

Sediments are formed when rocks on the land surface are broken down by rain, wind, and sunlight. Sediments consist of particles of minerals, and also loose pieces of rock. Streams and rivers move the sediments downstream toward the ocean. Some of the sediment is stored in large river valleys, but most of it reaches the ocean. Some is deposited in shallow water near the shore, and some is carried far out into the deep

Teacher Commentary

b) Sand generally yields the least detailed impressions.

c) Students should cite examples of detail that they observe in the impressions. For example, fine patterns of veins in leafs are often visible in clay impressions.

d) Reviewing predictions should not be a formality. When students form a prediction based on all the information and experience they have, they have a personal stake in the result. If their prediction proves correct, it can validate their reasoning. If the prediction proves incorrect, it challenges their reasoning and prompts them to reconsider their ideas. Either way, this can become a key learning moment for students.

6. Allow adequate time for students to consider the overall results of their investigations. Be alert to findings that stand out or seem inconsistent. Help everyone to reach conclusions that represent a fair analysis of their findings.

   a) Most classes will generalize that the finer the sediment size, the more detailed the resulting fossil impression. Classmates might disagree, and disagreements should be settled by reexamining the evidence.

   b) Answers may vary. Students might cite trace fossils or molds.

Students should note that the generalization for impressions should hold for other kinds of fossils. For example, fossil footprints in sandstone should provide less detail than fossil footprints made in clay-size sediment.

Assessment Tools

Journal-Entry Evaluation Sheet
Use this sheet as a general guideline for assessing student journals, adapting it to your classroom if desired.

Journal-Entry Checklist
Use this checklist as a guide for quickly checking the quality and completeness of journal entries.

Digging Deeper

This section provides text and photos that give students greater insight into the topics of sediment size and fossil formation. You may wish to assign the **As You Read** questions as homework to help students focus on the major ideas in the text.

As You Read...
Think about:
1. Mud is sediment made up of silt-size and clay-size particles. Silt is more coarse (is made of larger particles) than clay.

2. Sediments are particles of minerals and loose pieces of rock. Sediment forms when rocks at the Earth's surface are broken down by rain, wind, and sunlight. Sediment can also be formed when calcium carbonate minerals are precipitated from warm, shallow waters in the ocean.

3. Fossils are most common in limestones because most limestones consist partly or mostly of the shells of organisms.

4. Cast fossils and mold fossils are alike in that they are most often fossils from shells. Molds form when the shell dissolves, leaving behind an imprint of the shell in the rock. Casts form when the space that was occupied by the shell is filled with minerals precipitated by the water that flows through rock and the precipitated material takes the shape of the original shell.

Assessment Opportunity
You may wish to select questions from the **As You Read** section to use as quizzes, rephrasing the questions into multiple choice or true/false format. This provides assessment information about student understanding and serves as a motivational tool to ensure that students complete the reading assignment in an effort to comprehend the main ideas.

Teacher Commentary

NOTES

Investigation 2: Sediment Size and Fossil Formation

ocean. Most of the sediment deposited near the shore is coarse, and it gets finer farther away from the shore. Most of the sediment in the deep ocean is very fine mud.

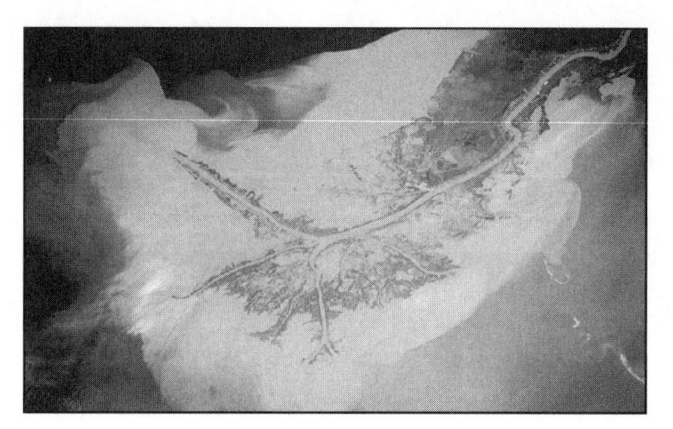

Sediments are also formed when calcium carbonate minerals are precipitated from warm, shallow waters in the ocean. Much of this is used by marine animals to make their skeletons. After the animals die, their skeletons become sediment. Where currents are weak, this sediment stays where the animals lived. Where currents are strong, the shells are moved along the bottom and are worn into rounded particles.

Fossils in Sedimentary Rocks

In certain conditions, and over a very long period of time, sediment becomes compacted and cemented into sedimentary rock. Fossils are more common in some kinds of sedimentary rocks than others. There are many factors that can contribute to the likelihood of an organism being preserved as a fossil. You investigated one of these, grain size, in this investigation. Fossils are most common in limestones. That is because most limestones consist partly or mostly of the shells of

Teacher Commentary

About the Photo

This aerial photograph of the Mississippi River delta shows sediment transport and deposition. Point out to students how the light brown discoloration in the water appears to fade as you look farther from the river channel. Typically, the coarsest sediment settles out closer to the river channel because of the loss in energy of transport when the river enters the ocean. The farther you move away from the mouth of the river, the finer the sediment that is carried and deposited.

INVESTIGATING FOSSILS

organisms. Sometimes, however, the shells are worn so much that they look like ocean sediment grains rather than "real" fossils. Fossils are also common in shales, which form from muds. As you have already learned, excellent imprint fossils can be formed in fine-grained sediments like muds. Only some shales contain fossils, however, because many areas of muddy ocean floor had conditions that were not suitable for animal life. In this case, only swimming or drifting organisms that die and fall into the mud have a chance to become fossilized. Although this does happen, it is a very rare occurrence. Some sandstones contain fossils as well. Most sandstones do not contain fossils, for various reasons. Water currents in the environment might have been too strong for animals to survive. Also, sands are very porous, so water seeping through the sand might have dissolved the shells away long before the sand was buried and changed into sandstone.

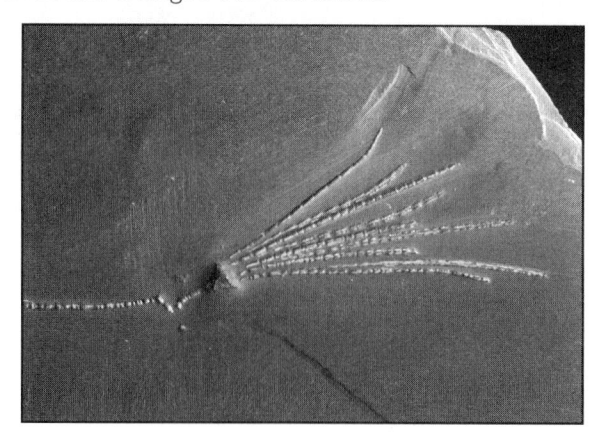

Kinds of Fossils

Sediments are home for many kinds of marine animals. Some animals live on the surface of the sediment, and some burrow into it. Some fossil shells are found mixed with the mud they lived in. Other fossil shells were

Teacher Commentary

About the Photos

The photo shows pyritized crinozoan from the Hunsrück Shale, Lower Devonian, Germany. Sometime after burial, the calcium carbonate shell of this crinoid (ancient "sea lily") was replaced by iron sulfide (FeS_2), which is the mineral pyrite and is sometimes called "fool's gold." Shale is a rock made from the lithification of clay. The fine sediment size can yield exceptional detail in fossils found in shale.

Investigation 2: Sediment Size and Fossil Formation

moved by strong currents and deposited along with sand or even gravel. If the shells are buried by more sediment before they are worn away or dissolved, they become fossilized.

Sometimes a fossil consists of original shell material. This is common in very young sediments that have not yet been turned into rock. Older sediments usually have been buried deeply by later sediments and turned into rock. Then it is more likely that the original shell has been dissolved away by water seeping through the pore spaces in the sediment. The fossil is left as an imprint of the original shell. An imprint like that is called a mold. Sometimes the space that was occupied by the shell is now empty. In other cases that space has been filled with later minerals that were precipitated by the flowing pore water. That material, which has the shape of the original shell, is called a cast.

Clams have shells that are in two parts, called valves. The valves are hinged along one edge. They are left and right, like your hands when you put them together along your little fingers. The clam can open its shell to feed and close its shell for protection. Think about what you might see when the clamshell is fossilized. Each valve has an outer surface and an inner surface. Depending on which valve you are seeing, and whether you are seeing the inside or the outside of it, and whether you are seeing its cast or its mold, eight different views are possible! Paleontologists have to be very careful to match up the fossils they see. Otherwise, they might think they are seeing fossils of several different kinds of animal rather than just one.

Teacher Commentary

About the Photos

The upper photograph shows fossil casts of brachiopods in limestone. Casts are formed when minerals are precipitated in the empty spaces inside of shells. The lower photograph shows molds of brachiopods in a fossiliferous limestone. Molds are the imprints of the original shells that remain after the shell has been dissolved by pore water in the sediment or rock. Ask students to look at the photographs carefully and distinguish between the fossil casts and molds.

INVESTIGATING FOSSILS

Review and Reflect

Review

1. Choose several objects from everyday life and compare them to the sizes of gravel, sand, and mud.
2. Give two reasons why fossils are relatively uncommon in sandstones.

Reflect

3. Think back to **Part B** of the investigation. Explain why you think that the clamshell made a better impression in fine-grained sediment than in the coarse-grained sediment.
4. From what you have learned in this investigation, do you think that a sandy beach is a good place for fossils to be preserved? Why or why not?

Thinking about the Earth System

5. Where do sediments come from? Describe any connections that you can make between the hydrosphere, the atmosphere, and the geosphere in the formation of sand and mud deposits. Note these on your *Earth System Connection* sheet.
6. How is the biosphere related to the formation of some sediments? Note any connections between the biosphere and sediment formation on your *Earth System Connection* sheet.

Thinking about Scientific Inquiry

7. How did you use mathematics in this investigation?
8. How did you support a prediction with evidence?
9. Describe how you modeled the process of fossilization in this investigation. In what ways was your model like the natural process of fossilization? In what ways was it different?

Teacher Commentary

Review and Reflect

Review

Before this investigation, many students might have had little idea about how sediment grain size might affect the chances of fossilization. You might need to remind students that smaller grains pack around an object more closely, thus increasing the definition of a fossil. One way to help reinforce this idea is to ask students to think about surrounding themselves with sports balls. For example, being buried in golf balls, which then are glued together, would produce quite a different result from being buried in basketballs in the same way.

Help your students to see that science investigations, while providing some answers to scientific questions, more often than not raise additional questions for investigation. Take time for students to talk about these possible questions.

1. Answers will vary. A reasonable comparison might be a house (gravel), tool shed (sand), and doll house (mud).

2. Fossils are less common in sandstone because water currents in places where sand is deposited might have been too strong for animals to survive. Another reason is that the high porosity of sands allows water to seep through sediment and rock, which leads to decomposition of soft tissue and dissolution of shells or bones.

Reflect

Give your students time to reflect on the nature of the evidence they have generated from their investigations. Help them to see that evidence is crucial in scientific inquiry.

3. Answers may vary. Students may suggest that grains of sand are too large to preserve fine detail or that grains of sand may not pack into the spaces between the ridges of the clamshell.

4. Students will most likely note that a sandy beach is not a good place for fossils to form. Sand tends not to preserve fine detail in fossils. When an organism dies on an exposed beach, it is more likely to be scavenged and scattered, or its footprints more likely to be erased (blown smooth) by the wind.

Thinking about the Earth System

Because the overall goal is for students to understand key aspects of the Earth system by the time they complete grade 8, they need time to make any connections they can between what they have done in this investigation and the Earth system. Ask students to revisit their *Earth Systems Connection* sheets. Encourage them to write in any new connections they have found. Remind them that they will be updating and adding to this sheet at the end of each investigation. Refer students to page Fx of their books as a means of exploring the Earth system further.

5. Students may refer to the satellite photograph of the river delta and note that rivers (the hydrosphere) can deposit sand and mud. The atmosphere plays a role in the deposition of sand and mud when strong winds pick up and deposit sediment. The atmosphere and hydrosphere thus act to sculpt and modify the geosphere, removing sediment in one place and depositing it somewhere else.

6. Some sediments consist entirely of material produced by the biosphere. Fossiliferous limestone, a sedimentary rock made up almost entirely of the shells of marine invertebrates, is such an example.

Thinking about Scientific Inquiry

In this investigation, your students have used mathematical ideas of measurement, scale, and ratio as scientific tools. Help them to understand the importance of mathematics for scientific inquiry. Students have also used a form of modeling to test the impression-forming properties of different grain sizes of clastic sediment. Spend time helping them to appreciate the value of modeling. In addition, help students to understand how they used other inquiry processes to find evidence to develop their ideas, and to prepare a presentation of their findings.

7. Answers will vary. Students should note the measured diameters, calculated ratios, and other numerical comparisons.

8. Students supported their predictions about the relationship between sediment size and the detail of fossil impressions using evidence gathered by making and comparing models of fossil impressions in sediments of different sizes.

9. See answer to **Question 8** above. Students should note that impressions are a type of fossil, so their models are very similar to a type of fossilization. The differences between the models and the real world include condensed time factor, use of plaster of Paris to make impressions, virtual absence of water in the model, and lack of disturbance (i.e., protection of the model during the fossilization process).

Assessment Tool
Review and Reflect Journal-Entry Evaluation Sheet
Use this evaluation sheet for assessing content and thoroughness of student work, whether you have students complete the work individually or within a group. Adapt and modify the sheet to meet your needs. Consider involving students in selecting and modifying the assessment criteria.

Teacher Commentary

NOTES

Teacher Review

Use this section to reflect on and review the investigation. Keep in mind that your notes here are likely to be especially helpful when you teach this investigation again. Questions listed here are examples only.

Student Achievement

What evidence do you have that all students have met the science content objectives?

Are there any students who need more help in reaching these objectives? If so, how can you provide this?

What evidence do you have that all students have demonstrated their understanding of the inquiry processes?

Which of these inquiry objectives do your students need to improve upon in future investigations?

What evidence do the journal entries contain about what your students learned from this investigation?

Planning

How well did this investigation fit into your class time?

What changes can you make to improve your planning next time?

Guiding and Facilitating Learning

How well did you focus and support inquiry while interacting with students?

What changes can you make to improve classroom management for the next investigation or the next time you teach this investigation?

Teacher Commentary

How successful were you in encouraging all students to participate fully in science learning? _____

_____

How did you encourage and model the skills values, and attitudes of scientific inquiry? _____

_____

How did you nurture collaboration among students? _____

_____

Materials and Resources

What challenges did you encounter obtaining or using materials and/or resources needed for the activity? _____

_____

What changes can you make to better obtain and better manage materials and resources next time? _____

_____

Student Evaluation

Describe how you evaluated student progress. What worked well? What needs to be improved? _____

_____

How will you adapt your evaluation methods for next time? _____

_____

Describe how you guided students in self-assessment. _____

_____

Self Evaluation

How would you rate your teaching of this investigation? _____

_____

What advice would you give to a colleague who is planning to teach this investigation? _____

_____

NOTES

Teacher Commentary

INVESTIGATION 3: CONDITIONS FOR FOSSIL FORMATION

Background Information

The Likelihood of Fossilization
Bones, teeth, shells, and other hard body parts are relatively easily preservable as fossils, although they may become broken, worn, or even dissolved before they are buried by sediment. The soft bodies of organisms, on the other hand, are relatively difficult to preserve. Special conditions of burial are needed to preserve organisms as delicate as, say, jellyfish. Sometimes such organisms fall to the muddy sea bottom in quiet water and are buried rapidly by more mud. Only in circumstances like that can such organisms be fossilized. For that reason, the fossil record of soft-bodied organisms is far less well known than the record of hard-bodied organisms. There is thus a strong bias in the fossil record. Some organisms rarely have the chance of becoming fossilized, but under very specific and geologically instantaneous circumstances, even these can become part of the fossil record. Other organisms or their body parts have a better chance of becoming part of the fossil record.

The fossil record is quite extensive: a few hundred thousand fossil species have been discovered and described. It has been estimated, however, that the total number of plant and animal species that exist today is four or five million. The average lifespan of species, from the time of origination to the time of extinction, is very poorly known but probably lies somewhere in the range from half a million years to five million years. Given the enormous duration of geologic time, the total number of species that have ever existed must be far greater than the number of species now living. This means that the fossil record represents a minuscule proportion of the total number of potentially fossilizable species. This underscores that body fossilization is an extremely rare event. Moreover, this is consistent with the general observation that a great many sedimentary rocks are loaded with trace fossils but contain few if any body fossils representing the organisms that generated the traces.

It is understandable that among the various groups of plant and animal species there are great differences in the potential for fossilization. It should seem almost like common sense to your students that something as durable as a clamshell has a much greater potential for fossilization than, say, a worm. In fact, the percentage of all species of robustly shelled organisms, like trilobites, mollusks, and brachiopods that are represented in the fossil record is fairly high, whereas the fossil record of worms is very scanty, even though there is good reason to believe that worm species have been abundant throughout the latter part of geologic time.

More Information...on the Web
Go to the *Investigating Earth Systems* web site www.agiweb.org/ies for links to a variety of other web sites that will help you deepen your understanding of content and prepare you to teach this module.

Investigation Overview

In this investigation, your students examine the school grounds for evidence of recently living things (animals and plants). They will assess the likelihood of any of these organisms ever becoming fossils. Evidence of recently living things should not be hard to find, certainly with plants. Of course, the chances of fossilization are very remote, but it is important that students understand the cycle of life, death, and decay. Following their field experience, student groups then model an example of how organic remains are buried in clastic sediment.

Goals and Objectives

As a result of this investigation, students will develop a better understanding of the conditions that favor the formation of fossils.

Science Content Objectives

Students will collect evidence that:

1. Fossils only form under certain conditions.
2. Conditions that retard decomposition contribute to fossil formation.
3. Fossil formation is a comparatively rare occurrence.
4. Fossil formation is connected to the biosphere, the hydrosphere, the atmosphere, and the geosphere.

Inquiry Process Skills

Students will:

1. Make observations about potential fossil-forming conditions around the school.
2. Generate questions about fossil formation.
3. Use models to investigate fossil-forming conditions.
4. Predict possible outcomes from the fossil-forming model.
5. Record observations from the model.
6. Make connections between the model and real-world conditions.
7. Communicate data and conclusions to others.

Connections to Standards and Benchmarks

In this investigation, your students will be investigating the conditions for fossil formation and the environments in which sediment is deposited and in which fossils can form. These observations will start them on the road to understanding the National Science Education Standards and AAAS Benchmarks shown on the next page.

Teacher Commentary

NSES Links

- Fossils provide important evidence of how life and environmental conditions have changed.
- Populations of organisms can be categorized by the function they serve in an ecosystem. Plants and some microorganisms are producers — they make their own food. All animals, including humans, are consumers, and obtain food by eating other organisms. Decomposers, primarily bacteria and fungi, are consumers that use waste materials and dead organisms for food.
- Models are tentative schemes or structures that correspond to real objects, events, or classes of events, and that have explanatory power. Models help scientists and engineers understand how things work.
- Landforms are the result of a combination of constructive and destructive forces. Constructive forces include crustal deformation, volcanic eruption, and deposition of sediment, while destructive forces include weathering and erosion.
- Some changes in the solid Earth can be described as the "rock cycle." Old rocks at the Earth's surface weather, forming sediments that are buried, then compacted, heated, and often recrystallized into new rock. Eventually, those new rocks may be brought to the surface by the forces that drive plate motions, and the rock cycle continues.
- Soil consists of weathered rocks and decomposed organic material from dead plants, animals, and bacteria. Soils are often found in layers, with each having a different chemical composition and texture.

AAAS Links

- Many thousands of layers of sedimentary rock provide evidence for the long history of the Earth and for the long history of changing life forms whose remains are found in the rocks. More recently deposited rock layers are more likely to contain fossils resembling existing species.
- Models are often used to think about processes that happen too slowly, too quickly, or on too small a scale to be observed directly, or that are too vast to be changed deliberately, or that are potentially dangerous.
- The cycling of water in and out of the atmosphere plays an important role in determining climatic patterns. Water evaporates from the surface of the Earth, rises and cools, condenses into rain or snow, and falls again to the surface. The water falling on land collects in rivers and lakes, soil, and porous layers of rock, and much of it flows back into the ocean.
- Many thousands of layers of sedimentary rock provide evidence for the long history of the Earth and for the long history of changing life forms whose remains are found in the rocks. More recently deposited rock layers are more likely to contain fossils resembling existing species.
- Two types of organisms may interact with one another in several ways: They may be involved in a producer/consumer, predator/prey, or parasite/host relationship.
- Over the whole Earth, organisms are growing, dying, and decaying, and new organisms are being produced by the old ones.

Preparation and Materials Needed

Preparation

This investigation requires about four to five 40-minute class periods to complete, depending on the depth of investigation and inquiry you have students pursue in **Investigate, Part A, Step 9**. If your school grounds do not provide access to grassy or wooded areas, consider having students complete **Part A, Step 1** at home under adult supervision.

- **Day One:** Have students address the **Key Question** and complete **Steps 1–2** of **Investigate Part A**, a study of potential fossilization on the school grounds.

- **Day Two:** Students can complete the modeling experiment in **Steps 3–8** of **Part A**. Assign the research project (**Step 9**) to students to complete over the next few days as a homework assignment.

- **Day Three:** Complete **Investigate Part B**, an activity on the factors that affect fossilization. Assign the **Digging Deeper** reading section and the **As You Read** questions for homework.

- **Day Four:** Review the main ideas of the reading. Ask students to present any results of research from **Part A**. Have students work through the **Review and Reflect** questions.

Before you take your students out on a walk around the school, be sure to check out the area yourself, so that you have a clear sense of where your students might find decaying matter. Suggestions can include:

- under stones, logs, and in the logs themselves
- under shrubs and trees
- in flower beds
- in compost heaps
- in gutters.

For **Investigate Part A (Steps 3–8)**, be sure that you set up the stream tables yourself ahead of time, so that you have a sense of how the activity works. You will need a supply of newspapers to put under the pans, and paper towels for spills. Small leaves and shells work best (large material may not be removed and transported down the stream table by the simulated rainfall and river currents). Use fine-grained sand. Coarse-grained sand will not work well with this model because it is not as easily eroded as fine-grained sand. Students can use watering cans with sprinkler attachments to simulate heavy rainfall. If your students pour a stream of water onto the sand too quickly, they will not get the same effect as a gentle sprinkling. They need to simulate rainfall, not a flood or cloudburst. It is important that the leaves be

Teacher Commentary

big enough to leave an impression but not so big that they cover too much of the sand. Make sure that the underwater leaf gets soaked ahead of time; otherwise it may float. Most small, delicate leaves can be used. Clamshells should be similar to the leaves in size. For the last step of the investigation, you might obtain copies of a local or regional topographic map so that students can relate their models of sediment deposition to a local real-world setting.

For **Part B** of the **Investigation**, make a photocopy of **Blackline Master** *Fossils* **3.1, Wheel of Fossilization** for each group. Students will use this as a cutout. You will need a supply of cardboard. To save time in the investigation, prepare the wheels yourself ahead of time and provide them to students.

Materials
Part A
- stream table, or similar setup
- wooden block (or books) to tilt stream table
- dry sand (as fine as possible)
- watering can
- water source
- 2 tree leaves, pre-soaked in water overnight
- 2 clamshells
- topographic map of your local area, or physical map of your region *

Part B
- photocopy of the "Wheel of Fossilization" on page F23 of the student text to use as a cutout, **Blackline Master** 3.1, **Wheel of Fossilization**.
- cardboard
- scissors
- sharpened pencil or dowel

* The *Investigating Earth Systems* web site (www.agiweb.org/ies/) provides suggestions for obtaining these resources.

Investigating Fossils – Investigation 3

Investigating Water as a Resource

Investigation 3: Conditions for Fossil Formation

Investigation 3:
Conditions for Fossil Formation

Key Question
Before you begin, first think about this key question.

Where can fossils form?

In the last activity you discovered that sediment size affects fossilization. Think about what you know about fossil formation. What other factors affect whether or not an organism becomes a fossil?

Share your thinking with others in your group and with your class. Keep a record of the discussion in your journal.

Materials Needed

For this investigation your group will need:
- stream table, or similar setup
- wooden block (or books) to tilt stream table
- dry sand (as fine as possible)
- watering can
- water source
- two tree leaves, pre-soaked in water overnight
- two clamshells
- topographic map of your local area, or physical map of your region
- cardboard
- set of compasses
- scissors
- protractor
- sharpened pencil or dowel

Investigate
Part A: Location, Location

1. With your group, examine your school grounds and, if possible, wooded or moist areas like stream banks, gullies, and along the shores of lakes. You may need to complete this part of the activity on a weekend at home or at a local park, under adult supervision.

Investigating Earth Systems
F 19

110 Investigating Earth Systems

Teacher Commentary

Key Question

Use this question as a brief warm-up activity to elicit students' ideas about the topic explored in the investigation. Tell students to write down their ideas in their journal. After a few minutes, hold a brief discussion. Emphasize thinking and sharing of ideas. Record all of the ideas on an overhead transparency or on the chalkboard.

Student Conceptions about Fossil Formation

Students should know that all living things eventually die. They may be less familiar with what happens to the remains of living things in the wild. In particular, they may be surprised at the amount of evidence of organic remains they can find, especially plant material. Animal remains may be harder to find. Although students may have seen animal road kills, they may not have seen animal remains in grassy or wooded areas. They may not realize how many of these remains quickly become food for other animals. Bear in mind that some students may find evidence of death and decay unpleasant. Looking upon this from a scientific point of view may help them to overcome this feeling.

Answer for the Teacher Only

Fossils are most likely to form in environments where the organism can be buried by sediment after death. The Earth-surface environments where sediments accumulate are highly varied. Sediments accumulate in lakes, in rivers, and in the ocean, both shallow and deep. You might suppose that because rivers are the principal means of erosion of the continents, they would not accumulate thick successions of sediments. In the lower courses of many river systems, however, the Earth's crust is undergoing slow subsidence, making way for continued deposition of sediment by the river. In some cases, thousands of meters of sediment can accumulate in this way. The greatest proportion of sediment is deposited in the oceans. Beaches, deltas, and broad continental shelves are important shallow depositional environments in the oceans. In the deep ocean, far from land, mostly fine sediment is deposited.

Assessment Tool

Key-Question Evaluation Sheet
Remind students to look at the criteria that outline the basic expectations for the warm-up activity. The evaluation sheet emphasizes that you want to see evidence of prior knowledge and that the students should communicate their thinking clearly.

> **About the Photo**
> Swamps provide an environment for preservation and fossilization of plant and animal life. The photograph provides abundant evidence of life and decay. Recently, one of the most complete fossil mastodons was discovered while a backyard pond in New York was being dredged. Paleontologists at the Paleontological Research Institution managed the excavation. For more information about the Hyde Park mastodon go to the *Investigate Earth Systems* web site www.agiweb.org/ies for a link to the Museum of the Earth web site.

Investigate

The investigation gives students the opportunity to study decomposition and preservation in the field and to model the erosion and deposition of sediments. The stream-table activity will help students to understand why fossils are most likely to form in environments where sediments are deposited (accumulating). **Part B** of the **Investigate** section is a simulation that explores additional factors that affect fossilization. Help students to connect these three related aspects of their investigations into a meaningful answer to the **Key Question**, "Where can fossils form?"

Teaching Suggestions and Sample Answers

Part A: Location, Location

Teacher Commentary

NOTES

Investigating Fossils

INVESTIGATING FOSSILS

⚠ When examining the school grounds or other areas, you should be supervised by a teacher, parent, or other responsible adult.

Do not handle any living or dead organisms or other litter you find.

Look for living plants and animals like birds, small mammals, and insects. Also look for evidence of death or decay, like leaf litter, carcasses, feathers, and bones. If this is not available, look for human-made litter (i.e., trash).

a) In your journal, keep careful notes about what you observe, and where you observed it. Draw a map of the area and mark on the map where you found the objects.

2. Upon return to the classroom, talk over your observations with your group and with your class.

a) Describe what you observed that indicates decay.

b) Describe what you observed that indicates preservation.

c) Did you find any potential fossils? What were they and why do you think they could become fossils?

d) If most dead organisms can become fossils, would you have expected to find more evidence for this on your outdoor excursion? What does this tell you about the likelihood of something becoming a fossil?

e) What new questions arose from this discussion?

Together, make a class list of key points and questions.

3. You will now build a model that may help you find answers to some of the questions you have generated. In particular, you will model how remains of certain organisms are more likely to be protected from decay than others.

Use a stream table or a large, flat, plastic container about one meter long. Tilt the container by using a book or wooden block at one end.

Teacher Commentary

1. If you have easy access to a small wooded area, you can complete the first step in the investigation within a 40-minute class period. Alternatively, you may wish to assign this as a weekend homework assignment and have students bring data to class.

   a) It is important that students begin to understand that marking where they find things (mapping) is an important paleontological tool. For paleontologists, finding a fossil is only part of the jigsaw. What also counts is where the fossil is found, and in what kind of rock. Paleontologists use this information to analyze and reconstruct the forms and relationships of ancient organisms, as well as the conditions of their preservation in the geological record. In this investigation, students model this process with recently living things.

2. Help students use these discussion questions to clarify their ideas about what can become a fossil, and under what conditions. By now, they should have enough experience from the previous investigations to do this. It is important that students have the opportunity to check their findings and ideas with other groups. You may find some differences among the explanations and ideas that different groups have. Try to lead all groups toward a common understanding of the chances of fossilization.

   a) Signs of decay include: loss of color; loss of shape; loss of rigidity; holes; bad odor; presence of insect larvae; exposure of skeleton; mold; and mildew. Ask your students to note similarities among all of the areas in which they find decomposing matter. Are all of the areas damp? Sheltered? Dark? Relatively warm? What do these things tell the students about the conditions that best support decomposition?

   b) Signs of preservation include hardened, dried wood or perhaps shells or bones. Signs of preservation will be far less extensive than signs of decomposition. This realization is an important first step in understanding why fossils are rare compared to the numbers of organisms that have lived on or in the Earth over time.

   c) Answers will vary. Most likely, students will note that preservation is most common where things have become buried by sediment and are not exposed at the surface. Whether or not they find these things depends in part upon how much excavation they do.

   d) Answers will vary. Students might have expected to find more evidence of fossilization, but by now many will recognize that just because most dead organisms can become fossils does not necessarily imply that they will become fossils. The scarcity of evidence of fossilization should reveal to students that the likelihood of a dead organism becoming a fossil is very small.

   e) Encourage students to formulate questions for research.

3. This model helps to show that fossils are most likely to form in lower areas, in places where sediment can be washed onto plant or animal remains. Organisms that die and fall to the ground at higher elevations have a greater chance of being exposed to the rainfall that washes away deposits and leaves the organism to decompose in the open air. Help students to see that, to form deposits, materials must be moved from one place to another. They may also need reminding that erosion is the wearing away of rock, and deposition is the placement of the worn-away particles in a new area.

Teaching Tip

Note that a sprinkler will work better for simulating rainfall than a pitcher of water. The diagram on page F20 of the Student Book shows only a point in time in the pouring of water; ideally, water should be poured back and forth across the sand so that it falls onto the shell and leaf at the upper end of the stream table.

Teacher Commentary

NOTES

Investigating Fossils

Investigation 3: Conditions for Fossil Formation

Conduct Investigations

Pour a little water into the lower end, and place a wet leaf and shell underwater on the container floor.

Put a pile of sand on the upper part of the container. Put a leaf and a shell on top of the sand.

4. Predict what will happen if you slowly add water to the upper end of the stream table, as if to model rain.

    a) Record your prediction. Include a reason for your prediction.

5. Slowly and carefully, model heavy rain falling on the land at the upper edge of your model. You may wish to use a watering can to apply the water to the sand.

Collect & Review

6. When you have completed your test, observe where the leaves and shells have ended up. Review your predictions and the reasons for them.

    a) Were your predictions correct? Did the results surprise you?

Consider Evidence

7. Think about the model and your trip outdoors.

    a) In nature, which of the two leaves would be more likely to become a fossil over time, and why?

Evidence for Ideas

    b) Which of the two shells would be more likely to become a fossil?

    c) Based on your model, what kind of places would fossils be more likely to form?

8. Look at the diagram and compare it to a topographic map of your local area.

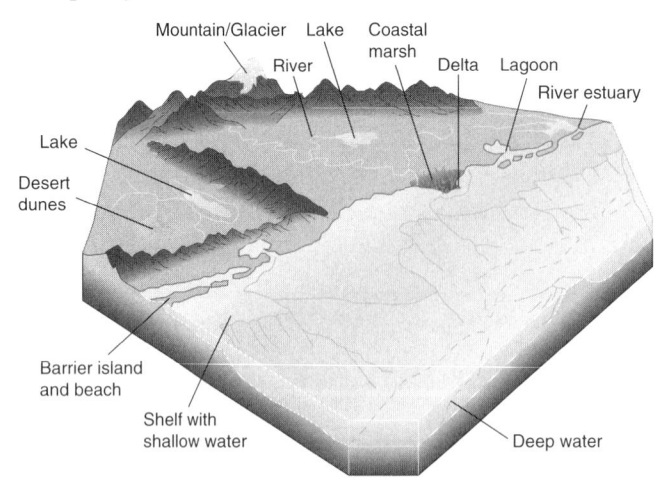

Labels on diagram: Mountain/Glacier, Lake, River, Coastal marsh, Delta, Lagoon, River estuary, Lake, Desert dunes, Barrier island and beach, Shelf with shallow water, Deep water

Inquiry
Models

Scientists and engineers use models to help them think about processes that happen too slowly, too quickly, or which cannot be directly observed. Choosing a useful model is one of the instances in which intuition and creativity come into play in science and engineering. In this investigation, you will build a model that will help to identify locations in which an organism is more likely to become fossilized.

Keep in mind that models are imperfect representations of natural processes. They are both like and unlike what they represent, in a number of ways.

F 21

Investigating Earth Systems

Teacher Commentary

4. This is another opportunity for students to make reasonable predictions of the most likely outcome of their experiment. Emphasize the importance of predictions in fair tests.

   a) Answers will vary. Students are most likely to predict that sediment will be washed "downstream" by the water that falls onto the sand at the upper end of the stream table. Ideally, they will cite the role of the energy of the falling water in dislodging and removing the sediment and the role of gravity in transporting the material.

5. Water need only be poured gently to simulate rainfall. Observe students' activities carefully. Watch for evidence of spills and have these mopped up quickly to prevent accidents.

6. Ensure that each group of students examines its results thoroughly. They should be encouraged to search for patterns and relationships. Students should understand that it is fine for their hypothesis not to prove correct. Explain that this happens more often than not in many scientific experiments. Stress that what is important is that the data are valid; that is, variables should be controlled and observations should be accurate.

   a) Although all groups have essentially completed the same experiment, the results may not all be identical. If this happens, help students to identify any reasons for differences. Most likely, differences will result from a variable that students failed to notice. Have students also consider differences in results in wider terms. They need to appreciate that controlled experiments must be done in a precise way, if the results are to be valid. You may want to consider allowing students to repeat their experiment with an improved design.

7. Give students the opportunity to discuss the results of their investigations. Help them to relate the model to their field-trip experience and to other real-world settings.

   a) The leaf at the lower end of the stream table is more likely to become a fossil over time because sediment is being piled on top of the leaf and burying it. The leaf at the upper end of the pan (on the land) is much more likely to decompose because it is exposed at the surface.

   b) Answers should be similar to those in **Question 7(a)**. This might be a good opportunity to ask students whether they think a terrestrial (land-dwelling) snail or a marine snail is more likely to become a fossil.

> ### About the Illustration
> The *IES* web site www.agiweb.org/ies/ provides links to web sites that provide further information about the environments of deposition shown in this schematic diagram.

c) Fossils are more likely to form in places where sediment is accumulating (depressions or other lower elevations) and less likely to form in places where sediment is being eroded (elevated regions).

8. Help your students make connections between the leaf activity (and its implications) and the diagram. You want your students to understand that water (and the particles it carries), moves from a high elevation to a lower elevation. You may want to have students look at this diagram in relation to their knowledge of how different sizes of particles form different types of fossils. This will help them to decide where well-defined fossils might be found. For example, they would not expect to find particularly well-defined fossils in a sandy desert, because sand has large particles, is blown about by the wind a great deal, and is in a very dry area.

> **Teaching Tip**
> Ask students to look at the photograph on page F15. Have them identify the environment of this photograph in the diagram on page F21.

Teacher Commentary

NOTES

Investigating Fossils

INVESTIGATING FOSSILS

a) Looking at the diagram, where on the land and under water do you think fossils might have formed in the past? Why?

b) Where do you think there is a chance that fossils might begin to form now?

c) What conditions would be necessary for fossils to begin to form now? What would have to happen?

d) Where do you think you might find conditions that lead to fossil formation in your local area or region?

Teacher Commentary

a) Sedimentary environments do change over time, but students are not likely to be aware of this fact. Students are most likely to suggest that fossils will have been more likely to form in areas of lower elevation, depressions, and other places where sediment is deposited. On land these include marshes and lakes; near the coast they include lagoons, deltas, and estuaries.

b) Students should note that fossils are most likely to be forming in areas of lower elevation, depressions, and other places where sediment is deposited.

c) An important condition for fossil formation is rapid burial by sediment.

d) Answers will vary. Try to obtain a local topographic map so that students can apply their knowledge to the local setting and examine a wider area than they did in their limited field excursion. Using the sample topographic map shown on page F22 of the Student Book as a guide, conditions that favor fossil formation include the river delta and the marshlands shown on the map.

About the Map
The map on page F22 is a part of a U.S. Geological Survey quadrangle that shows where the Nooksack River, in Washington State, enters the Puget Sound. Note how at its mouth the river breaks up into smaller channels called distributaries. In this area the land is characterized by salt marsh, as is indicated by the purple marsh symbols on the map. Ask your students to predict if they think that this would be a good area for fossil preservation. Why or why not?

Investigating Fossils – Investigation 3

Investigation 3: Conditions for Fossil Formation

Conduct Investigations

9. Test your ideas by conducting research on your local area and/or region.

Evidence for Ideas

   a) Did you find that there are fossils in your local area and/or region? Where were the fossils located? Were they abundant in the area that you thought they would be? If not, how do you explain this? Share your findings with your class.

Part B: "Wheel of Fossilization"

Explore Questions

1. Imagine that you observe a recently living organism in the ocean.

   a) What might happen to the remains?

   b) Will it leave behind any fossil evidence? Explain why or why not.

Conduct Investigations

2. To investigate the possible fates of different organisms, you will play a game using the "Wheel of Fossilization." First, your group will need to construct a "wheel," similar to the one shown in the diagrams.

   - Construct the wheel by cutting out a circle of cardboard.
   - Divide the circle into 12 roughly equal sections.
   - Number the sections 1-12.
   - Push a pencil through the center.

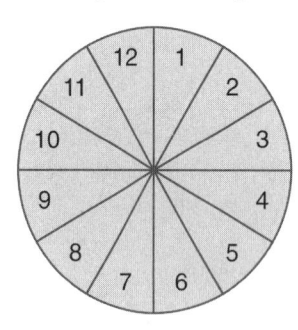

3. You will consider the position of a recently living organism, and the wheel will decide its fate. One of your group members will spin the wheel for you. The fate of the organism is determined by the number touching the desk when it stops spinning.

Teacher Commentary

9. Consider assigning this research project as an extra-credit project for students. It provides an important opportunity for students to apply what they have learned to their local area. The *IES* web site (www.agiweb.org/ies/) provides links to web sites that may provide further information about places to find fossils in your local area.

   a) Answers will vary. If students complete this project, be sure to provide them with the opportunity to share and discuss their findings with others.

> **Assessment Tools**
>
> **Investigation Journal-Entry Evaluation Sheet**
> Use this sheet as a general guideline for assessing student journals, adapting it to your classroom if desired. You should give the **Journal-Entry Evaluation Sheet** to students early in the module, discuss it with them, and use it to provide clear and prompt feedback.
>
> **Investigation Journal-Entry Checklist**
> Use this checklist as a guide for quickly checking the quality and completeness of journal entries.

Part B: "Wheel of Fossilization"

This second part of **Investigation 3** is designed to give your students a clear understanding of how rare it is for organic material to become fossilized.

1. Ask your students for their ideas about this question. The purpose of this question is to draw out your students' ideas about the factors that affect the likelihood of fossilization. Encourage all reasonable responses without seeking closure.

   a) Students might suggest that the remains will decompose or be scavenged by other organisms. They might also suggest that the remains might be buried over time by sediment.

   b) Answers will vary. Most likely, the dead organisms will not become fossils.

2. To save time, prepare the wheels ahead of time and distribute them to students. If you want students to make their own wheels, use photocopies of the **Blackline Master** *Fossils* **3.1: Wheel of Fossilization** as a cutout and distribute scissors and cardboard to students. Advise caution when pushing the pencil through the cardboard.

3. Observe students closely to prevent them from getting carried away with spinning the wheel. The wheel needs only to be spun sufficiently to produce reliable results.

INVESTIGATING FOSSILS

Possible Fates on the Wheel of Fossilization

1. You are a saber-toothed cat. Your body decomposes and your bones disintegrate in a field—NO FOSSIL
2. You are a shelled protozoan (a foraminiferan). Your body decomposes and your shell dissolves in the deep sea—NO FOSSIL
3. You are an oak tree. Your wood and leaves all decompose in a forest—NO FOSSIL
4. You are a snail. Your shell is preserved as a fossil, but rock erosion later destroys it—NO FOSSIL
5. You are a clam. Your shell is buried by mud in a quiet water setting—YOUR SHELL FOSSILIZES
6. You are a barnacle. Your body and shell are metamorphosed in an undersea lava flow—NO FOSSIL
7. You are a jellyfish. You have no hard skeleton, and your soft body decomposes—NO FOSSIL
8. You are a crab. You get eaten and your shell gets broken down into tiny bits in the process—NO FOSSIL
9. You are a tree fern. Your leaves are buried and preserved in swamp mud—YOUR TISSUES FOSSILIZE
10. You are a clamshell. Your body decomposes and your shell is broken to bits by waves—NO FOSSIL
11. You are a snail shell. Your body decomposes and your shell is recrystallized during mountain-building—NO FOSSIL
12. You are a *Tyrannosaurus rex*. Your footprint in mud is buried by sand along a river—YOUR TRACK FOSSILIZES.

4. Repeat so that each group member has three turns at the "Wheel."

   a) How many members of your group ended up becoming fossils?

   b) Did any one person become a fossil more than once?

   c) What happened to you, according to the fates given by the "Wheel?"

   d) Do you think this is a realistic game? Why or why not?

   Share the results of your group's discussion with the rest of the class.

   e) Keep a record of the discussion in your journal.

Teacher Commentary

> **Making Connections...*with Mathematics***
> There is an opportunity here for students to learn about "chance" as a mathematical concept. By carefully recording each spin of the wheel and the result, they can calculate the approximate chances of becoming a fossil. (In the case of the "Wheel of Fossilization," the chance of becoming a fossil is one in four, a much greater chance than occurs in nature.) You might want to consult with the students' mathematics teachers to see if any cross-curricular opportunities are possible.

4. A group of four students will yield 12 spins, or as many spins as there are possibilities on the wheel. Increasing the number of spins will improve the likelihood that the actual results will correspond to the probability of fossilization, as indicated by the selections on the wheel.

   a) Answers will vary. The actual probability is 25%, but results may vary significantly because of chance.

   b) Answers will vary. It is likely that this will happen to one student due to chance.

   c) Answers should be consistent with the descriptions of fossil fates given on the wheel. The purpose of this question is to make students record and think about these factors.

   d) On the basis of their experience on the field trip, where ample evidence of living or decaying matter was found compared to very few if any fossils, students should note that this game has a much higher probability of fossilization than would occur in nature.

   e) Check student work to find out what points of discussion students found to be salient.

Assessment Tools

Investigation Journal-Entry Evaluation Sheet
Use this sheet as a general guideline for assessing student journals, adapting it to your classroom if desired. You should give the **Journal-Entry Evaluation Sheet** to students early in the module, discuss it with them, and use it to provide clear and prompt feedback.

Investigation Journal-Entry Checklist
Use this checklist as a guide for quickly checking the quality and completeness of journal entries.

Investigating Fossils

Investigation 3: Conditions for Fossil Formation

Digging Deeper

THE LIKELIHOOD OF FOSSILIZATION

For a fossil to form, several conditions have to be met. First of all, the animal had to live in the given area! Animals live in many environments on Earth, but not everywhere. The water above many lake bottoms and some areas of the deep ocean bottom are stagnant. The bottom water is never exchanged with surface waters, so the water contains no dissolved oxygen. Animals cannot live without oxygen, so no animals live there. In these situations, the only possibility of fossilization is if a fish or other swimming or floating animal dies in oxygen-rich waters above, sinks down into the stagnant muddy bottom, and is buried by sediments.

Most environments on the land surface are populated with animals. Fossilization on land is very uncommon, however, because most areas of the land are being eroded. Unless there is deposition, fossils cannot be preserved. Deposition on land is common only in river valleys. Fossils are fairly common in sediments deposited on river floodplains.

Some ocean environments that support animal life are exposed to very strong currents and waves. After a shelled animal dies, the strong water motions cause the hard body parts to be broken and worn. Often the shells end up only as rounded grains of sand or gravel, which no longer look like fossils.

Evidence for Ideas

As You Read...
Think about:
1. Why are very few fossils found in rocks made from sediments that are laid down in deep ocean waters? What fossils would you expect to find in these rocks?
2. How does erosion affect the likelihood of fossilization? How does deposition affect the likelihood of fossilization?
3. Under what conditions are soft-bodied animals fossilized?

Investigating Earth Systems

F 25

Teacher Commentary

Digging Deeper

This section provides text and photos that give students greater insight into the topic of the likelihood of fossilization. You may wish to assign the **As You Read** questions as homework to help students focus on the major ideas in the text.

As You Read...
Think about:
1. Few animals live in some areas of the deep ocean because water is stagnant and does not support great quantities of life. The less life there is in a region, the lower the likelihood of fossilization. The only fossils that will form are those from animals and plants that live at shallower depths, fall to the ocean floor after death, and become buried before decomposing or being scavenged. Note: Many areas of the deep ocean also have very low rates of sedimentation, increasing the time needed for burial and decreasing the likelihood of fossil preservation.

2. Erosion decreases the likelihood of fossilization because it can break down even the hard parts of organisms, whereas deposition increases the likelihood of fossilization.

3. Rapid burial after death (or being buried alive) increases the likelihood of a soft-bodied organisms being fossilized.

> **Teaching Tip**
> The Burgess Shale, in Canada, is a rock formation that contains one of the most extensive collections of fossilized soft-bodied organisms. Paleontologists believe that the organisms were trapped in a submarine landslide that buried and protected the organisms from decomposition. Visit the *IES* web site (www.agiweb.org/ies/) for links to web sites that provide further information about this famous fossil locality and the paleontologists who have studied these fossils.

> **About the Photo**
> The photo shows a floodplain along the Yellowstone River in Yellowstone National Park, Wyoming. When the river floods the adjacent land it deposits a layer of sediment. Fossils can form in floodplains when animals die and the river buries the animals with new layers of sediment after each flood.

INVESTIGATING FOSSILS

For animals without skeletons, like worms or jellyfish, fossilization is a very rare event. When paleontologists find a well-preserved fossil of a soft-bodied animal, it's an occasion for celebration. For a soft-bodied animal to be fossilized, its body must be protected from decomposition. The body is usually exposed to air and water with a lot of oxygen, so it decomposes rapidly. The animal is likely to be fossilized only if it is buried soon after it dies (or when it is buried alive!). Even then, it is likely to decompose, because water that seeps through the sediment around it usually is rich in oxygen. Sometimes, however, the body is buried rapidly by fine mud. Water seeps through mud much more slowly than through sand, so the body does not decompose as fast. Mud often contains a lot of other organic matter as well, and that uses up oxygen faster. Some animal bodies then escape decomposition. Under just the right conditions, a delicate impression of the animal might be preserved.

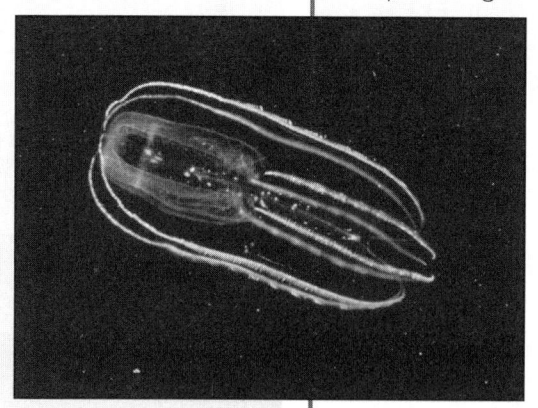

Paleontologists are sure that the fossil record is biased. That means that some kinds of organisms are much scarcer as fossils than they were when they were alive. Other kinds of organisms are much better represented by fossils. Animals with hard shells and skeletons are represented well in the fossil record. On the other hand, soft-bodied animals are probably represented very poorly. It's likely that most soft-bodied species that ever existed are gone forever without a trace. Land animals are probably very poorly represented as well. For example, most animals that are now alive, or have ever lived, are insects, but the fossil record of insects is poor.

Teacher Commentary

About the Photo

This photograph shows a lobate ctenophore, which shares some characteristics with jellyfish. A ctenophore is an example of the type of soft-bodied animal that is unlikely to be fossilized after it dies. Ask students if they have ever found a fossil. What were the characteristics of the fossil? What features could they identify?

Investigation 3: Conditions for Fossil Formation

Review and Reflect

Review

1. a) Why are low-lying areas more likely to accumulate fossils?

   b) Why is this not always true?

2. What are some factors that determine if a recently living organism ends up fossilized?

Reflect

3. Would you expect animals that lived in the oceans near a river delta to be better represented in the fossil record than animals that lived on land? Why or why not?

4. Would you be more likely to find a fossil of a freshwater fish or a hyena? Explain your reasoning.

5. Earth's earliest life was microscopic and soft-bodied. What challenges does this present for scientists who study early life on Earth?

6. What does it mean that the fossil record is biased? What causes it to be biased?

Thinking about the Earth System

7. On your *Earth System Connection* sheet, note how the things you learned in this investigation connect to the geosphere, hydrosphere, atmosphere, and biosphere.

8. What are some advantages and disadvantages of using the geosphere to understand the biosphere of the past?

Thinking about Scientific Inquiry

9. Scientists use evidence to develop ideas. What evidence do you have that becoming a fossil is rare?

10. How did you use a model in this investigation to investigate fossilization? How could you modify the model to make it more realistic?

Teacher Commentary

Review and Reflect

Review

It is important that you give your students enough time to review what they have learned from this investigation. This has been both a field study and a laboratory investigation. They might need help in relating the findings of the former to the latter.

1. a) Low-lying areas are more likely to accumulate fossils because they are more likely to be places where sediment is deposited. Burial by sediment (or other method of protecting organisms from decomposition or scattering) is an important condition for fossil formation.

    b) Organisms need to be present in or transported to the low-lying area for a fossil to form, no matter how much sediment is deposited.

2. Factors include burial and very slow decomposition.

Reflect

Students also need time to reflect on the nature of the evidence they have collected from their investigations. Help them to see that evidence is crucial in scientific inquiry.

3. Yes, animals that lived near a river delta would probably be better represented than animals that lived on land. Deltas are regions of sediment deposition, which increases the likelihood of fossilization.

4. A freshwater fish has much greater chances of becoming a fossil than a hyena. Hyenas live on land. In order to become fossilized, they must die in or near water or be buried by a landslide of some kind. Freshwater fish live in environments where rapid burial by sediment is far more likely.

5. Soft-bodied organisms are rarely fossilized. It takes a rare event to bury a soft-bodied organism.

6. That the fossil record is biased means that not all kinds of organisms are equally represented in the fossil record. The fossil record is biased toward animals with hard parts (bones, shells, and teeth) because these materials are more likely to be preserved.

Thinking about the Earth System

Students should revisit their *Earth System Connection* sheet and add anything new that they have learned about the idea of planet Earth as a collection of interacting systems. Ask students to refer to page Fx of their books and discuss how their investigative results connect with planet Earth. Ensure that students add their ideas to their *Earth System Connection* sheet.

7. Students should note that the formation of precipitation in the atmosphere contributes to river erosion and deposition. Erosion and deposition of sediment modifies the geosphere. Deposition of sediment helps preserve the record of life in the biosphere.

8. The biggest advantage is that the record of ancient life is found in the geosphere (the rock record). The disadvantage is that fossils are rarely preserved and that those fossils that remain are biased toward certain kinds of life. For example, most animals which are alive today and which have ever lived are insects, yet relatively few fossil insects have been found.

Thinking about Scientific Inquiry

This investigation exposed students to the idea of forming and testing a hypothesis. It is important that you give students time to understand how this approach to experimentation is a part of scientific inquiry. Students have also been using models as tools for investigation, exploring questions for scientific inquiry, and collecting and reviewing information. Help them to understand how they have used these processes in a scientific way by reviewing the list of **Inquiry Processes** shown on page Fxii in their book.

9. Evidence that students should cite includes the evidence from any of the few fossils found on their field trip and their study of possible sites of deposition. The simulation provided additional, albeit simulated, evidence for the rarity of fossil formation.

10. Students modeled the deposition of sediment in a river delta and the burial of dead organic material by that sediment. Ideas about how to modify the model to make it more realistic will vary. Accept all reasonable responses that improve the extent to which the model simulates the real-world processes.

Assessment Tool
Review and Reflect Journal-Entry Evaluation Sheet
Use the general criteria provided on this evaluation sheet to assess content and thoroughness of student work. Adapt and modify the sheet to meet your needs. Consider involving students in selecting and modifying the criteria.

Teacher Commentary

NOTES

Teacher Review

Use this section to reflect on and review the investigation. Keep in mind that your notes here are likely to be especially helpful when you teach this investigation again. Questions listed here are examples only.

Student Achievement

What evidence do you have that all students have met the science content objectives?

Are there any students who need more help in reaching these objectives? If so, how can you provide this?

What evidence do you have that all students have demonstrated their understanding of the inquiry processes?

Which of these inquiry objectives do your students need to improve upon in future investigations?

What evidence do the journal entries contain about what your students learned from this investigation?

Planning

How well did this investigation fit into your class time?

What changes can you make to improve your planning next time?

Guiding and Facilitating Learning

How well did you focus and support inquiry while interacting with students?

What changes can you make to improve classroom management for the next investigation or the next time you teach this investigation?

Teacher Commentary

How successful were you in encouraging all students to participate fully in science learning? _____

_____

How did you encourage and model the skills values, and attitudes of scientific inquiry? _____

_____

How did you nurture collaboration among students? _____

_____

Materials and Resources

What challenges did you encounter obtaining or using materials and/or resources needed for the activity? _____

_____

What changes can you make to better obtain and better manage materials and resources next time? _____

_____

Student Evaluation

Describe how you evaluated student progress. What worked well? What needs to be improved? _____

_____

How will you adapt your evaluation methods for next time? _____

_____

Describe how you guided students in self-assessment. _____

_____

Self Evaluation

How would you rate your teaching of this investigation? _____

_____

What advice would you give to a colleague who is planning to teach this investigation? _____

_____

Investigating Fossils – Investigation 3

NOTES

Teacher Commentary

INVESTIGATION 4: FOSSILS THROUGH GEOLOGIC TIME

Background Information

Species and Their Evolution

The species is the basic unit in the classification of plants and animals. The concept of a species has been around much longer than the Darwinian theory of organic evolution by natural selection. A species is defined as a population of organisms that can breed to produce fertile offspring. All of the members of a species are sufficiently closely related, in terms of their genetic makeup, to produce offspring that themselves can in turn produce fertile offspring. If two populations of generally similar organisms are not sufficiently closely related, they cannot interbreed, or if they do so, their offspring are infertile. The mule, which is the offspring of a male donkey and a female horse, is an example of the latter case: mules can't reproduce.

The members of a species are not genetically identical: the assemblage of genes, which determine the biological nature of the organism, differs slightly from individual to individual. Mutations to the genes occur at random all the time, owing at least in part to external influences like exposure to radiation or chemical substances. The slightly changed genes are then transmitted by sexual reproduction. According to the theory of evolution by natural selection, most mutations are harmful or fatal, but some give their carriers some advantage in life. Organisms carrying such a beneficial mutation then have some advantage in reproduction, and the beneficial gene tends then to be present in a greater and greater proportion of the species. Over the enormous number of generations during the lifespan of the species, which is ordinarily many hundreds of thousands of years if not millions of years, accumulation of the effects of beneficial mutations leads to fundamental changes in the species, even to the point at which a new species must be considered to have arisen.

New species also arise by isolation of one part of the population of a species from another part, owing to geographic isolation, climatic isolation, or some other circumstance that effectively prevents, or at least impedes, reproduction between the two groups of individuals. The different courses of genetic drift in the two groups, in response to at least slightly different environmental settings, leads eventually to two separate species by processes of natural selection.

In the modern world it is possible, at least in theory, to test, by means of breeding experiments, whether or not two groups of organisms constitute a single species. In the fossil record, however, it is obviously impossible to demonstrate by means of breeding experiments whether a collection of similar fossils were actually members of a single species. Paleontologists have to sidestep this problem by assuming that if the morphology (the form and structure of a plant or animal) of the fossil specimens is closely similar, they very likely did indeed belong to the same species.

The basic and very practical starting point in the initial study of a collection of fossils is to sort them by similarity in morphology. Commonly, the person doing the sorting is confronted immediately with the troublesome matter of making decisions about relative closeness of morphology. Personality tends to

Investigating Fossils – Investigation 4 **139**

rear its head in situations like this: are you a "lumper," meaning that you tend to group objects into a relatively small number of categories with a relatively large degree of variation within the categories, or are you a "splitter," meaning that you tend to group objects into a relatively large number of categories with a relatively small degree of variation within the categories? The only real guidance paleontologists have in this endeavor is by comparison with typical degrees of intraspecific (within-species) variation in known modern species.

The Geologic Time Scale
The development of ideas about geologic time had to await the first great revolution in geology, at the end of the eighteenth century, brought about by James Hutton's ideas about the development of the geological record by the action of processes like erosion, sedimentation, volcanism, and tectonism we can observe and study today. Two pioneers in the early years of the nineteenth century—William Smith in England and Georges Cuvier in France—laid the groundwork for dating sedimentary rocks by their fossil content. They were the first to perceive that there is a definite and nonrepeating succession of fossil species in the sedimentary rocks of the world, largely independent of the particular rock types that contain the fossils.

As geologists in the first part of the nineteenth century began their systematic study of the record of successions of ancient sedimentary rocks around the world, they were led on this basis to develop a chronology based on the fossil content of the rocks. For the sake of communication it became necessary to divide geologic time into manageable, named units. The boundaries between units were generally drawn where there were significant worldwide changes in the faunas contained in the rocks. By the late 1800s the result of these efforts, the relative geologic time scale, was largely in place. The adjective "relative" is used for this time scale, because absolute ages, in years, are not involved.

The relative geologic time scale involves a hierarchy of units, ranging from the longest spans of geologic time to the shortest. Eons are the broadest time units in general use. Almost all fossils recognizable with the unaided eye date from the Phanerozoic Eon, which began about 543 million years ago (and which, although unimaginably long by human standards, is only a small part of the Earth's more than four-billion-year history). The Phanerozoic is divided into three eras: the Paleozoic, the Mesozoic, and the

\multicolumn{3}{c	}{Life Through Time}
\multicolumn{3}{c	}{(boundaries in millions of years before present)}
Era	Period	Event
Cenozoic	Quaternary	modern humans
		1.8
	Tertiary	abundant mammals
		65
Mesozoic	Cretaceous	flowering plants; dinosaur and ammonoid extinctions
		145
	Jurassic	first birds and mammals; abundant dinosaurs
		213
	Triassic	abundant coniferous trees
		248
Paleozoic	Permian	extinction of trilobites and other marine animals
		286
	Pennsylvanian	fern forests; abundant insects; first reptiles
		325
	Mississippian	sharks; large primitive trees
		360
	Devonian	amphibians and ammonoids
		410
	Silurian	early plants and animals on land
		440
	Ordovician	first fish
		505
	Cambrian	abundant marine invertebrates; trilobites dominant
		544
Proterozoic		primitive aquatic plants
		2500
Archean		oldest fossils; bacteria and algae

Teacher Commentary

Cenozoic. Fossils are common from the very beginning of the Phanerozoic, for the somewhat circuitous reason that the beginning of the Phanerozoic was originally defined on the basis of the rather sudden appearance of shelled marine metazoans, whose potential for fossilization was far greater than for their soft-bodied predecessors.

When the relative time scale was developed, there was still no way to assign absolute ages to the rocks. That was to come much later, in the middle of the twentieth century, with the advent of radioisotopic dating methods. Soon after the discovery of natural radioactivity in the final years of the nineteenth century, geologists realized that the rate of decay of radioactive isotopes of some elements could be used to date rocks. This idea could not be exploited fully, however, until the middle of the twentieth century, with the advent of sophisticated devices, called mass spectrometers, that allow precise separation of the various isotopes involved. Generally, only igneous rocks are suitable for radioisotopic dating, so the sedimentary record must be dated either by a dating of beds of volcanic ash that in many places are interbedded with sedimentary rocks, or indirectly by a "bracketing" method whereby a date is obtained for two igneous intrusive bodies, one of which is overlain by sedimentary rocks and the other of which cuts through those same sedimentary rocks. By use of methods like these, absolute dates have gradually been associated with the relative time scale. The process continues today: only recently, the date of the beginning of the Paleozoic was changed from about 570 million years to 543 million years!

More Information…on the Web
Visit the *Investigating Earth Systems* web site www.agiweb.org/ies/ for links to a variety of other web sites that will help you deepen your understanding of content and prepare you to teach this module

Investigation Overview

In this investigation, your students focus upon geologic time. To do this, they first look at the vast magnitude of time involved using linear measurement as an analogy. They then use information as provided in "field notes" to model rock layers. This model, which represents the geologic record, demonstrates how geologists use the law of superposition along with fossils to correlate different rock sequences to determine the relative ages of the rocks and succession of fossil species.

Goals and Objectives

As a result of this investigation, students will develop a better understanding of geologic time and about how geologists interpret changes in life through time using fundamental scientific laws for interpreting strata.

Science Content Objectives
Students will collect evidence that:
1. The fossil record provides evidence of past life.
2. Fossil age is connected to the rock layers in which fossils are found.
3. In undisturbed rock, the oldest layers are deepest.
4. Fossil formation is connected to the biosphere, the hydrosphere, the atmosphere, and the geosphere.

Inquiry Process Skills
Students will:
1. Use mathematics to make a model to scale.
2. Use a model of rock layers to investigate how the fossil record is formed.
3. Collect and analyze data.
4. Compare model-produced data with other representations of the same data set.
5. Draw conclusions about life and geologic time from several models.
6. Communicate data and conclusions to others.

Connections to Standards and Benchmarks
In this investigation, your students will be investigating geologic time and how we interpret the fossil record. These observations will start them on the road to understanding the National Science Education Standards and AAAS Benchmarks shown on the following page.

Teacher Commentary

NSES Links

- Fossils provide important evidence of how life and environmental conditions have changed.

- Biological evolution accounts for the diversity of species developed through gradual processes over many generations. Species acquire many of their unique characteristics through biological adaptation, which involves the selection of naturally occurring variations in populations. Biological adaptations include changes in structures, behaviors, or physiology that enhance survival and reproductive success in a particular environment.

- Evolution is a series of changes, sometimes gradual, sometimes sporadic, that accounts for the present form and function of objects, organisms, and natural and designed systems. The general idea of evolution is that the present arises from materials and forms of the past.

- Extinction of a species occurs when the environment changes and the adaptive characteristics of a species are insufficient to allow its survival. Fossils indicate that many organisms that lived long ago are extinct. Extinction of species is common; most of the species that have lived on the Earth no longer exist.

AAAS Links

- Many thousands of layers of sedimentary rock provide evidence for the long history of the Earth and for the long history of changing life forms whose remains are found in the rocks. More recently deposited rock layers are more likely to contain fossils resembling existing species.

- Fossils can be compared to one another and to living organisms according to their similarities and differences. Some organisms that lived long ago are similar to existing organisms, but some are quite different.

- Fossil evidence is consistent with the idea that human beings evolved from earlier species.

Preparation and Materials Needed

Preparation
This investigation requires about three 40-minute class periods to complete, depending on the depth of investigation and inquiry you have students pursue.

- **Day One:** Have students address the **Key Question** and identify the first appearance of human life, as well as the first appearance of all life on Earth by looking at the chart of geologic time (**Part A, Step 1**). In order to get a better sense of the geologic time scale, students will construct their own time scale using a hallway, sidewalk, schoolyard, etc. This activity does not work well on a carpeted floor, so find a smooth surface. Chalk will work well if you use a sidewalk, but you may wish to use masking tape if you are conducting the activity in your hallway. (**Steps 2–6**). Also, photocopy the **Blackline Master** *Fossils* 4.2, **Data Table on Average Length of Steps** for each group ahead of time.

- **Day Two:** An important part of preparing for **Part B** of the investigation is to have an available space identified that has at least 100 feet. You may also wish to have 100 feet of rope (or distance on the floor) measured out before the activity for each group. Provide a photocopy of **Blackline Master** *Fossils* 4.1, **Life through Time**, for each group (**Steps 1–2**).

- **Day Three:** You need to prepare a "field" notebook containing a sequence of sedimentary rock layers for each group. (These field notes are available as a **Blackline Master 4.3, Stratigraphic Notebook.**) Photocopy the field notes for each group (each group will have notes from a different location) and collate them in a notebook. Each student group also needs a piece of poster board with blank columns (one column for each group), see **Blackline Master** *Fossils* 4.4, **Stratigraphic Cross Section.**

Materials

Part A
- metric measuring tape (as long as possible)
- chalk

Part B
- photocopy of chart showing dates when various kinds of animals first appeared in the fossil record (**Blackline Master** *Fossils* 4.1, **Life through Time**)
- chart paper
- calculator

Part C
- photocopy of **Blackline Master** *Fossils* 4.3, **Stratigraphic Notebook**
- photocopy of diagram on page F33 of the Student Book (**Blackline Master** *Fossils* 4.4, **Stratigraphic Correlation**)

Teacher Commentary

NOTES

Investigating Fossils

INVESTIGATING FOSSILS

Investigation 4:
Fossils through Geologic Time

Materials Needed

For this investigation your group will need:

- metric measuring tape (as long as possible)
- chalk
- chart paper
- calculator
- "stratigraphic" notebook with "fossils" (this can be made using the detailed instructions provided in the Teacher's Edition)

Key Question

Before you begin, first think about this key question.

How can we determine the age of a fossil?

Think about what you know about the conditions under which fossils form. If different fossils are found in different layers of rock, could you tell which fossils are the oldest? The youngest?

Share your thinking with others in your class. Keep a record of the discussion in your journal.

Investigate

Part A: Geologic Time

1. Geologists know that Earth is about 4.5 billion (4,500,000,000) years old. Primitive life evolved as much as 3.5 billion years ago, or more, but large and complicated life did not develop until much later. In terms of Earth's history, humans are very recent. Find them on the chart.

F 28 Investigating Earth Systems

Teacher Commentary

Key Question

Write this question on the board or on an overhead transparency. Have students record their answers in their journals. Emphasize that the date and the prompt (question, heading, etc.) should be included in journal entries. Tell them to think about and answer the question individually. Tell them to write as much as they know and to provide as much detail as possible in their responses.

Student Conceptions about the Age of Fossils

The passage of time is a relative concept. For example, if you ask your students to keep their eyes closed for one minute, many will open them much earlier, and some much later. Adults, also, often have difficulty estimating the passage of time. This difficulty is sharply magnified when students, and adults, try to envision the vast scale of geologic time. In addition, your students may have been seriously misled by fictional movies and other media, which distort life through time for entertainment. For example, the spectacle of humans fighting off dinosaurs may have led some students to think that dinosaurs and humans coexisted. In fact, nothing could be further from the truth, as the table on page F29 shows. Students may also have little idea of how fossils provide evidence not only of past animal life (the fossil record) but also of the age of rocks (geologic record). It is very important to use every opportunity to help students grasp the accepted scientific explanations and concepts as accurately as possible. They need to achieve this through an understanding of how scientists gather, analyze, interpret, and reconstruct the past.

Answers for the Teacher Only

The Earth is approximately 4.5 billion years old. This vast span of time is difficult for humans to comprehend. As science and technology advance, so too has human understanding of the Earth's age. In earlier times, most people believed that Earth's history could be measured in terms of thousands of years rather than millions and billions, but scientists have discovered that the Earth is much older than they first thought.

Rocks at the Earth's surface and within its crust record major events and life activity in the Earth's history. Unfortunately, this record is not complete. Instead of recording the history like a book reading from beginning to end, Earth's history must be pieced together by scientists mainly by using fossil evidence as their puzzle pieces. Using fossil evidence, scientists are able to construct a relative time scale by which to measure the age of the Earth.

About the Photo

This photograph shows a layer of clamshells in sandy sediment. The black ruler is for the relative scale of the shells. Scientists determined that these shells were deposited in the Cenozoic Era.

Assessment Tool
Key-Question Evaluation Sheet
Use this evaluation sheet to help students understand and internalize basic expectations for the warm-up activity. The **Key-Question Evaluation Sheet** emphasizes that you want to see evidence of prior knowledge and that students should communicate their thinking clearly. You will not likely have time to apply this assessment every time students complete a warm-up activity; yet, in order to ensure that students value committing their initial conceptions to paper and are taking the warm-up seriously, you should always remind them of the criteria. When time permits, use this evaluation sheet as a spot check on the quality of their work.

Investigate

Many of the concepts involved in this investigation cannot be discovered through hands-on activities. For this reason, students are asked to find ways of interpreting information through parallels and analogies, many of which are mathematical. It is important that students realize that this form of investigating is also part of scientific inquiry.

Teaching Suggestions and Sample Answers
Part A: Geologic Time
1. Students will look at the chart on page F29, showing life through time, and locate the time when humans first appeared on the Earth. Next, they will find the appearance of life on Earth and compare this length of time with the first human appearance.

Teacher Commentary

NOTES

Investigating Fossils

Investigation 4: Fossils through Geologic Time

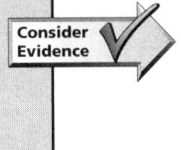

Consider Evidence

a) When did modern humans appear?
b) How does this compare to when life began on the planet?

Conduct Investigations

2. To get a better sense of this kind of time scale, your group is going to think of time as if it were distance.

   In a suitable place (a corridor or the schoolyard), mark a starting point with chalk. Next, each person should walk 10 normal paces, mark the distance with chalk, and put his or her name beside this point.

Use Mathematics

Major Divisions of Geologic Time
(boundaries in millions of years before present)

Era	Period	Event	
Cenozoic	Quaternary	modern humans	
			1.8
	Tertiary	abundant mammals	
			65
Mesozoic	Cretaceous	flowering plants; dinosaur and ammonoid extinctions	
			145
	Jurassic	first birds and mammals; abundant dinosaurs	
			213
	Triassic	abundant coniferous trees	
			248
Paleozoic	Permian	extinction of trilobites and other marine animals	
			286
	Pennsylvanian	fern forests; abundant insects; first reptiles	
			325
	Mississippian	sharks; large primitive trees	
			360
	Devonian	amphibians and ammonoids	
			410
	Silurian	early plants and animals on land	
			440
	Ordovician	first fish	
			505
	Cambrian	abundant marine invertebrates; trilobites dominant	
			544
Proterozoic		primitive aquatic plants	
			2500
Archean		oldest fossils; bacteria and algae	

⚠ Check for any hazards before pacing off your steps.

Investigating Earth Systems

F 29

Teacher Commentary

1. a) Students may use the chart on page F29 to infer that *Homo Sapiens* (modern humans) have existed on Earth for about 1.8 million years. The chart actually indicates only that modern humans came into being sometime during the Quaternary Period. In actuality, the species *Homo Sapiens* has existed on Earth for less than 100,000 years.

    b) Life appeared long before 2500 million years ago — in fact, as early as 3500 million years ago. Modern humans have existed for only a very small fraction of the time since life began on Earth.

> **Teaching Tip**
> The scientific explanation of evolution is now widely accepted within the scientific community. Many scientists do not see this as in conflict with Biblical explanations of the origins of life on Earth. Nevertheless, you will need to keep in mind that some of your students may belong to a religious community that bases its views on a literal interpretation of the Bible as an absolute truth. You will have to judge how to handle any issues that may arise from these conflicting ideas, traditions, and positions. It is important to respect the beliefs of others, and their right to hold such views. However, the authors of *Investigating Earth Systems*, along with the National Research Council and many other national and international science-education organizations, hold the position that scientific explanations of evolution cannot and should not be circumvented in school science curricula.

2. Linear measurement is more familiar and more concrete to students than temporal (time) measurement. This is why students are asked to use linear measurement as an analogy for time.

Investigating Fossils

INVESTIGATING FOSSILS

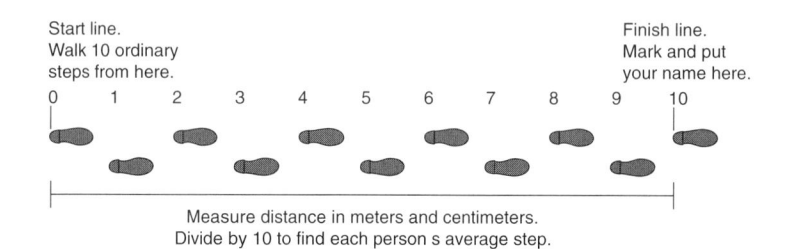

Start line.
Walk 10 ordinary
steps from here.

Finish line.
Mark and put
your name here.

0 1 2 3 4 5 6 7 8 9 10

Measure distance in meters and centimeters.
Divide by 10 to find each person's average step.

3. When everyone in your group has measured his or her 10-step distance, put the lengths on a chart like the one shown.

Names of Group Members	Distance of Steps (in meters and centimeters)	Average Step (total distance for each person divided by 10)
Total for Your Group (add each person's average)		T =
Average Group Step (divide total by number of persons in your group)		AGS =

4. Find the Average Class Step (ACS) by taking the Total (T) for each group, adding them all together, and dividing the total figure by the number of students participating. How does this number compare to the Average Group Step (AGS)?

   You may want to round the ACS figure up or down to make it into the nearest convenient number (for example, if it is 78 cm, round it up to 80 cm).

5. You will now apply your average distance to time.

   Think of one average step as representing 100 years of time. On this scale it means:

   - You have lived for about one-eighth of a step.
   - Your parents have probably lived for about one-third of a step.
   - Only someone at least 100 years old would have lived one step or more.

Use Mathematics

Teacher Commentary

3. Answers will vary. It is important to discuss methods of measurement because variations in methods, as well as accuracy of measurements, need to be accounted for when comparing and averaging data. Help students to appreciate this important aspect of scientific inquiry.

4. Because absolute measurements can be difficult to obtain in paleontology, paleontologists frequently use averages. For example, gauging actual fossil sizes is not possible because the paleontologist is dependent upon only those fossils that are found. By averaging the sizes of a collection of fossils of the same species, it is possible to estimate the relative size of a species of fossil. It may be useful to consult with your students' mathematics teachers to explore any cross-curricular opportunities.

5. Some students may have difficulty in converting this linear measurement to a time measurement. Watch for any who need help, and assist them in understanding the relationship.

Investigation 4: Fossils through Geologic Time

Look again at the Major Divisions of Geologic Time chart.

In your group, figure out how many steps would represent life through time for the beginning of each of the periods starting with the Cambrian Period, when a great many different kinds of animals become common in the fossil record. How many steps would be required to represent all of the time that life has been on Earth (about 3.5 billion years)?

6. To get another sense of the huge scale of geologic time, use some mathematical calculations. Imagine that you want to make a movie that will include life through time starting from the origin of the Earth to today. Suppose this movie is going to be 24-h long!

a) How long would humans be on the screen?

Share your answer, and the calculations you used to get it, with the rest of the class.

Part B: Life through Geologic Time

1. On a long gymnasium floor, a corridor, or a parking lot, measure out a distance of at least 100 ft (about 30 m).

   Use a 100-foot tape measure or lay out a 100-foot piece of rope between the beginning and end of that distance. This will represent all of geologic time.

2. Your teacher will give you a chart that shows the dates when various kinds of animals first appeared in the fossil record. Plot these dates along the line. To do that, you will have to form a ratio. For each kind of animal, divide the date of appearance by the total length of geologic time. Use that ratio to figure out where to put the point along your 100-foot line. If you are not sure how to do this, your teacher will help you.

   a) Where would a point be that stands for your age?

   b) Where would a point be that stands for your grandparent's age?

   c) Where would a point be that stands for the beginning of recorded human history (about 4000 years)? How does that compare with the time since the dinosaurs became extinct?

Teacher Commentary

6. Some students may also have difficulty in converting geologic time to a smaller time scale. You may need to provide additional assistance to those students who have trouble understanding this relationship. If 4.5 billion years is equivalent to 24 hours, then the equivalent of 1.8 million years is approximately 35 seconds at this scale.

Assessment Tools

Investigation Journal-Entry Evaluation Sheet
Use this sheet as a general guideline for assessing student journals, adapting it to your classroom if desired. You should give the **Journal Entry-Evaluation Sheet** to students early in the module, discuss it with them, and use it to provide clear and prompt feedback.

Investigation Journal-Entry Checklist
Use this checklist as a guide for quickly checking the quality and completeness of journal entries.

Part B: Life through Geologic Time

In **Part A** of the investigation, students explored the relative time scale for geologic time and got a sense of the vastness of the history of life on Earth. Now, in **Part B**, students create a more accurate measure of geologic time by constructing their own time scale. Students calculate the first appearances of various kinds of animals in the fossil record and plot these along a 100-foot line. By doing this investigation, students learn how a human day, year, or even a lifetime seems minuscule compared to the duration of Earth's history.

This investigation will take one class period to complete. Students will have an easier time conducting the activity if you provide them with an overview of the investigation before you take them outside of the classroom.

1. In a long hallway, gymnasium floor, parking lot, etc. (an area stretching at least 100 feet or longer), measure out a 100-foot rope or line for each group.

2. Provide student groups with the photocopies of the **Blackline Master 4.2, Data Table on Average Length of Steps.**

    a) As students compare their ages to the geologic time scale, they get a sense of Earth's age. Students will realize that it will be hard to mark their lifespan accurately on the time scale. If the 100 feet represent 2.5 billion years, then a student's lifespan (~ 12 years) would be represented by 0.000006 inches at this scale!

Investigating Fossils – Investigation 4   **155**

b) Students will realize that the human lifespan does not hold a significant place on the geologic time scale.

c) Human existence on this planet is an extremely small fraction of the entire geological time scale. At the same 2.5 billion years equals 100 feet scale, the ~ 4000 years of recorded human history would be represented by about 0.002 inches! Human history is only 0.01% of the time since the dinosaurs became extinct (about 65 million years ago). Students will realize that by this standard even the appearance of the first dinosaurs is considered young.

Assessment Tools

Investigation Journal-Entry Evaluation Sheet
Use this sheet as a general guideline for assessing student journals, adapting it to your classroom if desired. You should give the **Journal Entry-Evaluation Sheet** to students early in the module, discuss it with them, and use it to provide clear and prompt feedback.

Investigation Journal-Entry Checklist
Use this checklist as a guide for quickly checking the quality and completeness of journal entries.

Teacher Commentary

NOTES

Investigating Fossils

INVESTIGATING FOSSILS

Part C: Figuring out the Fossil Record

1. Your teacher will give each group a special notebook. Think of the notebook as a sequence of sedimentary rock layers. Geologists call this a stratigraphic section. You might see such a section in a highway cut, a river bank, or a sea cliff. Each page stands for a single layer in the sequence.

   Each notebook comes from some place around the world. Each one is different. The number of layers is not the same from notebook to notebook, and the layers themselves are different.

   Some of the layers contain fossils. Some do not. The names of the different fossils are shown by capital letters on the pages. These letters have nothing to do with the age of the fossils.

   You need to keep three important things in mind.

   - Sedimentary rock layers are originally deposited one on top of another in horizontal layers. The oldest layer is at the bottom of the stack, and the youngest is at the top.

     The first part of this statement (that sedimentary rock layers are deposited one on top of another) is called the "Law of Superposition."

     The second part of the statement (about originally being in horizontal layers) is called the "Law of Original Horizontality."

     Combined, these two ideas are very important, because they provide a means to tell which rock layers (and fossils in those rock layers) are older than others.

   - Different kinds of plants and animals are called species. A species appears at a certain time and most become extinct at a later time. Once a species becomes extinct, it never appears again.

Inquiry
Laws in Science

In science and nature, the word "law" is given a very special status. A scientific law or a law of nature is generally accepted to be true and universal. Laws are accepted at face value because they have been so strongly tested, and yet have always been observed to be true. A law can begin as a hypothesis, but only after years and even decades of testing can a hypothesis become a law. It can become a law only if it has been shown to be true over and over again, without exception. A law can sometimes be expressed in terms of a single mathematical equation, but laws don't always need to have complex mathematical proofs.

F 32
Investigating Earth Systems

Investigating Earth Systems

Teacher Commentary

Part C: Figuring out the Fossil Record

This investigation should take one class period to complete. If you give students an overview of the investigation before they get started on the activity, things will go much more smoothly.

You need to prepare a "field" notebook containing a sequence of sedimentary rock layers for each group. (The field notes are available as a **Blackline Master** *Fossils* 4.3, **Stratigraphic Notebook**.) Photocopy the field notes for each group (each group will have notes from a different location) and collate them in a notebook.

1. Students will take the field notes for their location and plot the information in the column labeled for their group on the poster board.

> **About the Photo**
> This photograph shows alternating layers of sandstone and shale near Arkadelphia, Arkansas. The sandstone is the greenish brown color. The shale is the blackish gray layer. Using the trees that are visible at the top of the picture for perspective, it appears the sandstone layers are on top of the shale layers. Therefore, it is fairly safe to assume that each sandstone layer is younger than the shale layer below it and older than the shale layer above it.

Investigating Fossils

Investigation 4: Fossils through Geologic Time

- Geologists didn't know beforehand the succession of fossil species through geologic time. They had to figure that out from the succession of fossils in stratigraphic sections all around the world. You're going to do the same thing in this investigation.

Conduct Investigations

2. You will use the data from each group's notebook to figure out the succession of fossil species. Each group has a sheet of poster board with blank columns (one for each group). On each sheet of poster board, plot your succession of layers in one of the columns. In the column, show the contacts between the layers with horizontal lines. If a layer contains one or more kinds of fossils, label them in the column.

Inquiry

Reporting Findings

In this investigation you are mirroring what paleontologists do. Findings are reported by many different paleontologists and are added to the fossil record.

Group 1 Group 2 Group 3 Group 4 Group 5 Group 6

Teacher Commentary

2. Students should include on their poster board the depths of each layer, fossils found contained within each layer, and any additional information in the field notes. (Note: The fossils are shown by capital letters. Help students to understand that the letters do not represent the ages of the fossils.) There may be more than one kind of fossil in one layer. Students should draw the contacts between the layers with horizontal lines. After they transfer their information to the poster board, students should pass their board to the other groups. This means that each student group will have to plot their information as many times as there are groups.

INVESTIGATING FOSSILS

3. The time interval when one or more species existed is called a zone. Your job is to figure out the "standard" succession of zones, worldwide. To help you do this, draw light pencil lines between the columns, to match up times when fossils A to Z lived. Erase lines and change them as needed.

4. When you are satisfied that you have figured out the succession, write it down in a vertical column on a blank sheet of paper, with the oldest at the bottom and the youngest at the top.

5. As a class, compare the succession of fossil zones from all of the groups.

   a) Are each group's results the same? If not, discuss the reasons why. Then agree on the single acceptable succession.

   b) Why do some layers contain fossils but other layers have no fossils?

   c) There are two basic reasons why a particular fossil zone might be missing from one or more of the columns. What are these reasons?

   d) How would you use the results of this investigation to tell the ages of the rock layers in a new stratigraphic section?

   e) Imagine that you are studying a newly discovered stratigraphic section somewhere in the world. You find an entirely new fossil species in one of the layers. Would that change your thinking about the standard succession of fossil zones? If not, why not? If so, how?

Teacher Commentary

3. Once all groups have a poster board with completed information from all the other groups, they use all of the fossil information to interpret the standard succession of zones all over the world. (Note: Students should use pencils to draw in the lines of succession.) For the example data given in **Blackline Master** *Fossils* 4.3: **Stratigraphic Notebook,** the standard succession of zones is S, A, D, N, Z, B.

4. After each group has completed their standard succession, they will take the information to write down the succession in a vertical column on a blank sheet of paper. The oldest layer will be at the bottom and the youngest at the top.

5. The idea here is to mirror what paleontologists do. Findings are reported by many different paleontologists and added to the fossil record. Make sure that this is understood by students, as they compile their own class fossil record.

   a) Some groups will not draw their lines correctly. Help students develop strategies on how to draw distinct lines on the basis of the evidence in their field notes.

   b) Fossils are commonly found in particular kinds of sedimentary rocks, not in all rocks. (Just as one would not expect to see a particular species living in all sedimentary environments, everywhere today, one should not expect to see a fossil species represented in all sedimentary rocks from an ancient time.)

   c) Students may suggest that erosional processes can wipe away stratigraphic layers or that sediments are not always deposited at any particular location and time.

   d) Students should suggest that they could identify the appearance and/or disappearance of particular fossils and place these events within the standard succession of zones.

   e) Students may suggest that the geologic-time scale could be altered to reflect this newly discovered stratigraphic section. However, many statigraphic sections that can be interpreted on the basis of the standard succession also contain unique or less well-known fossils. The appearance of a new fossil therefore does not negate the standard succession of zones. If the paleontologist found one of the index fossils used in the standard succession in a time zone that was unexpected, this might necessitate a reevaluation of the succession.

Assessment Tool

Group-Participation Evaluation Sheets I and II
Use these two evaluation sheets to provide students with an opportunity to assess group participation. Do not use the results of this evaluation as the sole source of assessment data. Rather, it is better to assign a weight to the results of this evaluation and factor it in with the other sources of assessment data. (If you have not done this before, you may be surprised to find how honestly students will critique their own work, often more intensely than you might do.)

Investigating Fossils

Investigation 4: Fossils through Geologic Time

Digging Deeper

TELLING GEOLOGIC TIME

Species

Every plant or animal belongs to a species. A species is a population of plants or animals that can breed to produce offspring that can then produce offspring themselves.

Biologists believe that new species evolve from existing species by a process called natural selection. Here's how it works. Genes are chemical structures in the cells of the organism. The nature of the organism is determined by its genes. The organism inherits the genes from its parents. Occasionally, a gene changes accidentally. That's called a mutation. The changed gene is passed on to the next generation. Most mutations are bad, some are neutral but some mutations make the organism more successful in its life. Organisms that inherit that favorable new gene are likely to become more abundant than others of the species.

Sometimes the population of a species becomes separated into two areas, by geography or by climate. Then the two groups no longer breed with each other. The two groups then slowly change by natural selection. Each group changes in different ways. Eventually, the two groups are so different that they can't breed to produce offspring any more. They have become two different species.

As You Read…
Think about:
1. What is a species?
2. How do species change through time?
3. What are index fossils? How are they used in stratigraphic correlations?
4. How has radioactivity been used to refine the geologic time scale?

Evidence for Ideas

Investigating Earth Systems

F 35

164 Investigating Earth Systems

Teacher Commentary

Digging Deeper

This section provides text and photos that give students greater insight into the topic of fossils in geologic time. You may wish to assign the **As You Read** questions as homework to help students focus on the major ideas in the text.

As You Read...

Think about:

1. A species is a population of plants or animals that can breed to produce offspring that can themselves breed and reproduce.

2. Environmental pressures and genetic variation either allow species to evolve and fill new ecological niches or force species into extinction. Generation after generation, individuals least suited for the changing environment are eliminated through the process known as natural selection. The result of this natural selection process allows species to evolve.

3. Index fossils are used to identify and date the strata in which they are found. Important qualities of index fossils are that they are common in the rock record, have a wide geographic distribution, and existed for a short period of time. Scientists use index fossils for comparing stratigraphic sections from around the world.

4. Radiometric dating allows scientists to refine the relative ages of rocks and to identify an absolute age, sometimes as great as hundreds to thousands of millions of years.

Assessment Opportunity

You may wish to rephrase selected questions from the **As You Read** section into multiple choice or true/false format to use as a quiz. Use this quiz to assess student understanding and as a motivational tool to ensure that students complete the reading assignment and comprehend the main ideas.

About the Photo

The photograph on page F35 shows two different peppered moths against a tree trunk. One is white with gray specks and one is black. In England during the 1800s, most peppered moths were white with gray specks. However, at the end of the century, industrial activity in most cities polluted the air with soot and smog. The gray-speckled moth was more visible against the tree trunks and easier for birds to prey upon. In contrast, the black-peppered moths were less vulnerable to being eaten by birds because their darker color camouflaged them against the darker tree trunks tainted by air pollution. By 1900, the population of the black-peppered moths had nearly replaced the population of the gray-speckled peppered moths. As air quality improved over time, the tree trunks returned to their natural color and the gray-speckled peppered moth again had the advantage against predators. Students can read more on the recent discoveries about the evolution of the peppered moths by going to the *IES* web site.

INVESTIGATING FOSSILS

Species eventually become extinct. That means that the population gets smaller and smaller, until no more organisms of that species are left alive. Species become extinct for various reasons. If the environment changes too fast, the species might not be able to adapt fast enough. Also, a new species might evolve to compete with an existing species. Biologists are sure that once a species becomes extinct it never appears again.

In the modern world, biologists can identify species by seeing whether the organisms can breed with one another. Paleontologists have much more trouble with fossil species, because the organisms are no longer around to breed! All that can be done is to match up shells or imprints that look almost identical and then assume that they represent a species. The features of an organism are controlled by its genetics. Thus, similar-looking fossil organisms had similar genetic composition.

The Fossil Record

Paleontologists want to know the history of evolution and extinction of fossil species through geologic time. To do that, they try to study all of the fossils that have been preserved in sedimentary rocks. That's called the fossil record. Paleontologists have been collecting fossils from sedimentary rock layers around the world for

Teacher Commentary

About the Photo
The leopard shown in this photograph is native to regions of Asia and Africa. Leopards are hunted for their fur and are in danger of extinction. What other animals do students know that are in danger of become extinct in their lifetime?

Investigating Fossils

Investigation 4: Fossils through Geologic Time

over 200 years. Their goal is to figure out the succession of species through all of geologic time. Once that succession is known, it serves as a scale of geologic time. Then, if you find a particular fossil in a rock, you know where that rock fits into the geologic time scale.

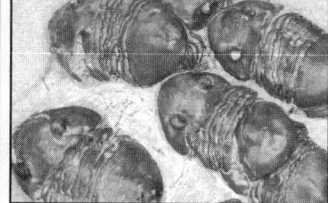

Cambrian trilobites   Ordovician trilobites   Devonian trilobites

There's a big problem in figuring out the succession of species through geologic time. You ran into this problem in the investigation. You don't know beforehand what the succession of species is! All you have are many stacks of sedimentary rocks (called stratigraphic sections) around the world to look at. No single stack spans all of geologic time, and no single stack has nearly all of the species that ever lived. You have to compare all of the stacks against one another to get the best approximation to the real succession. That's what you did in **Part C** of this investigation. You compared all of the stacks to one another and matched them up to figure out the succession of fossils. Paleontologists are still refining their ideas about the succession, as new fossils are found.

Stratigraphic Correlation

As you probably figured out already, matching up stratigraphic sections from around the world can be very difficult. If there were no fossils and you could only use the characteristics of the rock layers it would be even harder! This is because at any given time, very

Investigating Earth Systems

Investigating Earth Systems

Teacher Commentary

About the Photos

From left to right, these photos show trilobites from the Cambrian, Ordovician, and Devonian periods of geologic time. Over tens of millions of years, characteristics of the trilobites changed in appearance. What features do students notice changed the most?

INVESTIGATING FOSSILS

different types of sediments can be deposited in different places. It is these sediments that will eventually become the sedimentary rock layers making up the stratigraphic sections. At any given time, mud may be slowly collecting in some places while in other places sand is piling up rapidly. In other places, maybe there is nothing collecting at all! So you see, very different looking rock layers may mark the same time interval in different stratigraphic sections. The process of matching up equivalent "time layers" of rocks in different places is called stratigraphic correlation. One of the best (and oldest) tools for correlating strata around the world is the use of special fossils called index fossils.

Index fossils have two important characteristics. First, they must have been widely distributed around the world. Second, they must have existed for only relatively short periods of geologic time before becoming extinct. Consider a fossil of an organism that lived only in one place, or that existed for very long periods of geologic time. It would be of little use in matching up layers of rock that were deposited far from one another over the same limited span of time.

Dating Rocks

Knowing the fossil record lets a geoscientist place a particular fossiliferous rock layer into the scale of geologic time. But the time scale given by fossils is only a relative scale, because it does not give the age of the rock in years, only its age relative to other layers. Long after the relative time scale was worked out from fossils, geologists developed methods for finding the absolute ages of rocks, in years before the present. These methods involve radioactivity. Here's how one of the important ones works.

Teacher Commentary

NOTES

Investigation 4: Fossils through Geologic Time

Some minerals contain atoms of the radioactive chemical element uranium. Now and then, an atom of uranium self-destructs to form an atom of lead. Scientists know the rate of self-destruction. They grind up a rock to collect tiny grains of minerals that started out containing some uranium but no lead. Then they use a very sensitive instrument, called a mass spectrometer, to measure how much of the uranium has been changed to lead. Using some simple mathematics, they can figure out how long ago the mineral first formed. Rocks as old as four billion years can be dated this way.

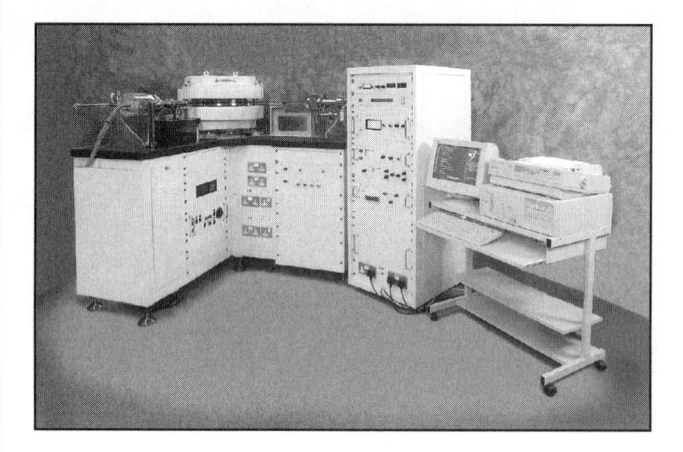

Absolute dating of rocks has provided many "tie points" for the relative time scale developed from fossils. The result is an absolute time scale. When you collect a fossil from a rock, you can place it in the relative time scale. Then you also know about how old it is in years (or usually millions, or tens of millions, or hundreds of millions of years). Even though modern technology makes it possible to date some rocks, the relative time scale is still very important. This is because it takes a lot of time and money to obtain an absolute date, and most rocks cannot be dated using radioactivity.

Teacher Commentary

About the Photo

This photograph shows a mass spectrometer. It is a highly sensitive instrument that uses a magnetic field to separate atoms by mass. A mass spectrometer is especially useful because it can be used to measure very minute quantities of elements and can even distinguish between different kinds of atoms (called isotopes) of the same element. Many of the different techniques used to quantitatively date rocks are based on this method of distinguishing the different isotopes of an element.

INVESTIGATING FOSSILS

Review and Reflect

Review

1. According to the chart in this investigation, how long have modern humans (*Homo sapiens*) been on Earth?
2. How are fossils used to match or correlate rock layers deposited in different places at the same time?
3. Why do geologists not use the characteristics of the rocks themselves to identify different rock layers that were deposited at the same time?

Reflect

4. In your own words, explain why you think that geologists still find the relative time scale to be a very useful tool.
5. Why is it that a scientist must look in many places to determine the succession of fossil species through geologic time?

Thinking about the Earth System

6. On your *Earth System Connection* sheet, note how the things you learned in this investigation connect to the geosphere, hydrosphere, atmosphere and biosphere.

Thinking about Scientific Inquiry

7. How did you model the fossil record?

Teacher Commentary

Review and Reflect

Review

Students should be given ample time to review what they have learned from this investigation. In particular, they need to review what they have learned about the role of time in *Investigating Fossils* as well as the appearance and disappearance of different life forms throughout Earth's history.

1. Students may use the chart on page F29 to infer that *Homo Sapiens* (modern humans) have existed on Earth for about 1.8 million years. The chart actually indicates only that modern humans came into being sometime during the Quaternary Period. In actuality, the species *Homo Sapiens* has existed on Earth for less than 100,000 years.

2. Fossils that are widely distributed, common in the rock record, and lived for a short period of time are used by scientists to match and compare layers of sedimentary rocks from around the world.

3. At any given time, many different kinds of sediments are constantly being deposited at many locations on the Earth's surface. For example, just because limestone formed at a particular time in Earth's history does not mean that the conditions are the same all over the world for limestone to develop elsewhere at the same time. For this reason, the kind of rock is generally not a good measure to use to tell time in the geologic record. Fossils are used because they provide information on both time and what the environment was like at a particular time on Earth.

Reflect

Students need time to reflect on the nature of the evidence they have collected from their investigations. Help them to see that evidence is crucial in scientific inquiry.

4. Answers may vary. It is not always necessary to know *exactly* when in Earth's history a particular event occurred or a life form existed. In addition, not all rocks can be dated using absolute (quantitative) dating methods like radioactive decay. For those that can, the dating process requires a lot of time, effort, and expensive laboratories and equipment. The relative time scale is useful because it is an approximation to when similar species existed and major events occurred on Earth, and interpreting it requires only some knowledge and skill, and not necessarily expensive laboratories and equipment.

5. Answers may vary. Students should explain that additional strata are needed because no single example gives scientists an accurate approximation of the appearance and disappearance of particular species on Earth. Environmental conditions on Earth have varied greatly throughout geologic time and are never

the same everywhere on Earth at any particular time. So any one stratigraphic column may not contain all of the necessary rock layers, or if the layers are there, each one may not contain the right kinds of fossils.

Thinking about the Earth System

Have students again revisit their *Earth System Connection* sheet and update it. As a result of their investigations, your students should, by now, have learned enough to make some clear connections between the parts of the Earth system. In particular, they should be able to discuss how the geosphere preserves a record of changes in the biosphere over time. Be alert to the questions and reasoning that students use in considering this wider set of issues. Refer students to page Fx of their books as a means of exploring the Earth system further.

6. Students should note the interaction between the biosphere and the geosphere, and also note how the presence of fossils depends greatly on the environment of deposition and the type of rock containing the fossil. Additionally, the atmosphere and the hydrosphere play important roles in creating the environmental pressures that contribute to the processes of extinction and evolution.

Thinking about Scientific Inquiry

Remind the students that the science inquiry processes that they used in this investigation will help them find information and approach problems throughout their lives. Point out to them that this will be especially useful when, as adults, they will need to use evidence to make decisions. Have the students think back on where and how they used inquiry processes in this investigation.

7. Student answers will vary. Students will likely discuss how they created a timescale in **Part B** that organized events in Earth's history by their relative times. They used mathematical ratios to develop a good approximation of when events occurred and various life forms appeared. Students also used fossil data from several locations to simulate how a real succession of species is developed.

Assessment Tool
Review and Reflect Journal-Entry Evaluation Sheet
Use the **Review and Reflect** part of the investigation to assess individual or collective understandings about the concepts and inquiry processes explored. You can use the general criteria provided on this evaluation sheet to assess content and thoroughness of student work, whether the students worked individually or in groups. Adapt and modify the sheet to meet your needs. Consider involving students in selecting and modifying the assessment criteria.

Teacher Commentary

NOTES

Teacher Review

Use this section to reflect on and review the investigation. Keep in mind that your notes here are likely to be especially helpful when you teach this investigation again. Questions listed here are examples only.

Student Achievement
What evidence do you have that all students have met the science content objectives?

Are there any students who need more help in reaching these objectives? If so, how can you provide this?

What evidence do you have that all students have demonstrated their understanding of the inquiry processes?

Which of these inquiry objectives do your students need to improve upon in future investigations?

What evidence do the journal entries contain about what your students learned from this investigation?

Planning
How well did this investigation fit into your class time?

What changes can you make to improve your planning next time?

Guiding and Facilitating Learning
How well did you focus and support inquiry while interacting with students?

What changes can you make to improve classroom management for the next investigation or the next time you teach this investigation?

Teacher Commentary

How successful were you in encouraging all students to participate fully in science learning? _____

_____

How did you encourage and model the skills values, and attitudes of scientific inquiry? _____

_____

How did you nurture collaboration among students? _____

_____

Materials and Resources

What challenges did you encounter obtaining or using materials and/or resources needed for the activity? _____

_____

What changes can you make to better obtain and better manage materials and resources next time? _____

_____

Student Evaluation

Describe how you evaluated student progress. What worked well? What needs to be improved? _____

_____

How will you adapt your evaluation methods for next time? _____

_____

Describe how you guided students in self-assessment. _____

_____

Self Evaluation

How would you rate your teaching of this investigation? _____

_____

What advice would you give to a colleague who is planning to teach this investigation? _____

_____

Investigating Fossils – Investigation 4

NOTES

Teacher Commentary

INVESTIGATION 5: COMPARING FOSSILS OVER TIME
Background Information

Fossils through Geologic Time

Does it come as a surprise to you that the fossil record extends almost as far back in geologic time as the record of the Earth's rocks? The broadest subdivisions of geologic time in common use among geoscientists are the Archean, before 2500 million years ago, the Proterozoic, from 2500 million to 543 million years ago, and the Phanerozoic, from 543 million years ago until the present. The oldest rocks found so far have been dated at about 4000 million years. Fossils of primitive single-celled organisms, called cyanobacteria, as old as 3500 million years have been found in a number of places in the world. The organisms are of a kind called prokaryotes. In contrast to more modern organisms, called eukaryotes, the cells of prokaryotes do not have a nucleus, and their DNA is not organized into chromosomes. Prokaryotic cells also lack the various other internal organ-like structures that are characteristic of more advanced life forms.

Prokaryotic organisms reproduce asexually, and the pace of evolution during the Archean and for a large part of the Proterozoic was extremely slow. During the Proterozoic, about 1800 million years ago, single-celled organisms with eukaryotic cells first made their appearance. The fossil record of these eukaryotic organisms is not abundant, but it is clear that by the end of the Proterozoic a multitude of rather complex single-celled organisms had evolved. The most useful of these for the purposes of dating later Proterozoic rocks are called acritarchs, which are globular or spiky single-celled organisms that are thought to have been akin to dinoflagellates, which are an important group of planktonic algae today. (Planktonic organisms are those that float freely and passively in the near-surface waters of lakes and oceans.)

The first multicellular organisms made their appearance near the end of the Proterozoic. Exotic faunas of a greater variety of soft-bodied and rather complex organisms, of macroscopic rather than microscopic size, have been found in excellent preservation in shales in several places around the world. Most of these have no evident relationship to the later phyla of Phanerozoic time. It is possible that during the final few hundred million years of the Proterozoic there were "false starts" in the evolution of metazoans (multicellular organisms). Coincident with the appearance of these body fossils of soft-bodied organisms, trace fossils (track, trails, and other indirect evidence of the life activities of organisms) become abundant in the sedimentary record beginning about 600 million years ago.

Fossils of organisms with hard skeletal materials, which, of course, make the organisms potentially much more preservable, make their appearance in the sedimentary record very abruptly at the beginning of the Phanerozoic, about 550 million years ago. With advances in precision of radioisotopic dating of rocks, it is now becoming apparent that most of the phyla of marine invertebrates appeared within the short space of several million years! This spectacular episode in evolution has been called the "Cambrian explosion" (the Cambrian being the first time period of the Phanerozoic). The dynamics of this extremely rapid period of organic evolution are still unclear. After the beginning of the Phanerozoic, the fossil record is much more abundant, because of the better preservability of invertebrates with solid skeletons or shells of calcium carbonate or chitin. (Chitin is a solid polysaccharide compound. It is the main constituent of the exoskeletons of arthropods, like crabs and lobsters.) Of course, soft-bodied organisms, like worms, must have been abundant as well, but because of their low preservability, their fossil record is poor. Single-celled organisms, even the very primitive prokaryotes, have continued successfully to the present: it's not a matter of more complex life forms displacing the earlier ones; it's a matter of adding the more complex forms to the existing web of life.

Your students are likely to be much more exposed to, and conscious of, a number of later major milestones in the history of life during the Phanerozoic. Multicellular plants first invaded the land in the Silurian, a bit more than 400 million years ago, and lush forests became established by the Devonian, more than 350 million years ago. Coal, which is formed by lush growth of trees in coastal swamps, is very scarce before the Devonian. Fish became abundant in the oceans by the Silurian, and the first amphibians evolved in the Devonian. The appearance of fishes and amphibians marked the beginning of the long evolutionary history of the vertebrates. The oldest known reptiles are from the Pennsylvanian Period, about 300 million years ago. Reptiles, in the form of the dinosaurs (with which most young people are familiar today!) attained their dominance in the Jurassic and Cretaceous Periods, from about 200 million years ago to about 65 million years ago, at which time they suffered a very abrupt extinction, for reasons that are still controversial. Thereafter, reptiles have played a minor part in the Earth's faunas. Mammals seem to have evolved in the Triassic Period, over two hundred million years ago, but they remained small until the demise of the dinosaurs, after which they underwent great diversification to develop the wide range of adaptations and body sizes seen today.

The pace of evolution and extinction during the Phanerozoic has not been smooth. Long periods of steady evolution and extinction of species has been punctuated by several major, even catastrophic episodes of mass extinction. The greatest of these was at the end of the Permian Period, when over ninety percent of all known species became extinct. The cause (or causes) of that great extinction is now being debated. Another major mass extinction occurred at the end of the Cretaceous Period. It is now widely believed that that extinction was caused, or at least triggered or augmented, by the impact of a giant asteroid. After each such mass extinction, the remaining life forms underwent explosive evolutionary radiation, whereby large numbers of new species evolved to fill the many ecological niches that had been vacated by the mass extinction.

More Information...on the Web
Visit the *Investigating Earth Systems* web site www.agiweb.org/ies/ for links to a variety of other web sites that will help you deepen your understanding of content and prepare you to teach this module.

Teacher Commentary

Investigation Overview

In this investigation, your students will be comparing today's clams to ancient clams. Clams first developed almost 600 million years ago. They are one of nature's greatest survivors in life through time, and offer students the opportunity for a wonderful hands-on investigation into fossils.

Goals and Objectives

Science Content Objectives
Students will collect evidence that:
1. Living things have changed over time.
2. Fossils are a record of how living things have changed over time.
3. There are similarities and differences between fossil and modern organisms.
4. Fossil formation is connected to the biosphere, the hydrosphere, the atmosphere, and the geosphere.

Inquiry Process Skills
Students will:
1. Observe and describe fossils.
2. Use measurements to describe fossils.
3. Make accurate representations of fossils.
4. Interpret data.
5. Compare and contrast fossils with modern organisms.
6. Use multiple resources to research fossils.
7. Share information about fossils.
8. Communicate data and conclusions to others.

Connections to Standards and Benchmarks
Students make a comparative study between fossil clams and shells of recent clams. They use this to study evidence of how species evolve over time. Reading the **Digging Deeper** section of the activity will help students to better understand the process of identifying fossils and what the fossil records reveals about the evolution of life. These observations and information will start them on the road to understanding the National Science Education Standards and AAAS Benchmarks shown on the following page.

NSES Links

- Evolution is a series of changes, sometimes gradual, sometimes sporadic, that accounts for the present form and function of objects, organisms, and natural and designed systems. The general idea of evolution is that the present arises from materials and forms of the past.

- Biological evolution accounts for the diversity of species developed through gradual processes over many generations. Species acquire many of their unique characteristics through biological adaptation, which involves the selection of naturally occurring variations in populations. Biological adaptations include changes in structures, behaviors, or physiology that enhance survival and reproductive success in a particular environment.

- Millions of species of animals, plants, and microorganisms are alive today. Although different species might look dissimilar, the unity among organisms becomes apparent from an analysis of internal structures, the similarity of their chemical processes, and the evidence of common ancestry.

- Form and function are complimentary aspects of objects, organisms, and systems in the natural and designed world. The form or shape of an object is frequently related to use, operation, or function.

AAAS Links

- Many thousands of layers of sedimentary rock provide evidence for the long history of the Earth and for the long history of changing life forms whose remains are found in the rocks. More recently deposited rock layers are more likely to contain fossils resembling existing species.

- Fossils can be compared to one another and to living organisms according to their similarities and differences. Some organisms that lived long ago are similar to existing organisms, but some are quite different.

- Small differences between parents and offspring can accumulate (through selective breeding) in successive generations so that descendants are very different from their ancestors.

- A great variety of living things can be sorted into groups in many ways, using various features to decide which things belong to which group.

- In classifying organisms, biologists consider details of internal and external structures to be more important than behavior or general appearance.

- Many thousands of layers of sedimentary rock provide evidence for the long history of the Earth and for the long history of changing life forms whose remains are found in the rocks. More recently deposited rock layers are more likely to contain fossils resembling existing species.

Teacher Commentary

Preparation and Materials Needed

Preparation
This investigation requires about five 40-minute class periods to complete, depending upon the depth to which you have students conduct research on their own questions about the evolution of clams (**Step 8** of **Investigate**):

- **Days One and Two:** Have students address the **Key Question** and complete their observations and descriptions of fossil and recent clam shells (**Steps 1–7** of **Investigate**). Have students begin their research project (**Step 8**) as a homework assignment during the first two days.

- **Days Three and Four:** Have students finalize their research on clams and present their findings to the class. Assign the **Digging Deeper** reading section and the **As You Read** questions for homework.

- **Day Five:** Review the main concepts from the investigation and have the students complete the questions in **Review and Reflect**.

You will need to obtain enough fresh clams from your local grocery or fish store to have at least one per group. Steaming the clams in their shells is the easiest way of removing the flesh from the shell. It also removes any potential health risks.

It is strongly suggested that each group have a real fossilized clamshell with which to make comparisons. Alternatives are imitation fossil clams or photographs, but, in both cases, these offer students far less opportunity for study. Try to ensure that the fossil collection is varied. Have clam fossils that represent different time periods, or different specimens from the same time period.

Materials
- fossil clamshell
- hand lens
- eight index cards
- metric ruler, or tape measure
- pencil and other drawing implements
- paper clip or a stapler
- fresh clamshells (with clams removed)

Investigating Fossils

Investigation 5: Comparing Fossils over Time

Investigation 5:

Comparing Fossils over Time

Key Question
Before you begin, first think about this key question.

How are modern organisms different from ancient organisms?

Think about the age of the Earth. How has life changed since the first organisms appeared?

Share your thinking with others in your class. Keep a record of the discussion in your journal.

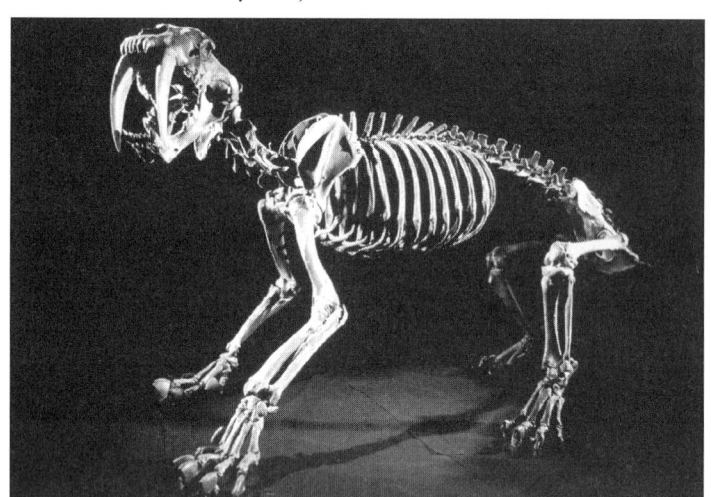

Materials Needed

For this investigation your group will need:
- fossil clamshell
- hand lens
- eight index cards
- metric ruler or tape measure
- pencil and other drawing implements
- paper clip or a stapler
- fresh clamshells (with clam removed)

Investigate

1. Each group will receive a fossil clamshell.

   Observe the fossil in detail, noting all its characteristics. Remember to observe it from all angles, both inside and out. Each group will have a fossil clamshell. At first glance, they all look very similar. If you look closely, however, you will see fine differences.

Teacher Commentary

Key Question

Instruct students to respond to this question in their journals. Allow a few minutes of writing time. Have them share their ideas with a neighbor, then with the rest of their group, and finally, the entire class. Make a list of ideas on the board. Accept student ideas uncritically, even if they appear undeveloped (or are simply not correct). However, do not praise wrong ideas. The point of this exercise, as with all the **Key Questions**, is to provoke thought and prepare for the investigation. Instruct students to make a "master list" in their journal of ideas and new questions.

Student Conceptions about Changing Life

Students generally appreciate several key differences, including the fact that early organisms were less complex and that life was less diverse long ago than it is today. The idea that a kind of organism (pelecypod, algae, etc.) can have a long history may be hard for students to appreciate at first.

Answer for the Teacher Only

Some ancient organisms are very similar to the same kinds of organisms today (algae, for example). See the **Background Information** at the beginning of this investigation in this Teacher's Edition for a general overview related to this question.

> **Assessment Tool**
> Key-Question Evaluation Sheet
> Use this evaluation sheet to help students understand and internalize basic expectations for the warm-up activity.

> **About the Photo**
> This photograph shows a saber-toothed cat, *Smilodon californicus*. The species first appeared during the Oligocene and became extinct in the Pleistocene. They are recognized by the long, curving, upper canine teeth.

Investigate

The investigation gives students the opportunity to study and describe fossil clams and to compare ancient clams to modern clams. The experience examining features of fossils that record changes in life through time is further developed in the reading and through research that students conduct on the evolution of clams.

Teaching Suggestions and Sample Answers

1. Distribute materials to students. Encourage students to make as many observations as possible of the fossil clamshell. They should look for even the tiniest detail, and record it.

   Encourage students to make any measurements they can. These can include linear measures in centimeters and millimeters, mass, angles, surface area, or volume (water displacement).

Teacher Commentary

NOTES

Investigating Fossils

INVESTIGATING FOSSILS

Think about any measurements you could make of the fossil clamshell.

Look for any distinguishing features.

Are there any parts or markings that you can use to help you recognize your fossil clamshell among other fossil clamshells?

Pay attention to size and shape. Take lots of measurements. Look for places where muscles might have been attached, where feeding organs may have protruded from the shell, how the animal moved, and any other aspects of "living" that you can suggest.

Collect & Review

2. Obtain four index cards.

On one index card, describe the fossil as if you were sending the description to someone who had never seen it before. Include all the observations and any measurements you have made.

Teacher Commentary

2. Allow students to describe their fossils in any way they see fit. In **Step 3**, the accuracy of their recordings will be tested. Remind students to label their index cards with their names and any other information that you see fit.

Investigation 5: Comparing Fossils over Time

On the other three index cards, make as accurate drawings of the fossil as you can, from three different angles.

Outside view of clamshell fossil

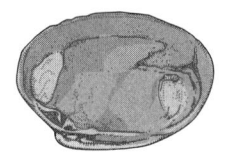

Inside view of clamshell fossil

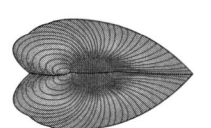

Side view of clamshell fossil

You will need to collaborate on this task. Share the work between your group members. Keep your index cards safe, because you will need them for the next step.

3. All the clam fossils will now be collected, mixed up, and then displayed for all to visit and study. They will be placed in a random order.

    Using your index cards as a guide, try to find your fossil in the collection.

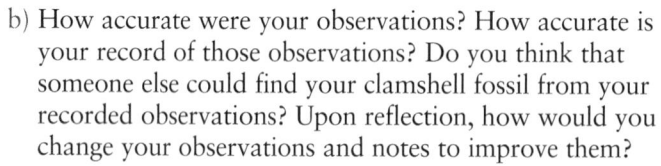

    a) How difficult was it to find your fossil clam? What made it easy or difficult to find?

    b) How accurate were your observations? How accurate is your record of those observations? Do you think that someone else could find your clamshell fossil from your recorded observations? Upon reflection, how would you change your observations and notes to improve them?

4. Fasten your index cards together. Use a paper clip or a staple. Write your names on the top of the first card.

    All the sets of cards will be collected. They will be redistributed so that each group has another group's cards.

    Once again, the clamshell fossils will be displayed, this time in a different order.

    Using the data on the set of index cards you have been given, search and find the clamshell fossil it describes.

    When you think you have identified the clam fossil correctly, check the names of the group members on the first card. Ask that group to verify that you have the correct one.

5. When each group has identified and verified the correct fossil, take time to discuss differences between the clam fossils.

Evidence for Ideas

Inquiry
Recording Observations

Scientists are very careful about recording observations. They try not to miss any detail that may turn out to be important later.

They also record their observations in a way that others can see and understand. This will also be important for you to do, because other groups are going to use your records later.

Teacher Commentary

> **About the Illustration**
>
> The illustration shows the outside, inside, and side view of a fossil clam.
>
> You can make an overhead transparency of this illustration using **Blackline Master** *Fossils* 5.1: **Sample Illustrations of Fossils** to facilitate classroom discussion.

3. Collect the fossils, mix them up, and then lay them out in a place where students can look at them. The idea here is to test students' accuracy in recording by using the index cards to find the fossil.

    a) Answers will vary, depending upon the skill your students have with describing objects and the nature of the fossil clams — the more similar they are, the more challenging it will be to identify the fossils on the basis of the first attempts at describing them. Artistic talent is also a factor that can affect how easy it is for others to find the fossil using only a diagram and description.

    b) Students should note ways that they can improve their descriptions, including the accuracy and quality of their drawings. Students might add measurements and note distinguishing features of the particular fossil.

4. Collect the fossils, and again mix them up and lay them out so that students can see them. This time, each group will try to find a fossil on the basis of another group's records. This will be more challenging because the first time around, students may have just recognized their fossil on sight. Now, others must find the fossil using the descriptions, which makes the quality and accuracy of descriptions even more important.

    Students need to understand that observations should be recorded in a way that others can understand. This is a fundamental part of scientific investigation. It is also a reason why scientists use agreed-upon measures like the metric system. Alert your students to the importance of these ideas.

5. Hold a class discussion (or encourage group discussion) about differences and similarities between the fossil shells.

Investigating Fossils

INVESTIGATING FOSSILS

Record the results of your discussion in your journal.

a) How are all the clamshell fossils the same? How are they different?

b) What features can be measured, or counted?

c) What characteristics can help to sort one clamshell fossil from another?

d) Make a list of items that could be helpful for future study of clamshells.

This diagram will help you with your observations:

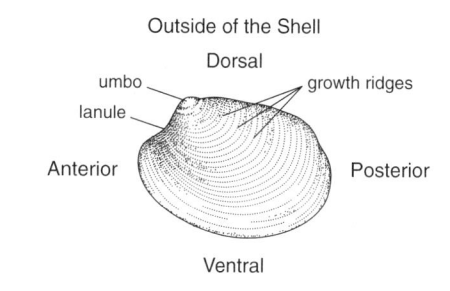

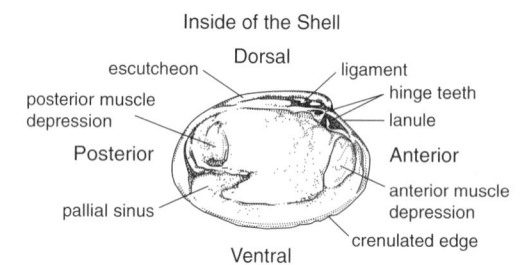

Outside of the Shell

- Dorsal
- umbo
- lanule
- growth ridges
- Anterior
- Posterior
- Ventral

Inside of the Shell

- Dorsal
- escutcheon
- ligament
- hinge teeth
- posterior muscle depression
- lanule
- Posterior
- Anterior
- pallial sinus
- anterior muscle depression
- crenulated edge
- Ventral

6. Your group will now be given a modern clamshell.

Once again, you will use four index cards to make a record of your observations.

You will also repeat the display-and-find process as before, using another group's index-card data to identify their clamshell and verify it.

7. Now, revisit your original fossilized clamshell, and the observations you made on index cards. Lay these alongside the modern clamshell and its set of observations.

Teacher Commentary

a) Here, students are introduced to the key features of clamshells, including the names of their parts. The shells have several features in common, including growth ridges and other features noted in the diagram on page F44 of the Student Book.

b) Growth ridges and the number of hinge teeth can sometimes be counted. Lengths of various parts of the shell can be measured, along with the length, width, and height of the shell.

c) Have students identify all these parts/characteristics on their fossil sample.

d) See the answer above and the features noted in the diagram on page F44 of the Student Book.

> **About the Illustration**
> The illustration shows parts of a fossil clam.
>
> You can make an overhead transparency of this illustration using **Blackline Master** *Fossils* **5.2: Diagram of Parts of a Clamshell** to facilitate classroom discussion.

6. Here, students use the experience they have had with fossil clamshells in comparing modern clamshells with ancient ones. Help the students to find similarities and differences between modern clams and ancient clams.

Investigation 5: Comparing Fossils over Time

Compare the two. Answer the following questions:

a) How are the two clamshells (ancient and modern) similar? How are they different?

b) Is there any way of telling that one is a fossil and the other is not? If so, how?

c) How can you tell that the fossilized clamshell may be a very ancient relative to the modern clamshell?

Discuss these questions, and any others you think important, first in your group, and then with all other groups. Try to reach an agreement about the similarities and differences between fossil clams and modern clams.

8. By now, you have discovered quite a lot about clams. Spend some time researching them. You will need to use all the resources available to do this.

The school library can be searched for reference books.

If you have access to computers, try CD-ROM encyclopedias, or log onto the Internet and search under "clams" (also try "pelecypods" and "bivalves," which are technical terms for clams) for further information.

a) When your group has completed its research, organize your information in a clear and understandable form. Try to be creative about this. Use any pictures you can find to make your presentation attractive and interesting to others.

Hold a whole-class session, in which each group shows what it has found out about clamshells.

9. When you have shared all the information you have collected about clams, think about other organisms that have existed through time. Review the Major Divisions of Geologic Time chart on page F29.

As you do so, discuss and answer these questions:

a) What other kinds of organisms besides clams have survived for millions of years?

b) What organisms have become extinct over time?

c) What might have given some organisms a better chance of survival than others?

Use any other resources you have available to help find answers to these questions.

Inquiry

Using References as Evidence

When you write a science report, the information you gather from books, magazines, and the Internet comes from scientific investigations. Just as in your investigations, the results can be used as evidence. Because evidence, like an idea, is important, you must always list the source of your evidence. This not only gives credit to the person who wrote the work, but it allows others to examine it and decide for themselves whether or not it makes sense.

Teacher Commentary

7. **a)** Answers will vary depending upon the particular species of clam. Similar features include growth ridges, posterior muscle depressions, hinge teeth, and other parts of the clamshell as shown in the diagram on page F44.

   b) Answers will vary. It is not always easy to distinguish between fossil clamshells and modern clamshells. Well-preserved fossil clamshells can be in better condition than shells that have been recently weathered by the action of ocean waves.

   c) The general similarities between the shells provide important clues to the evolutionary link between the two species.

> **Teaching Tip**
> Hold a general discussion of students' experiences with shelled animals in general, and clams in particular. Some students may have seen clams in their natural habitats, or fishermen bringing them to market. Most likely, students will have seen them only at the store or at home.

8. Students need to understand that finding and gathering information is an important scientific process. They need to know that scientists use a variety of tools like databases, reference books, scientific reports, and so on to do this. Allow your students to consider what resources they could use, and where information might be available. Finding information for themselves is an important part of this investigation. Students should be encouraged to find out how a clam and other similar creatures live, get their food, and protect themselves from predators.

   a) Students need to understand that scientists disseminate their findings to others. Pooling the information that different groups have acquired will broaden everyone's knowledge and understanding. For this reason, students should think about how to organize their information in a way that others can easily see and understand.

   You will need to organize this in a way that works for your students. Some students might need access to a computer and to the Internet to show their information most effectively.

9. Students can now apply their knowledge of ancient and modern clams to other organisms. This should give them a better sense of the nature of evolution, the emergence of new species, and the extinction of others over time.

   a) Fish, amphibians, sharks, and reptiles are examples of organisms that have survived for millions of years.

   b) Trilobites, dinosaurs, and ammonites are examples of organisms that have become extinct.

Investigating Fossils – Investigation 5

c) Students might find from their research that lack of predators or ability to adapt to changing environments have been important to the survival of groups of organisms over time.

Assessment Tools

Journal-Entry Evaluation Sheet
Use this sheet as a general guideline for assessing student journals. Remind students about the criteria for evaluating journals.

Journal-Entry Checklist
Use this checklist for quickly checking the quality and completeness of journal entries.

Investigation Journal-Entry Evaluation Sheet
Use this sheet to help students to learn the basic expectations for journal entries that feature the write-up of investigations. It provides a variety of criteria that both you and students can use to ensure that student work meets the highest possible standards and expectations. Adapt this sheet so that it is appropriate for your classroom. You may also wish to make modifications to tailor a sheet specific to a given investigation.

Teacher Commentary

NOTES

Investigating Fossils

INVESTIGATING FOSSILS

As You Read...
Think about:
1. Why do paleontologists use geometric shape to analyze a collection of fossils?
2. According to fossil records, how have organisms evolved during geologic time?
3. When did the first multicellular organisms appear in the fossil record?

Digging Deeper

FOSSILS THROUGH GEOLOGIC TIME
Identifying Fossils

When you sorted fossils by the features of their geometry, you were doing exactly what paleontologists do. A paleontologist collects as many fossils as possible from a rock or sediment. Once the fossils are prepared by scraping and cleaning, they are sorted by geometry. Fossils with very similar geometry are assumed to belong to a single species. That is because an organism's geometry is controlled by its genetics. Fossils with somewhat different geometry are assumed to belong to a different species. Usually, the fossil species has already been studied and named. Sometimes, however, the species is a new one. Then the paleontologist writes a detailed description of the new species, gives the new species a name, and publishes the description for others to read and use in their own work. Not much excites a paleontologist more than discovering a new species!

Sorting fossils is tricky business, for several reasons. Some organisms died when they were young and still developing, and some died when they were old. Some were male and some were female. Also, most species show a lot of natural variability. You know that from looking at other members of your own species! It's often impossible for paleontologists to

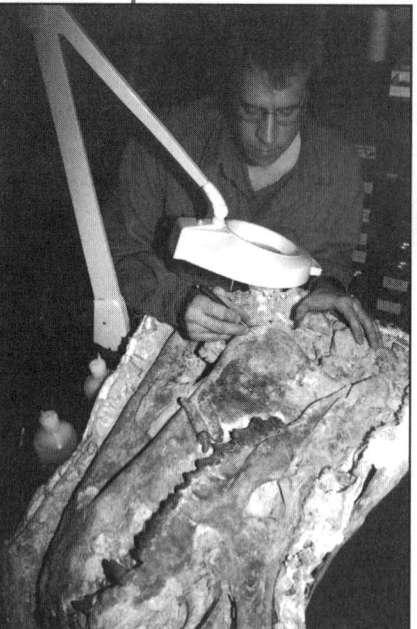

F
46   Investigating Earth Systems

Teacher Commentary

Digging Deeper

This section provides text and photos that give students greater insight into the topics of fossils through time and fossil identification. You may wish to assign the **As You Read** questions as homework to help students focus on the major ideas in the text.

As You Read...

Think about:

1. An organism's geometry is controlled by genetics, which makes geometric shape an important area of study for evolutionary paleontologists.

2. The oldest fossils date back to 3.5 billion years before the present.

3. Multicellular organisms began to evolve a little more than a half a billion years ago.

Assessment Opportunity

You may wish to select questions from the **As You Read** section to use as a quiz, rephrasing the questions into multiple choice or true/false format. Use this quiz to assess student understanding, and as a motivational tool to ensure that students complete the reading assignment and comprehend the main ideas.

About the Photo

In this photograph, a scientist cleans and examines the head of a dinosaur skeleton called a brontothere. Dinosaur skeletons in museums are often casts of the original fossil. The cast is made by taking a mold of the original fossil like the one shown in this photo. Have the students ever seen a dinosaur skeleton in a museum? What differences did they notice between the various types of dinosaurs?

Investigation 5: Comparing Fossils over Time

decide whether they are looking at a single species with a lot of variability, or two similar species.

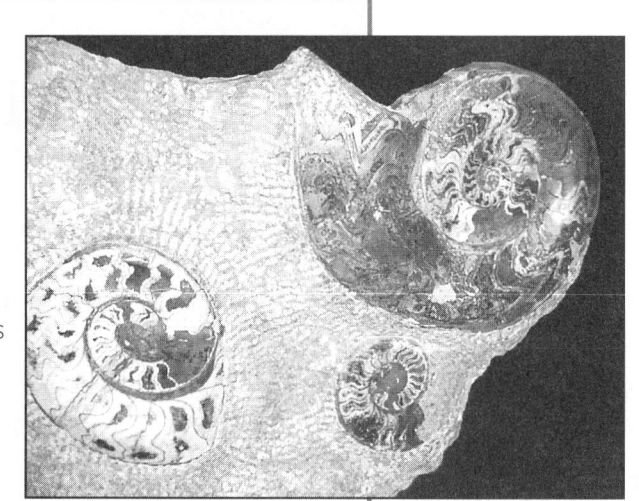

Evolution in the Fossil Record

The oldest fossils are more than 3.5 billion years old. They are simple unicellular (single-celled) algae, very similar to algae that still exist today. Evolution was very slow until about 700 million years ago, when unicellular organisms with larger and more complex cells evolved. Not long after that, a little more than half a billion years ago, multicellular (many-celled) organisms appeared. Instead of consisting of just a single cell, multicellular organisms have an enormous number of cells, grouped according to their function. Several kinds of multicellular organisms evolved in a very short time, geologically. Paleontologists still do not understand very well how this happened. Many of these early kinds of multicellular organisms, like clams, snails, and corals, are still abundant today. More complex kind of animals, like reptiles, birds, and mammals, evolved even more recently in geologic time.

Teacher Commentary

About the Photos

The upper photograph shows ammonite fossils of different sizes. What reasons can students give for the differences in size? It could be from a difference in the maturity of each individual. The apparently smaller ammonite could also have been larger, but a portion of it was not preserved with the rest. A paleontologist's job is to find answers to these and other questions.

The lower photograph shows a fossilized coral. Corals are an example of multicellular organisms that evolved relatively quickly. Given the previous investigation about the preservation of soft-bodied animals, are the students surprised to see a photograph of a fossilized coral?

INVESTIGATING FOSSILS

Review and Reflect

Review

1. What do fossil clams have in common with modern clams?
2. What kind of organism is the oldest found in the fossil record?

Reflect

3. How can you tell that the very ancient clam is related to the modern clam?
4. What are some of the difficulties in identifying fossils?
5. From what you've learned in this investigation, do you think that paleontologists have overestimated or underestimated the number of different species observed in the fossil record? Explain your answer.

Thinking about the Earth System

6. On your *Earth System Connection* sheet, note how the things you learned in this investigation connect to the geosphere, hydrosphere, atmosphere, and biosphere.

Thinking about Scientific Inquiry

7. Why is it important to take good observations?
8. Why is it important in a scientific investigation to record your observations and procedures carefully in a way that is easily understood by others?

Teacher Commentary

Review and Reflect

Review
Allow your students ample time to pull all their evidence together and arrive at conclusions and explanations. Help them to make all the connections based upon their data.

1. Fossil clams share several features with modern clams, including growth ridges, posterior muscle depressions, hinge teeth, and so on.

2. Single-celled (unicellular) algae are the oldest fossils found in the geologic record.

Reflect
Give students time to reflect on the nature of the evidence they have generated from their investigations. Again, help them to see that evidence is crucial in scientific inquiry.

3. Similarities in geometric shapes tie ancient and modern clams together as related through evolution.

4. Sometimes an organism has died at a young age (not fully developed), which makes it difficult to identify (just think how different you looked as a baby than you do today!). Natural variability in species can also make fossils difficult to identify.

5. Students might claim that paleontologists have underestimated the number of species in the fossil record because so few fossils survive and even fewer have been discovered.

Thinking about the Earth System
6. Encourage students to look at the bigger picture of the Earth System. Ensure that they update their *Earth System Connection* sheet with any new knowledge.

Thinking about Scientific Inquiry
Ask students to reflect on how they used the inquiry processes as they worked through this investigation.

7. Careful observations are an important part of making accurate descriptions. If you do not observe something carefully, you are more likely to miss important features of characteristics of an object or process.

8. Clear, accurate descriptions of observations and procedures make it easier for others to understand what you have done or seen (or for you to understand what you have written when you revisit your work later). If someone wishes to duplicate your efforts to test your ideas, they need to know exactly what you did.

> **Assessment Tool**
>
> **Review and Reflect Journal-Entry Evaluation Sheet**
> Use the **Review and Reflect** part of the investigation to assess individual or collective understandings about the concepts and inquiry processes explored. You can use the general criteria provided on this evaluation sheet to assess content and thoroughness of student work, whether the students worked individually or in groups. Adapt and modify the sheet to meet your needs. Consider involving students in selecting and modifying the assessment criteria.

Teacher Commentary

NOTES

Teacher Review

Use this section to reflect on and review the investigation. Keep in mind that your notes here are likely to be especially helpful when you teach this investigation again. Questions listed here are examples only.

Student Achievement

What evidence do you have that all students have met the science content objectives?

Are there any students who need more help in reaching these objectives? If so, how can you provide this?

What evidence do you have that all students have demonstrated their understanding of the inquiry processes?

Which of these inquiry objectives do your students need to improve upon in future investigations?

What evidence do the journal entries contain about what your students learned from this investigation?

Planning

How well did this investigation fit into your class time?

What changes can you make to improve your planning next time?

Guiding and Facilitating Learning

How well did you focus and support inquiry while interacting with students?

What changes can you make to improve classroom management for the next investigation or the next time you teach this investigation?

Teacher Commentary

How successful were you in encouraging all students to participate fully in science learning? _____

_____

How did you encourage and model the skills values, and attitudes of scientific inquiry? _____

_____

How did you nurture collaboration among students? _____

_____

Materials and Resources

What challenges did you encounter obtaining or using materials and/or resources needed for the activity? _____

_____

What changes can you make to better obtain and better manage materials and resources next time? _____

_____

Student Evaluation

Describe how you evaluated student progress. What worked well? What needs to be improved? _____

_____

How will you adapt your evaluation methods for next time? _____

_____

Describe how you guided students in self-assessment. _____

_____

Self Evaluation

How would you rate your teaching of this investigation? _____

_____

What advice would you give to a colleague who is planning to teach this investigation? _____

_____

Investigating Fossils – Investigation 5

NOTES

Teacher Commentary

INVESTIGATION 6: ADAPTATIONS TO A CHANGING ENVIRONMENT

Background Information

The **Background Information** section of Investigation 4 discussed the concept of a species and the theory of evolution by natural selection but did not address the external forces that facilitate and drive natural selection leading to the adaptation of an organism to its environment. Evolutionary adaptation of an organism to its environment and the circumstances that facilitate adaptation and the evolution of species is the focus of **Investigation 6**.

Life has colonized nearly every environment on Earth, ranging from the deep ocean floor (even within the ocean crust!) to the frozen polar regions. The great diversity of species on the Earth and their ability to thrive in the most extreme of environments are a testament to evolution and the ability of organisms to adapt over time to survive in an ever-changing environment. It is environmental pressure that drives natural selection and determines whether some change or mutation in an individual of a species will be beneficial to that individual's chance of success. In evolutionary terms, success is really measured not only by an organism's ability to live and thrive in its environment but more so by an organism's ability to successfully reproduce and continue its line in the gene pool of its species. Very few characteristics of an organism do not contribute, on the whole, to the success of an organism. Many of these adaptations are easily seen, like the long neck of a giraffe or the keen eyes of an eagle. Often times the advantage that they give to the organism is apparent. In the aforementioned examples, both of these adaptations help the organism to successfully compete for food. In other cases, however, both the nature of the adaptation and the advantage it provides is less clear. Several categories and examples of adaptations are listed on page F50 of the Student Book. In many cases the advantage that these adaptations provide to the organism can be easily reasoned out. Others that are less obvious are briefly discussed in this Teacher's Edition within the **Investigate** section of this investigation.

The surrounding environment and availability of ecological niches is one of the strongest factors that can influence the evolution and adaptation of species. An ecological niche is the position of an organism or population in its environment. One can consider an ecological niche to be a role within an ecosystem. Events or conditions that cause change to an environment cause changes in the ecological niches that the environment has to offer. Examples of such change range from gradual climatic change to catastrophic events that cause the extinction of large numbers of species. Climate change can affect not only the climate and weather but also the distribution and kinds of plant life. This change affects the entire food web, often making available a great many ecological niches in the process. This creates opportunities that organisms take advantage of by adapting to the new conditions and fulfilling a new role in the ecosystem. The evolution of horses is an excellent example of this.

The earliest known horse ancestors lived in North America more than 50 million years ago. This early horse, called *Hyracotherium*, more closely resembled a dog than the horse that lives today. It was small, about 0.4 m tall at the shoulder, had an arched back, and had padded feet with four toes. It lived in thickly wooded areas, which dominated much of North America at the time, and ate leafy vegetation. Over time, North America became more arid, and as grasses evolved the expansive forests gave way to more and more grassland. During this time the horse was changing. Its leg bones and feet became more adapted to sprinting over open terrain, it grew taller, and the position of its eye sockets gradually changed to provide greater peripheral vision. As grasses became more abundant the nature of its teeth also adapted to be more attuned to grinding tough grasses.

The degree to which the evolutionary line of horses is represented in the fossil record is one of the best in paleontology (the study of life in the past). Imagine having fossils of only the earliest and the modern horse! It would be difficult to recognize that they are of the same evolutionary line. Fossils that bridge the gap between early and later forms of an evolutionary line are called transitional fossils. Transitional fossils are one of the important clues that help paleontologists piece together the puzzle of evolutionary history. Unfortunately, most evolutionary lines are not as well documented by transitional fossils as the line of horse evolution. Another potentially important transitional fossil is shown on page F57 of the Student Book. This photograph is of an *Archeopteryx* fossil taken from rocks formed in the latter part of the Jurassic Period. Many clues have led paleontologists to suggest that modern birds have evolved from dinosaurs. *Archeopteryx* fossils are believed by some to be a transitional fossil that represents a transition from reptiles to birds.

Another clue that paleontologists can use to reconstruct evolutionary history is vestigial structures. Vestigial structures are evolutionary "holdovers" that some organisms have inherited from their evolutionary ancestors. These structures are one of the few examples where a part of an organism serves no apparent function to helping it be successful in its environment. The photo on page F55 shows one such example, a dog's dew claw. Another example is the human appendix. On the basis of the presence of a vestigial hip bone found in whales, scientists have proposed that the evolutionary ancestors to whales were land-dwelling creatures. The hip bone serves no apparent purpose to whales in the marine environment, but this evolutionary "holdover" provides the essential evolutionary clue to the whale's distant land-dwelling past. It explains, in part, the presence of marine mammals in an environment otherwise dominated by different life forms.

More Information...on the Web
Visit the *Investigating Earth Systems* web site www.agiweb.org/ies/ for links to a variety of other web sites that will help you deepen your understanding of content and prepare you to teach this module.

Teacher Commentary

Investigation Overview

At the beginning of this investigation, students are asked to consider why any given plant or animal looks the way it does, and to consider if the organism has always looked so. This question suggests that the traits of organisms serve a function, and challenges students to consider the role that any given characteristic may play in the life of the organism. This prepares students for the next step in this investigation, which is to consider the specific function of a number of different animal characteristics. This investigation is extended when students consider two possibilities for eye placement within the skull, and they propose a hypothesis to explain the possible causes and an experiment to test this hypothesis. The investigation culminates in students being randomly assigned some specific environmental conditions and designing an animal adapted to survive in those conditions. Each adaptation must be justified; thus in this investigation students are challenged to further consider the theory of evolution by natural selection and to consider ecological niches and some of the forcing mechanisms that drive adaptation and the natural selection process. The **Digging Deeper** reading section reviews some adaptations, the concept of the ecological niche, and the concept of vestigial organs and structures. The evolution of the modern horse is used to illustrate how environmental conditions can affect evolution, and how the process of evolution is preserved in the fossil record.

Goals and Objectives

As a result of this investigation, students will understand that environmental conditions help to determine which adaptations are beneficial to an organism and enhance its likelihood of survival and reproduction. Students will also understand how environmental changes guided the evolution of a modern species and how that evolution has been recorded in the fossil record.

Science Content Objectives

Students will collect evidence that:

1. Characteristics and behaviors of organisms enable them to survive and reproduce in their habitat.
2. Organisms evolve and adapt to a changing environment through natural selection.
3. An ecological niche is the overall role of a species in its environment.

Inquiry Process Skills

Students will:

1. Consider questions for inquiry.
2. Relate characteristics of organisms to the role each plays in its survival.
3. Develop a hypothesis.

4. Propose an experiment or study to test a hypothesis.
5. Apply their knowledge and understanding to design an organism that reflects successful adaptation to environmental change.
6. Communicate findings and ideas to others.

Connections to Standards and Benchmarks

In **Investigation 6** students learn about adaptations of organisms, and the control on those adaptations exerted by their environment. In so doing, they learn about a process integral to the Theory of Evolution by Natural Selection. Students' also learn about the preservation of evolutionary history in the fossil record. Students' formulate hypotheses and propose experiments to test them. This investigation will start them on the road to understanding the National Science Education Standards and the AAAS Benchmarks shown below, along with other standards and benchmarks related to the history and nature of science.

NSES Links

- Fossils provide important evidence of how life and environmental conditions have changed.
- Biological evolution accounts for the diversity of species developed through gradual processes over many generations. Species acquire many of their unique characteristics through biological adaptation, which involves the selection of naturally occurring variations in populations. Biological adaptations include changes in structures, behaviors, or physiology that enhance survival and reproductive success in a particular environment.
- Millions of species of animals, plants, and microorganisms are alive today. Although different species might look dissimilar, the unity among organisms becomes apparent from an analysis of internal structures, the similarity of their chemical processes, and the evidence of common ancestry.
- Extinction of a species occurs when the environment changes and the adaptive characteristics of a species are insufficient to allow its survival. Fossils indicate that many organisms that lived long ago are extinct. Extinction of species is common; most of the species that have lived on the Earth no longer exist.
- Evolution is a series of changes, sometimes gradual, sometimes sporadic, that accounts for the present form and function of objects, organisms, and natural and designed systems. The general idea of evolution is that the present arises from materials and forms of the past.
- Form and function are complementary aspects of objects, organisms, and systems in the natural and designed world. The form or shape of an object is frequently related to use, operation, or function.
- The Earth processes we see today, including erosion, movement of the lithospheric plates, and changes in atmospheric composition, are similar to those that occurred

Teacher Commentary

in the past. Earth history is also influenced by occasional catastrophes, such as the impact of an asteroid or comet.

- Scientists formulate and test their explanation of nature using observations, experiments, and theoretical and mathematical models. Although all scientific ideas are tentative and subject to change and improvements in principle, for most major ideas in science, there is much experimental and observational confirmation.

- Models are tentative schemes or structures that correspond to real objects, events, or classes of events, and that have explanatory power. Models help scientists and engineers understand how things work.

AAAS Links

- A great variety of living things can be sorted into groups in many ways using various features to decide which things belong to which group.

- Changes in an organism's habitat are sometimes beneficial and sometimes harmful.

- In all environments — freshwater, marine, forest, desert, grassland, mountain, and others — organisms with similar needs may compete with one another for resources, including food, space, water, air, and shelter. In any particular environment, the growth and survival of organisms depend upon the physical conditions.

- Individuals of the same kind differ in their characteristics, and sometimes differences give individuals an advantage in surviving and reproducing.

- Fossils can be compared to one another and to living organisms according to their similarities and differences. Some organisms that lived long ago are similar to existing organisms, but some are quite different.

- Small differences between parents and offspring can accumulate (through selective breeding) in successive generations so that descendants are very different from their ancestors.

- Individuals with certain traits are more likely than others to survive and have offspring. Changes in environmental conditions can affect the survival of individual organisms and entire species.

- Many thousands of layers of sedimentary rock provide evidence for the long history of the Earth and for the long history of changing life forms whose remains are found in the rocks. More recently deposited rock layers are more likely to contain fossils resembling existing species.

- Models are often used to think about processes that happen too slowly, too quickly, or on too small a scale to be observed directly, or that are too vast to be changed deliberately, or that are potentially dangerous.

- Physical and biological systems tend to change until they become stable and remain that way unless their surroundings change.

Preparation and Materials Needed

Preparation
No advance preparation of materials is required for this investigation. You should, however, try this investigation before teaching it. Students will likely be interested in what sort of "better beast" you have designed. Examine the list of adaptive characteristics shown on page F50 and consider how these traits are useful to the animals that have them. Additional information regarding some of these characteristics and the advantages they provide can be found on the *Investigating Earth Systems* web site. Additionally, information regarding horse evolutionary history and other topics covered in the **Digging Deeper** reading section can be found there.

Materials
- gaming die
- poster board
- colored pencils or markers

Teacher Commentary

NOTES

Investigating Fossils

Investigation 6: Adaptations to a Changing Environment

Investigation 6:
Adaptations to a Changing Environment

Key Question
Before you begin, first think about this key question.

Why does any given plant or animal look the way it does, and has it always looked that way?

Think about a specific plant or animal and about what characteristics it may have that helps it to survive in this world.

Share your thinking with others in your class. Keep a record of the discussion in your journal.

Materials Needed
For this investigation your group will need:
- gaming die
- poster board
- colored pencils or markers

Investigate
Part A: Building a Better Beast

1. Look at the lists of different types of animal characteristics given on the next page. Each of these characteristics is an adaptation that can

Investigating Earth Systems

F
49

218   Investigating Earth Systems

Teacher Commentary

Key Question

Give students a few minutes to write down their responses to this question in their journals. Hold a brief discussion, emphasizing thinking and sharing of ideas. Record all of the ideas on an overhead transparency or on the chalkboard. Have students record this information in their journals.

Student Conceptions about Adaptations

The **Key Question** focuses on the organism's appearance. Students' experience with adaptations, however, is likely based on recognizing how they have adapted to meet challenges that they have experienced. Thus, they may associate "adaptations" with changes that are deliberately made by an organism during its lifetime, rather than associating the term with a natural process that occurs over geologic time scales and can affect things like physiology, over which an organism has no control.

Answers for the Teacher Only

Adaptation, as a result of the process of natural selection, occurs when certain random mutations or changes that occur within a species become preferentially passed on to offspring because they provide some advantage to the organism's survival and chance for successful reproduction. Over time, this process causes certain characteristics to become preferentially incorporated into a species population and gene pool. Given the expanse of geologic time, a lot of opportunity for "fine-tuning" of a species' characteristics can occur. The theory of evolution by natural selection suggests that most of the characteristics of any given organism do (or did in the past) contribute to an organism's chance for survival and successful reproduction. Though it is not always obvious, most of the characteristics of any given organism (both behavioral and physical) have a reason for being.

About the Photo

Giraffes are one example of an animal that looks very distinct because it has adapted to survive in its environment. A giraffe's long neck helps it to eat leaves from high up in trees, where it doesn't have to compete with many other animals for the food. Many adaptations of other animals are also very clear to see, but others are not. Can you think of a more subtle aspect about some animal's appearance that helps it to survive in its environment?

Assessment Tool

Key-Question Evaluation Sheet
Remind students to look at the criteria that outline the basic expectations for the warm-up activity. Use the evaluation sheet to emphasize that you want to see evidence of prior knowledge and that students should communicate their thinking clearly.

Investigating Fossils

INVESTIGATING FOSSILS

help different animals to survive in the many different habitats on the Earth. For example, ducks have webbed feet to help them swim and dive for food, and they have a layer of down to keep them warm in the water. As a class, discuss some of these characteristics and how they are useful.

Now think about an animal that you may know of or perhaps may have even seen before.

a) What characteristics of that animal help it to adapt to its environment and thrive?

b) Look again at the list of different characteristics given below. Which of those characteristics does your animal have?

c) Share your thinking with your group. As a group, develop a list of animals and their characteristics or adaptations.

Animal Characteristics		
Eyes Forward in head On sides of head **Feet** Webbed Clawed Padded Hooved **Mouth** Beak Tearing teeth Grinding teeth Cutting teeth	**Covering** Fur Feathers Scales Skin Shell **Coloration** Camouflage Bright **Movement** Running Flying Climbing Swinging Leaping	**Homes** Trees Caves Underground Water **When Animals Eat** Day Night Dawn or Dusk **Dealing with Heat and Cold** Body Covering Active/Feeding Times Homes **Other Defenses** Bad Smell or Taste Size

Teacher Commentary

Investigate

Teaching Suggestions and Sample Answers
Part A: Building a Better Beast

> **Teaching Tip**
> You may wish to use an overhead transparency of **Blackline Master** *Fossils* 6.1, **Animal Characteristics** when discussing the animal characteristics listed on page F50.

1. Answers will be highly variable depending on the animal chosen by the student (or group of students). Many of the characteristics shown in the list on page F50, like webbed feet, have obvious advantages. In this case they are one adaptation that helps a bird to move and hunt in the water. Others, like eye position, are not as obvious. Eyes in the forward part of the head are a characteristic typical of predators, and this position helps provide better depth perception and focuses the field of vision more directly in front of the animal, where stalked prey are likely to be. Alternatively, grazers often have eyes set back farther in the skull, to the sides of the head. This provides a greater field of vision with which to spot potential predators. Hooves are adaptations well suited to moving quickly over open, hard ground, whereas padded feet are better suited to quiet stalking over a wider range of terrains. In general, students should be encouraged to use their imaginations in examining this list and to justify their reasoning. There is not necessarily one correct answer for each item on the list. In some cases similar adaptations may provide different advantages to different kinds of organisms.
An example follows.

   The following example is for a grizzly bear:

   a) It is a large animal with a thick coat of fur, eyes in the forward part of its skull, padded feet with sharp claws, and teeth designed for both tearing and grinding. It lives in caves and hibernates during the winter. The thick coat of fur and hibernation helps the bear to survive the long, cold winters that are typical in the areas in North America where it lives. Its home in caves helps to protect it when it is hibernating, and its large size also helps to protect it against other predators. The bear is itself a predator, and its eye position, padded feet, large claws, and tearing teeth help it to hunt. The bear also eats other things, like nuts and berries, and so it also has grinding teeth.

   b) Eyes forward in head, padded feet, tearing teeth, grinding teeth, fur, lives in caves, and is inactive during cold times.

   c) The list will vary depending on the animals chosen by the students, but should include details similar to (though perhaps not as comprehensive) as those provided for **Step 1(a)**.

Investigating Fossils

Investigation 6: Adaptations to a Changing Environment

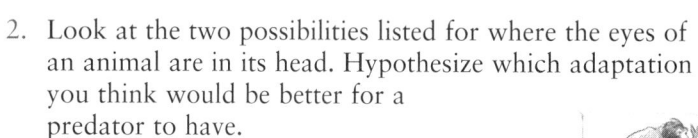

2. Look at the two possibilities listed for where the eyes of an animal are in its head. Hypothesize which adaptation you think would be better for a predator to have.

   a) Propose an experiment or study that could test your hypothesis. Write your proposed test down in your journal.

   b) Repeat this same thought process for another of the categories listed. Hypothesize what the advantage for a particular adaptation is and propose a means of testing your hypothesis.

Teacher Commentary

2. Student hypotheses will likely vary, but their reasoning for the hypotheses should be logical. One possible hypothesis/explanation for the relative advantages of different eye positions is given above in the answer to **Step 1**.

   a) Student experiments should test their hypotheses and should be possible to execute (though not necessarily by them, given the resources available). Experiments do not necessarily have to be experiments in the classical sense. For example if the student or group hypothesizes that eyes in the forward part of the skull are an advantage to a hunter, then they could examine different kinds of predators and prey and compile data on their eye socket position in order to look for a pattern or relationship in the data. Alternatively, if a student (or group) hypothesized that eye sockets set farther back and to the sides of the skull improved peripheral vision, then that student (or group) should design a controlled experiment to test different animal's peripheral vision. One possibility would be testing different animals by placing a visual stimulus in a specific location relative to the animal and seeing if there is a difference between the responses of animals with forward-looking eyes and those with eye sockets farther back in the skull.

   b) See the Example given for **Step 2(a)**.

About the Photo
There are many different habitats and conditions to which animals have become adapted on this planet. Some are shown in the photographs on page F51; they include open grasslands, forests, fresh and salt water, and high mountain tops. There are other habitats not shown on page F51. Organisms manage to survive in some very extreme conditions. What extreme habitats can you think of, and what organisms live there?

Assessment Tool
Investigation Journal-Entry Evaluation Sheet
Use this evaluation sheet to provide students with a variety of criteria that they can use to ensure that their work meets the highest possible standards and expectations.

INVESTIGATING FOSSILS

3. It is now your group's job to "build a better beast." Using the table below, roll a die to see what environment your animal will live in.

   Now, roll the die again to see if your animal will be a carnivore (meat eater), a herbivore (plant eater), or an omnivore (both a plant and meat eater).

No.	Habitat	No.	Animal Type
1	open grassland/savanna	1	herbivore
2	tropical rainforest	2	herbivore
3	temperate forest	3	carnivore
4	mountains	4	carnivore
5	desert	5	omnivore
6	wetlands	6	omnivore

4. Work together with your group to design an animal that would have the adaptations necessary to survive given the conditions dictated by your rolls of the dice. To do this, you should first make a list of some of the characteristics of the habitat in which your animal lives.

   You can pick adaptations from the categories listed below. You can also invent your own adaptation.

   a) Draw a picture of your creature and give it a name. Also list each adaptation, and describe how each adaptation will be of benefit to your creature.

5. Participate in a class discussion about each group's animals and adaptations.

Teacher Commentary

3. You may wish to set up additional constraints to more specifically guide your students' imaginations. For example, an additional roll of the die could determine the animal's size.

4. Students' "beasts" and their adaptations should strongly reflect the conditions randomly set upon them by the rolls of the gaming die. All adaptations should be explained along with the advantage that the adaptation provides to the organisms survival and chance of successful procreation.

    a) Pictures should reflect the adaptations discussed and show some imagination and creativity. An example is given in the drawing on page F52.

5. Encourage an active discussion and probe students' thinking to explain why and how the adaptations they chose will help their animal to survive. Even if an adaptation is beneficial to an organism on the whole, there may be some drawbacks as well. Ask students to consider any potential drawbacks that the adaptation will have for the organism.

Investigation 6: Adaptations to a Changing Environment

Digging Deeper

ADAPTATIONS

Living organisms are adapted to their environment. This means that the way they look, the way they behave, how they are built, or their way of life makes them suited to survive and reproduce in their habitats. For example, giraffes have very long necks so that they can eat tall vegetation, which other animals cannot reach. The eyes of cats are like slits. That makes it possible for the cat's eyes to adjust to both bright light, when the slits are narrow, and to very dim light, when the slits are wide open.

Behavior is also an important adaptation. Animals inherit many kinds of adaptive behavior. In southern Africa there are small animals called meerkats, which live in large colonies. The meerkats take turns standing on their hind legs, looking up at the sky to spot birds of prey. Meanwhile, the meerkats in the rest of the colony go about their lives. You can probably think of many other features of body or behavior that help animals to lead a successful life.

As You Read...
Think about:
1. Describe in your own words what it means that an organism is adapted to its environment.
2. What is an ecological niche?
3. What is a vestigial structure? Provide an example.

Teacher Commentary

Digging Deeper

This section provides text and photos that give students greater insight into the topic of adaptations. You may wish to assign the **As You Read** questions as homework to help students focus on the major ideas in the text.

As You Read…
Think about:

1. An organism is adapted to its environment when it has developed specific characteristics, in response to its surrounding environment, that help it to survive and reproduce.

2. An ecological niche is the overall role of an organism in its environment. Environments have many ecological niches.

3. A vestigial structure is some part of an organism that is no longer used by the organism or needed by the organism to survive in its environment. A vestigial structure provides evidence that a species is still changing. The structure is inherited from an organism's evolutionary ancestors. Examples of vestigial structures include a dog's "dew" claws and the human appendix.

About the Photo
Not all adaptations of organisms to their environment are physical adaptations. Some are behavioral adaptations. This photograph shows meerkats in southern Africa standing on their hind legs watching out for predators. What behavioral adaptations can you think of that have been made by other organisms?

Assessment Opportunity
You may wish to select questions from the **As You Read** section to use as a quiz, rephrasing the questions into multiple choice or true/false format. Use this quiz to assess student understanding, and as a motivational tool to ensure that students complete the reading assignment and comprehend the main ideas.

Investigating Fossils

INVESTIGATING FOSSILS

In biology, an ecological niche refers to the overall role of a species in its environment. Most environments have many niches. If a niche is "empty" (no organisms are occupying it), new species are likely to evolve to occupy it. This happens by the process of natural selection, which you learned about in **Investigation 4.** By natural selection, the nature of the species gradually changes to become adapted to the niche. If a species becomes very well adapted to its environment, and if the environment does not change, species can exist for a very long time before they become extinct.

The Modern Horse and Some of Its Ancestors

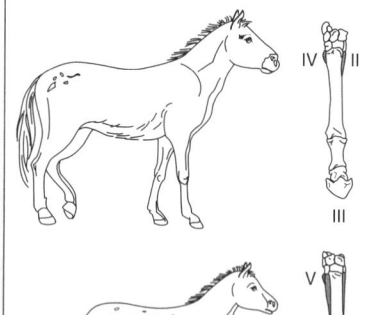

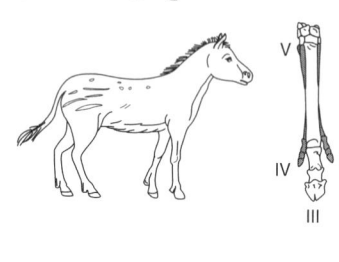

Equus
- Lived from about 5 million years ago to the present
- Lives in areas of the grassy plains
- Eats grasses and is classified as a grazer
- Is about 1.6 m tall at the shoulder
- Has 1 hoofed toe on each of its front and rear limbs.

Merychippus
- Lived from about 17 to 11 million years ago
- Lived in areas with shrubs and on the grassy plains
- Ate leafy vegetation and grasses and is classified as a grazer (the first in the line of horses)
- Was about 1.0 m tall at the shoulder and had a long face and legs making it appear much like a modern horse.
- Had 3 hoofed toes on each of its front and rear limbs. The central toe was much larger than the others.

Miohippus
- Lived from about 32 to 25 million years ago
- Lived in less thickly wooded areas
- Ate leafy vegetation and is classified as a browser
- Was about 0.6 m tall at the shoulder (about the size of a German shepherd dog) and had padded feet.
- Had 3 toes on each of its front and rear limbs.

Hyracotherium-Oldest known horse
- Lived from about 55 to 45 million years ago
- Lived in thickly wooded areas
- Ate leafy vegetation and is classified as a browser
- Was about 0.4 m tall at the shoulder (about the size of a small dog) and had padded feet.
- Had 4 toes on each of its front limbs and three on each of its rear limbs.

Teacher Commentary

> **Teaching Tip**
> You may wish to make an overhead transparency of **Blackline Master** *Fossils* 6.2, **The Modern Horse and Some of Its Ancestors** to discuss the fossil record of horse evolution, and how changes in climate can result in the evolution of new species.

About the Photos

The diagram shown on page F54 illustrates and explains a few of the adaptations that have occurred in the evolutionary line of the modern horse. The earliest known horse ancestor is over 50 million years old, and looked very different from the modern horse. Many of these adaptations can be related to the shrinking forests in North America and the expansion of grasslands. As the grasslands expanded, horses evolved to fill the new ecological niches that developed. Horses are one of the best examples in the fossil record where many different fossils have been discovered that connect the modern horse to its earliest ancestors. Note that the modern horse still has vestigial remnants of its earliest ancestors' "extra" toes.

The photo on page F55 shows the "dew" claw of a dog. This is a more obvious example of an "evolutionary leftover" or vestigial structure. At one point, the modern dog's ancestors probably needed this toe, but it is not used by the modern dog.

Investigation 6: Adaptations to a Changing Environment

Horses are an excellent example of an animal evolving to fill a niche. Many fossils of different kinds of horses have been discovered, and paleontologists think that the earliest ancestor of the modern horse lived in North America more than 50 million years ago. This animal was a small padded-foot forest animal about the size of a dog. If you saw one next to a modern horse, you might not even think the two were related! As time passed, the climate of North America became drier, and the vast forests started to shrink. Grasses were evolving, and the area of grassland was increasing. Horses adapted to fill this new grassland niche. They grew taller, and their legs and feet became better adapted to sprinting in the open grasslands. Their eyes also adapted to be farther back on their heads to help them to see more of the area around them. Each of these adaptations helped the evolving grassland horses to avoid predators. Their teeth also changed to be better adapted to grinding tough grassland vegetation.

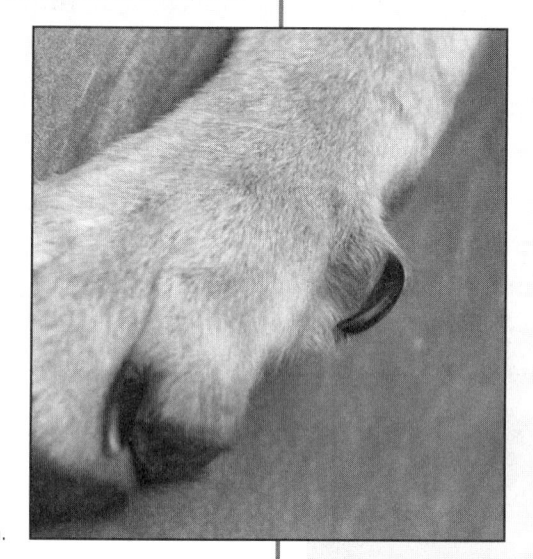

Have you ever wondered what purpose the "dew" claw on the inside of a dog's paw serves? The claw is the dog's thumb. Because a dog runs on the balls of its feet and four digits, the claw no longer serves a purpose. Organs or parts of the body that no longer serve a function are called vestigial structures. They provide evidence that the species is still changing. Even humans have vestigial structures. The human appendix is one such example. It used to store microbes that helped to digest plant matter, but it is no longer needed in the human.

Teacher Commentary

NOTES

Investigating Fossils – Investigation 6

INVESTIGATING FOSSILS

Review and Reflect

Review

1. Are all animal adaptations physical adaptations? Explain your answer.
2. Pick an animal living today and describe two adaptations that help it to survive in its environment.
3. Describe three ways that horses have changed over the past 50 million years.

Reflect

4. Describe how adaptation relates to the process of natural selection that was described in the **Digging Deeper** reading section of **Investigation 4**.
5. What advantage might there be in a predator having soft, padded feet?
6. Examine the diagram on page F29 showing the major divisions of geologic time. How can the concept of ecological niches explain the rapid increase in the number of mammals since the end of the Cretaceous Period?

Thinking about the Earth System

7. What correlation did you make in this investigation between changes in the atmosphere/climate system and changes in the biosphere?

Thinking about Scientific Inquiry

8. How did you use the processes of scientific inquiry in this investigation?

Teacher Commentary

Review and Reflect

Review

Your students should have gathered enough evidence to provide a reasonable answer to the **Key Question** for **Investigation 6**. You need to stress that it is evidence that counts. They may have difficulty in understanding what constitutes evidence as opposed to opinion or inference. This is an opportunity to clarify both the nature and importance of evidence in scientific inquiry.

1. Not all adaptations are physical adaptations. Some adaptations are behavioral adaptations like, for example, meerkats that stand up on their hind legs so they can watch out for predators.

2. Answers will vary. One example is a goose. Geese have adapted to a water environment by developing webbed feet and a thick layer of down that keeps them warm and dry.

3. Horses have adapted in many ways since their earliest ancestors lived more than 50 million years ago. They have become much taller, their foot structure has changed from having padded feet with four toes to being hoofed with only one toe, and the position of their eye sockets has moved farther back in their skull.

Reflect

4. When a change or mutation happens in a species, it can help or hurt the organism's chance of survival in its environment. If the change is beneficial, then the change can be passed on to its offspring. Over time, this change can become a trait of all of the individuals in a population or species. When this happens, this change becomes an adaptation of the species to its environment.

5. Soft padded feet can help a predator to quietly sneak up on its prey, giving the predator an advantage in the hunt.

6. At the end of the Cretaceous Period a great many species became extinct. Because these extinct species were no longer fulfilling their role in the ecosystem, many ecological niches were no longer filled. All of the available niches allowed other kinds of organisms (mammals, for example) to adapt and evolve to fill these niches, causing a rapid increase in the number of new species.

Thinking about the Earth System

7. One example of how changes in the atmosphere–climate system correlated to changes in the biosphere is how both the plants and horses changed in response to drier climates in North America. As the climate in North America became drier, areas covered largely by forests became open grasslands and savannas. Horses changed to adapt to this new environment by developing adaptations that allowed them to run quickly over open terrain and to spot predators more easily.

Thinking about Scientific Inquiry

Help students understand the relevance of inquiry processes to their lives by asking them to think of everyday examples of when they use inquiry processes (finding out where a misplaced book has gone; forming an opinion about a new TV show; winning an argument).

8. Several times in this investigation students formed questions, posed hypotheses, and proposed experiments to test those hypotheses.

Assessment Tool
Review and Reflect Journal-Entry Evaluation Sheet
Use the **Review and Reflect** part of the investigation to assess individual or collective understandings about the concepts and inquiry processes explored. You can use the general criteria provided on this evaluation sheet to assess content and thoroughness of student work, whether the students worked individually or in groups. Adapt and modify the sheet to meet your needs. Consider involving students in selecting and modifying the assessment criteria.

Teacher Commentary

NOTES

Teacher Review

Use this section to reflect on and review the investigation. Keep in mind that your notes here are likely to be especially helpful when you teach this investigation again. Questions listed here are examples only.

Student Achievement

What evidence do you have that all students have met the science content objectives?
_____

Are there any students who need more help in reaching these objectives? If so, how can you provide this? _____

_____

What evidence do you have that all students have demonstrated their understanding of the inquiry processes? _____

_____

Which of these inquiry objectives do your students need to improve upon in future investigations? _____

_____

What evidence do the journal entries contain about what your students learned from this investigation? _____

_____

Planning

How well did this investigation fit into your class time? _____

_____

What changes can you make to improve your planning next time? _____

_____

Guiding and Facilitating Learning

How well did you focus and support inquiry while interacting with students?

_____

What changes can you make to improve classroom management for the next investigation or the next time you teach this investigation? _____

_____

Investigating Earth Systems – Investigating Fossils

Teacher Commentary

How successful were you in encouraging all students to participate fully in science learning? _____

_____

How did you encourage and model the skills values, and attitudes of scientific inquiry? _____

_____

How did you nurture collaboration among students? _____

_____

Materials and Resources

What challenges did you encounter obtaining or using materials and/or resources needed for the activity? _____

_____

What changes can you make to better obtain and better manage materials and resources next time? _____

_____

Student Evaluation

Describe how you evaluated student progress. What worked well? What needs to be improved? _____

_____

How will you adapt your evaluation methods for next time? _____

_____

Describe how you guided students in self-assessment. _____

_____

Self Evaluation

How would you rate your teaching of this investigation? _____

_____

What advice would you give to a colleague who is planning to teach this investigation? _____

_____

Investigating Fossils – Investigation 6

NOTES

Teacher Commentary

INVESTIGATION 7: BEING A PALEONTOLOGIST
Background Information

Geologic Maps
A geologic map is a map that shows the distribution of bedrock that is exposed at the Earth's surface or buried beneath a thin layer of surface soil or sediment. A geologic map is more than just a map of rock types: most geologic maps show the locations and relationships of rock units. Rock units are bodies or masses of rock that have a high degree of uniformity relative to adjacent rock units. Rock units are large: their minimum dimensions are almost always several meters or tens of meters, and their maximum dimensions may be as great as many tens or even hundreds of kilometers.

Each rock unit is identified on the map by a symbol of some kind, which is explained in a legend or key, and is often colored a distinctive color as well. Part of the legend of a geologic map consists of one or more columns of little rectangles, with appropriate colors and symbols, identifying the various rock units shown on the map. There is often a very brief description of the units directly in this part of the legend. The rectangles for the units are arranged in order of decreasing age upward. Usually, the ages of the units, in terms of the standard relative geologic time scale, is also shown.

All geologic maps convey certain other information as well. They show the symbols that are used to represent such features as folds, faults, and attitudes of planar features like stratification or foliation. They have information about latitude and longitude, and/or location relative to some standard geographic grid system. They always have a scale, expressed both as a labeled scale bar and as what is called a representative fraction, 1:25,000 for example. In the representative fraction the first number is a unit of distance on the map and the second number is the corresponding distance on the actual land surface.

All geologic maps (except perhaps very special-purpose maps that show all the details of an area that might be the size of a small room!) involve some degree of generalization. Such generalization is the responsibility of the geologist who is doing the mapping. Obviously, it is not practical to represent features as thin as a few meters on a map that covers many square kilometers: the width of the feature on the map would be far thinner than the thinnest possible ink line. The degree of generalization necessarily increases as the area covered by the map increases. You could easily see this for yourself if you have access to a geologic map of some small area together with the corresponding geologic map of the entire state: the detail of the small area on the state map would be much less than on the full map of that small area.

More Information…on the Web
Go to the *Investigating Earth Systems* web site www.agiweb.org/ies for links to a variety of web sites that will help you deepen your understanding of content and prepare you to teach this investigation.

Investigation Overview

In this investigation, your students use what they have learned about life through time to research an "unknown" fossil. They act as paleontologists, searching for information about their fossils from any and all resources available. As they acquire information about their fossils, they begin to prepare a "portrait" of it. Eventually, they prepare a display of their portrait for others.

Goals and Objectives

The purpose of this activity is to review science content and inquiry processes that have been used throughout the module. It can be used as a final assessment, review for a final test, or both. As a result of carrying out **Investigation 7**, students will develop a better understanding of what fossils can tell us about life through time, and about the work that paleontologists do to decipher the fossil record. Students will also learn how geologic maps and cross sections summarize important information about the geologic history of a region.

Science Content Objectives

Students will collect evidence that:

1. Information about fossil formation can be deduced from a fossil itself.
2. Fossils can be traced to particular geographic areas.
3. Fossil formation is connected to the biosphere, the hydrosphere, the atmosphere, and the geosphere.

Inquiry Process Skills

Students will:

1. Deduce information from a fossil.
2. Use maps and other tools to research a fossil.
3. Use a number of resources to research a fossil.
4. Collate information about a fossil.
5. Create a display communicating information about a fossil.

Connections to Standards and Benchmarks

All the content standards and benchmarks students have been working to understand come together in this final investigation. Remember, these are statements of what students are expected to understand by the time they complete eighth grade. What they have been doing throughout this module on fossils is just part of that ultimate learning outcome. Your students will have developed their understanding of some of these ideas, at least in part, but many students will require additional experiences.

Teacher Commentary

As your students work through **Investigation 7**, keep these standards and benchmarks in mind and note the general level of understanding evident in what students discuss and do. Be especially alert to any confusion that a simple question from you might clarify, but do not attempt to teach these standards directly. Your role here is to guide students gently from the ideas they have toward a more complete understanding.

Preparation and Materials Needed

Preparation
In this final investigation, your students put everything they have discovered to make a fossil portrait, applying their knowledge of fossils and how they form.

You and your students will have gathered some of the information and data that are relevant for this investigation through earlier activities. Students will need access to reference materials and computers for Internet research. Be sure to schedule computer time in your media center in advance. Students may also need to go to their local libraries. Local colleges and universities may have geologists or paleontologists who can help you obtain fossils and research materials.

If you are using this as a final individual assessment for each student, your students should work on their resource trails individually. If, however, you are using it as a group assessment, you will need to set up criteria so that each student can demonstrate accountability for a particular part of the resource trail.

You can make an overhead transparency of **Blackline Master** *Fossils* **7.1: Geologic Map and Cross-Section** to help students better understand the information and scale of a geologic map and cross-section.

Materials
- unknown fossil
- metric ruler and measuring tape
- fossil record charts
- set of known fossil samples
- state or regional geologic map*
- access to research material**
- materials to create a display

* The *Investigating Earth Systems* web site www.agiweb.org/ies/ provides suggestions for obtaining these resources.

** The *Investigating Earth Systems* web site www.agiweb.org/ies/ provides topical Internet sites and a list of resources that will aid student research.

Teacher Commentary

NOTES

Investigating Fossils

Investigation 7: Being a Paleontologist

Investigation 7:
Being a Paleontologist

Putting It All Together

Key Question
Before you begin, first think about this key question.

What can fossils tell you about life through time?

Think about what you have learned so far. What kinds of clues can fossils give about Earth history and changing life?

Share your thinking with others in your class. Keep a record of the discussion in your journal.

Materials Needed

For this investigation you will need:

- unknown fossil
- metric ruler and measuring tape
- fossil record charts
- set of known fossil samples
- state or regional geologic map
- access to research material
- materials to create a display

Investigate

1. You will be given an unknown fossil and a geologic map from its state of origin. Examine the fossil carefully.

   a) Write down your first thoughts about it in your journal. Think about these things:

   • What could have made this fossil?

244 Investigating Earth Systems

Teacher Commentary

Key Question

Allow students time to answer this question. Discuss students' ideas as a class. Tell students that the final investigation will be to develop a "portrait" of a fossil that is based on their research and portrays information about not only the fossil, but also the time and environment in which it lived.

Student Conceptions about Fossils and Life through Time

Help your students to see that all the previous investigations are relevant for this final one. From the previous investigations, your students should have a solid understanding of fossils and life through time. Many of their initial informal ideas will be closer to commonly accepted scientific concepts and explanations. Keep in mind that understanding geologic time might still be a difficulty for some students.

Assessment Tool

Key-Question Evaluation Sheet
Use this evaluation sheet to help students understand and internalize basic expectations for the warm-up activity.

Investigate

Teaching Suggestions and Sample Answers

In this final investigation, students are asked to use inquiry processes in their investigation as they deem appropriate. They may need reminders about this, especially if the work they are doing is engaging. Their recognition and use of inquiry processes is an important part of understanding scientific inquiry. Review the processes before students begin their work, and give reminders throughout their investigations.

1. Again, it is very important that actual fossils be used, if possible. Have a variety available, so that each group has something different. It will help if the fossils are well defined, of whole organisms (rather than parts), include animals and plants, and, together, represent different stages of the fossil record. You might need to check your fossils against the information resources you have for students to use. A fossil that is extremely hard to identify and date in the fossil record will diminish students' opportunities for research. Although this investigation is set up so that each group is working on one fossil, you might give each student his or her own fossil as an alternative. If you do this, let your students work in groups, each helping the others with their fossil research.

Teaching Tip

Students will be given a geologic map that relates to the fossil they have been given. You might want to make an overhead transparency of the geologic map on page F61 (**Blackline Master** *Fossils* **7.1, Geologic Map and Cross-Section**) and review some of the basic features of maps and cross-sections with students prior to the onset of this investigation. See the **Background Information** section of this investigation for a discussion about the basic features of geologic maps.

a) Answers will vary greatly depending on both the student and the fossil that they are examining. Student guesses of what creature made the fossil should be based on something that they may know exists in the world today (in accordance with the principle of uniformitarianism, which essentially states that the present is the key to the past). They should recognize that the rock that contains the fossil is a sedimentary rock, and they may even be able to further distinguish the rock type. The estimate of how old the fossil is should reflect an understanding of geologic process. Accordingly, an answer like a few centuries old or anything younger than that would be inappropriate. Similarly, a guess of several billion years old would also be inappropriate.

About the Photo

The photograph on page F57 shows a fossil of an *Archaeopteryx* that lived during the Jurassic Period. Paleontologists debate whether or not the *Archaeopteryx* is in fact the first bird, but they recognize it as a form that is transitional from bird to reptile. In contrast to modern birds, *Archaeopteryx* had a full set of teeth, a rather flat, long, bony tail, and three claws on the wing which could have still been used to grasp prey (or maybe trees). To date, paleontologists have found several *Archaeopteryx* fossils around the world.

Assessment Tools

Assessing the Final Investigation

Students' work throughout the module culminates with this final investigation. To complete it, students need a working knowledge of previous investigations. The last investigation is a good review and a chance to demonstrate proficiency because it refers to the previous steps. For ideas about using the last investigation as a performance-based exam, see the section in the back of this Teacher's Edition. If you chose to use it as a scoring guide, review it with students before they begin their work.

Teacher Commentary

NOTES

INVESTIGATING FOSSILS

- What kind of rock is it in?
- How old might it be?

Inquiry
Using Maps as Scientific Tools

Scientists collect and review data using tools. You may think of tools as only physical objects like shovels and hand lenses. However, forms in which information is gathered and stored are also tools. In this investigation you are using a geologic map as a scientific tool.

You will have the opportunity to conduct research on your fossil, so that you can compare what you think about it now, to what you think about it later on.

2. Using all of your knowledge and resources about fossils, including your geologic map, find out as much as you can about your fossil.

   Later, you can summarize this to give a "portrait" of your fossil sample. This can be in the form of: a model, a poster, a web page, a magazine article, a newspaper article, a brochure, a diorama, a free-standing display, any other method that you choose.

3. Information that you may be able to find out about your fossil should include:
   - what kind of organism it represents;
   - what the organism looked like when it was alive;
   - what parts of the organism were fossilized and what were not (and why);
   - where the organism might have come from originally;
   - what kind of rock the fossil is in;
   - during what time period the fossil organism lived;

Teacher Commentary

> **About the Photo**
> The photograph on page F58 shows a fossil of a bass from the Eocene Green River Formation near Kemmerer, Wyoming. In the small town of Kemmerer, people have found more than 113,000 fossil fish. Ask students what type of environment might have allowed so many fish to be preserved in the fossil record. Are they surprised to see the quality of the fish preserved as a fossil?

2. Students need to access as many different sources of information as possible. Apart from normal school resources such as the library, reference books, textbooks, videos, CD-ROMs, and the Internet, encourage students to locate out-of-school resources such as home computers and books at home and community libraries. It might be possible to consult specialists in local universities and colleges, organizations, hobby clubs, and museums.

3. It is important that students identify their "audience" when considering how to present their fossil portraits. There are opportunities here for students to use their creative skills, especially if the audience extends beyond the class (to other classes or to parents). Have students consider these options from the start. Knowing how they are going to present their information will help them to be selective about resources.

Investigation 7: Being a Paleontologist

- detailed description of the fossil itself (dimensions, visual description, texture).

Review the resources that you have in your classroom, in your school, and in your community. Decide what would be the most useful ones, and collect these as you need them.

4. Do your research on your fossil, carefully recording what you find out in your journal, as well as the resources you have used.

5. When you have finished your research, construct your fossil portrait, using one of the methods listed in **Step 2**, or a presentation method of your own.

   Be sure that your portrait covers as many of the questions in **Step 3** as possible.

   Using both pictures and words, make the portrait appealing to your target audience.

6. When all of the fossil portraits are completed, you will have the opportunity to present your work.

   Be prepared to answer questions about your research, the sources of your information, how recent they are, and how reliable they are. Be prepared, also, to ask other students in your class questions about their fossil portraits when they present.

Inquiry

Presenting Information

Scientists are often asked to provide information to the public. In doing so, they need to consider both the information they wish to present and the best method of presenting the information. In this investigation you will need to choose the method of presentation that you think will be the most effective.

Be sure your teacher approves your plan before you begin.

Teacher Commentary

4. Encourage students to share resources. It is quite likely that information resources that one group of students finds will be helpful to other groups. Make sure that groups do not compete with each other. Explain that scientists generally work in collaboration, sharing findings, information, and techniques, so that scientific understanding can be advanced for the benefit of all.

5. It is important that students do not skimp on time in preparing their presentations. Encourage a high quality of presentation. Remind students that this is the final investigation for this module, and that what they produce will have value for them, and others.

6. You will need to judge how to organize this, depending upon the forms of presentation your students have chosen. However you organize the session, keep in mind that students need adequate time to present their fossil "portraits" to others in a meaningful and complete way. This is an opportunity for students to look back on how they have conducted their research. Help them to make any connections they can.

Assessment Tool

Student-Presentation Evaluation Form
Use the **Student-Presentation Evaluation Form** as a simple guideline for assessing presentations. Adapt and modify the evaluation form to suit your needs. Provide the form to your students and discuss the assessment criteria before they begin their work.

Group-Participation Evaluation Forms I and II
Use these forms to provide students with an opportunity to assess group participation. Do not use results of this evaluation as the sole source of assessment data. Rather, it is better to assign a weight to the results of this evaluation and factor it in with other sources of assessment data.

Investigating Fossils

INVESTIGATING FOSSILS

As You Read...
Think about:
1. What kind of information does a geological map contain?
2. What is a rock unit?
3. Look at the map and cross section on page F61.
   a) What rock layer is the youngest? Explain your answer.
   b) What rock layer is the oldest? Explain.
   c) How do you know the layers were deformed by pressure?

Digging Deeper

GEOLOGIC MAPS AND CROSS SECTIONS

Geologic maps show the distribution of the solid rock (bedrock) at the Earth's surface. In some places this rock is exposed and in other areas it is buried beneath a thin layer of surface soil or sediment. The number of different kinds of rock in the Earth's crust is enormous. However, the bedrock over a large area is usually the same type. That is because rocks are originally formed in large volumes by a specific process. The rock bodies formed during the same process are called rock units.

A geologic map is more than just a map of rock types. Most geologic maps show the locations and relationships of different rock units. Each rock unit is identified on the map by a symbol of some kind. The symbol is explained in a legend or key, and is often given a distinctive color as well. Part of the legend of a geologic map consists of one or more columns of little rectangles, with appropriate colors and symbols. The rectangles identify the various rock units shown on the map. There is often a very brief description of the units in this part of the legend. The rectangles for the units are arranged in order of decreasing age upward.

Geologic maps show other information as well. They show the symbols that are used to represent such features as folds or faults. They have information about latitude and longitude. They always have a scale, expressed both as a labeled scale bar and as a ratio—1:25,000, for example. The first number is a unit of distance on the map and the second number, after the colon, is the corresponding distance on the actual land surface.

Geologic maps present a general picture of the rock units present. Such generalization is the responsibility of

Evidence for Ideas

Investigating Earth Systems

Teacher Commentary

Digging Deeper

This section provides text and photographs that give students greater insight into geologic maps and cross sections. You may wish to assign the **As You Read** questions as homework to guide students to think about the major ideas in the text.

As You Read...
Think about:
1. A geologic map provides information about the distribution of bedrock at the Earth's surface. It gives information on the kinds of rocks that constitute the different rock units and also their age relative to one another. Geologic maps also provide information about geologic structures like folds and faults, and sometimes also include a vertical cross section that shows what the rock units would look like in an imaginary vertical plane downward from some line on the land surface. Other information, like latitude, longitude, and a scale are also included on the map.

2. A rock unit is a rock body formed by some process over some period of time. Note: Because a rock body was formed during the same process does not necessarily mean it was formed by a single event or over a very short period of time.

3. **a)** The rock unit Ow is the youngest rock unit. This information can be gotten from the description of rock units in the map legend which, by convention, lists the youngest rock unit at the top of the legend in the left most column (if there is more than one). Note: Although unit €p€ev appears to be uppermost (and therefore youngest) unit shown in the cross section at the bottom of the figure on page F61, this is misleading because the older Lower Cambrian to Precambrian unit named the Everett Formation (€p€ev) has been thrusted on top of the younger Upper to Middle Ordovician Walloomsac Formation (Ow). Most of the older Everett Formation has been eroded away in this area, but a small section is still exposed at the surface.

    b) The oldest layer is the Everett Formation. See notes for **Step 3(a)** for an explanation for how this is known. Once again, this may be confusing for students because geologic processes have thrust the oldest formation on top of the younger ones.

    c) These units are all sedimentary rock units (with the exception of the Everett Formation, which is a metamorphosed sedimentary rock). Most sedimentary rocks are originally deposited in approximately horizontal layers, but those shown on the map are folded. Because these rocks must have originally been nearly horizontal, they must have been deformed by pressure. Note: This conclusion is not expressly stated in the **Digging Deeper** text, and must be reasoned out on the basis of what students have learned thus far in this module.

Assessment Opportunity

You may wish to rephrase selected questions from the **As You Read** section into multiple choice or true/false format to use as a quiz. Use this quiz to assess student understanding and as a motivational tool to ensure that students complete the reading assignment and comprehend the main ideas.

Teacher Commentary

NOTES

Investigating Fossils

Investigation 7: Being a Paleontologist

the geologist doing the mapping. The amount of generalization increases as the area covered by the map increases.

Most geologic maps are accompanied by one or more vertical cross sections. These are views of what the geology would look like in an imaginary vertical plane downward from some line on the land surface. The geologist constructs these cross sections after the map is completed. Their locations are selected so as to best reveal the three-dimensional nature of the geology. The degree of certainty about the geology shown on the cross section decreases downward with depth below the surface.

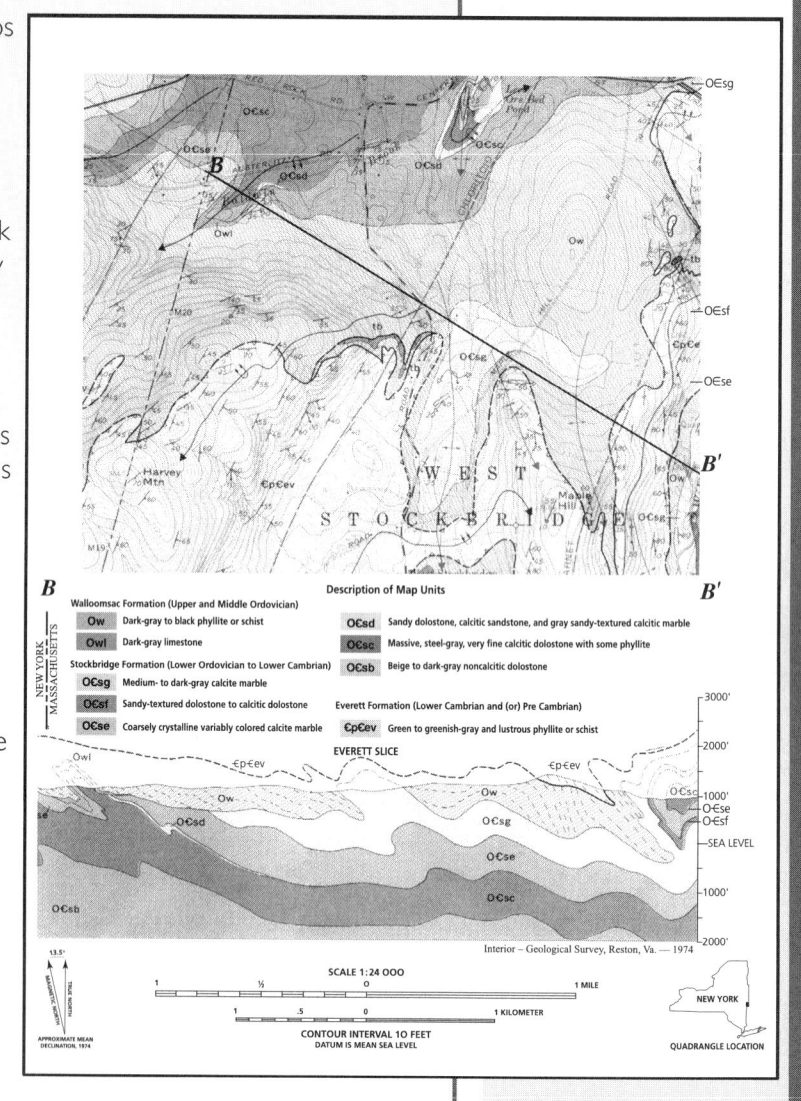

Teacher Commentary

About the Illustration

This geologic map is for West Stockbridge, Massachusetts, near the border with New York. The dark line across the map that is labeled B and B´ marks the location of the plane shown in the vertical cross section. The dotted lines above the surface indicate where rock layers used to be but have since been eroded away.

INVESTIGATING FOSSILS

Review and Reflect

Review

1. What were the names of the fossils in your classmates' fossil portraits?

Reflect

2. What useful information about fossils could be found on a geologic map?
3. What information on a geologic map could be verified using the fossil record?
4. What have you discovered from this investigation to add to your understanding of life through time?
5. How does the study of fossils help geologists understand life through time?
6. How might understanding Earth's history be useful to humans now and in the future?
7. Think back on the entire research experience with your unknown fossil.
   a) How difficult was it to find the information you wanted?
   b) What resource was most helpful in finding out about your fossil? Why was that?

Thinking about the Earth System

8. How can you use the type of rock that your fossil was in along with information about the fossil animal itself to interpret the environment in which it lived?

Thinking about Scientific Inquiry

9. How did you collect evidence in this investigation?
10. How did you present your findings to others? Why was this important?

Teacher Commentary

Review and Reflect

Review
1. The fossil names will vary depending on the portraits given. However, the names should be suitably scientific, like brachiopod, for example, and not proper names like "Fred."

Reflect
Give your students time to reflect on the nature of the evidence they have generated from all their investigations and how this has been used in this final investigation. Help them to see that the concepts they have been investigating throughout the module have enabled them to create an informative presentation. It may be best to organize a class discussion of these questions, asking each group to contribute its part of the answer. If groups have been given a variety of fossils that cover a broad span of geological time, the class should be able to find some well-informed answers and explanations. From their research, your students should have gathered enough evidence to provide a reasonable answer to the **Key Question**. Again, emphasize that it is evidence that counts.

2. If the rock units from which the fossils were recovered are known, the map can provide age information on the rock units and therefore the fossils. The descriptions of the rock units themselves often state if the units are fossiliferous (fossil-bearing), and the type of rock can provide information about the nature of the environment in which the fossilized organism once lived.

3. Answers will vary. One likely answer is that the ages of the fossiliferous rock units as stated in the map legend could be corroborated using the fossil record.

4. Answers will vary.

5. The study of fossils helps geologists understand the general evolution of life on Earth, the time scales over which this evolution occurs, the forces that cause this evolution, and even the specific evolutionary history of individual kinds of organisms.

6. By understanding Earth's history, people can better understand things that they observe on Earth today. Understanding Earth's history helps in understanding how important aspects of the Earth system came to be, and also what the future might hold in store.

7. a) Answers will vary.

    b) Answers will vary.

Thinking about the Earth System

Allow time for all students to compare their completed *Earth System Connection* sheets. As they have built this up over time, it should indicate they understand that:

- The fossil record is found in the geosphere (rock layer) of the Earth.
- Most of the sediments that form fossils are carried by water (part of the hydrosphere) to the places where they are deposited.
- Sediments can also be carried by wind (atmosphere).
- The living things that form the fossils are part of the Earth's biosphere.
- The Earth's systems are closely intertwined in the formation of fossils.

8. Fossils occur in sedimentary rocks, and sedimentary rocks are made from sediments. There are many different kinds of sediment, and different kinds of sediments are deposited (and eventually turned into a sedimentary rock) in different environments. For example, mud is deposited in still-water environments like lakes, lagoons, or the deep ocean. So, the kinds of sediments that constitute the sedimentary rock provide information about the sediment. Additionally, the structures of the fossil organism itself may impart some information about the environment in which it lived. For example, was it a freshwater or a marine environment? Was the environment in deep or shallow water?

Thinking about Scientific Inquiry

Help students understand the relevance of inquiry processes to their lives by asking them to think of everyday examples of when they use processes (finding out where a misplaced book has gone; forming an opinion about a new TV show; winning an argument).

9. Answers will vary. Students will likely cite the research they did in assembling their fossil portraits.

10. Answers will vary, but students will likely discuss the presentation of the fossil portraits. They should recognize the importance of relaying their findings to others so that others can both consider them with regard to accuracy and learn from each others' research.

Assessment Tool
Review and Reflect Journal-Entry Evaluation Sheet
This section provides text, graphs, and a photo that give students greater insight into the topic of fossils and life through time. You may wish to assign the **As You Read** questions as homework to help students focus on the major ideas in the text.

Teacher Commentary

NOTES

Teacher Review

Use this section to reflect on and review the investigation. Keep in mind that your notes here are likely to be especially helpful when you teach this investigation again. Questions listed here are examples only.

Student Achievement

What evidence do you have that all students have met the science content objectives?

Are there any students who need more help in reaching these objectives? If so, how can you provide this?

What evidence do you have that all students have demonstrated their understanding of the inquiry processes?

Which of these inquiry objectives do your students need to improve upon in future investigations?

What evidence do the journal entries contain about what your students learned from this investigation?

Planning

How well did this investigation fit into your class time?

What changes can you make to improve your planning next time?

Guiding and Facilitating Learning

How well did you focus and support inquiry while interacting with students?

What changes can you make to improve classroom management for the next investigation or the next time you teach this investigation?

Teacher Commentary

How successful were you in encouraging all students to participate fully in science learning? _____

How did you encourage and model the skills values, and attitudes of scientific inquiry? _____

How did you nurture collaboration among students? _____

Materials and Resources

What challenges did you encounter obtaining or using materials and/or resources needed for the activity? _____

What changes can you make to better obtain and better manage materials and resources next time? _____

Student Evaluation

Describe how you evaluated student progress. What worked well? What needs to be improved? _____

How will you adapt your evaluation methods for next time? _____

Describe how you guided students in self-assessment. _____

Self Evaluation

How would you rate your teaching of this investigation? _____

What advice would you give to a colleague who is planning to teach this investigation? _____

NOTES

Teacher Commentary

NOTES

Reflecting

Evidence for Ideas

Back to the Beginning

You have been studying fossils in many ways. How have your ideas changed since the beginning of the investigation? Look at the following questions and write down your ideas in your journal:

- What is a fossil?
- How are fossils are formed?
- How can we find out how old a fossil is?
- What can fossils tell you about how life changed through time?
- What are some things that you want to understand better about fossils and changes in life through time?

How has your thinking about fossils changed?

Thinking about the Earth System

Consider what you have learned about the Earth system. Refer to the *Earth System Connection* sheet that you have been building up throughout this module.

- What connections between fossils and the Earth system have you been able to find?

Thinking about Scientific Inquiry

You have used inquiry processes throughout the module. Review the investigations you have done and the inquiry processes you have used.

- What scientific inquiry processes did you use?
- How did scientific inquiry processes help you learn about fossils?

A New Beginning

Not so much an ending as a new beginning!

This investigation into fossils is now completed. However, this is not the end of the story. You will see the importance of fossils where you live, and everywhere you travel. Be alert for opportunities to observe the importance of fossils and add to your understanding.

Reflecting

This is the point at which your students review what they have learned throughout the module. This review is very important. Allow students time to work on this in a thoughtful way.

Back to the Beginning

These five questions presented here were used as a pre-assessment (see **Blackline Master** *Fossils* P.1). Encourage students to complete this final review without looking at their journal entries from the beginning of the module. Their initial entries may influence their responses.

When students have completed their writing, encourage them to revisit their initial answers from the pre-assessment. Compare their writings at the end of the unit to their writings at the beginning. It is important that students are not left with the impression that they now know all there is to know about fossils and life through time. Emphasize that learning is a continuous process throughout our lives.

> ### Assessment Opportunity
> Comparisons between students' initial answers to these questions (in the pre-assessment at the beginning of the module) and those they are now able to give provide valuable data for assessment.

Thinking about the Earth System

Now that your students are at the end of this module, ask them to make connections between fossils and the Earth System. You may want to do this through a concept map. This is an opportunity for you to gauge how well students have developed their understanding of the Earth System for assessment purposes.

Thinking about Scientific Inquiry

To help students understand the relevance of these processes to their lives, ask them to think of everyday examples of when they use these processes (finding out where a misplaced book has gone; forming an opinion about a new TV show; winning an argument).

NOTES

Appendices

Investigating Fossils
Alternative End-of-Module Assessment

Part A: Matching
Write the letter of the term from Column B that best matches the description in Column A.

Column A	Column B
1. the timescale based upon fossil evidence	A. Cast
2. fossil imprint of a trilobite	B. Species
3. worm burrows	C. Index fossil
4. the role of an organism in its environment	D. Body fossil
5. a tool for correlating strata from around the world	E. Ecological niche
6. a population of plants or animals that can breed to produce fertile offspring	F. Vestigial structures
	G. Absolute time scale
	H. Relative time scale
	I. Trace fossil

Part B: Multiple Choice

Provide the letter of the choice that best answers the questions or completes the statement.

7. In undisturbed layers of sedimentary rock the _____ rock is on top, the _____ on the bottom.
   A. thickest / thinnest
   B. thinnest / thickest
   C. youngest / oldest
   D. oldest / youngest

8. Fossils are found mainly in what kind of rocks?
   A. igneous
   B. sedimentary
   C. metamorphic
   D. volcanic

9. The law that states that undisturbed sedimentary layers get progressively younger from bottom to top is called the Law of _____.
   A. Uniformitarianism
   B. Horizontality
   C. Superposition
   D. Crosscutting relationships

10. The oldest fossils found on Earth are approximately how old?
    A. 3.5 thousand years old
    B. 3.5 million years old
    C. 3.5 billion years old
    D. 3.5 trillion years old

11. Which of the following would be more likely to aid in the preservation of a fossil?
    A. rapid burial by sediments
    B. an oxidizing environment
    C. dissolution by pore water
    D. high rates of mechanical weathering

12. Dinosaur footprints are:
    A. trace fossils
    B. cast fossils
    C. body fossils
    D. index fossils

13. Dinosaurs were most abundant during during which geologic era?
    A. Cenozoic
    B. Mesozoic
    C. Paleozoic
    D. Precambrian

14. Relative dating involves all of the following EXCEPT?
    A. comparing fossils found in rock layers
    B. placing events in their proper sequence or order
    C. using the law of superposition
    D. using radioactivity to find the age of a rock

15. You are a fossil hunter looking for shells of an extinct species of coral. Which of the following rocks will you look for to begin your search for coral fossils?
    A. shale
    B. granite
    C. limestone
    D. conglomerate

16. Which of the following is NOT a characteristic of index fossils?
    A. index fossils are extinct today
    B. index fossils lived for a relatively short period of time
    C. index fossils are found in few locations around the world
    D. index fossils are widely distributed

17. You are a scientist who is trying to figure out the absolute age of a rock. Which of the following elements could help to determine its age?
    A. Uranium
    B. Nitrogen
    C. Oxygen
    D. Nickel

18. Once fossils are found and cleaned, geologists most commonly sort them by which of the following characteristics?
    A. Color
    B. Size
    C. Orientation
    D. Shape

19. What percentage of Earth's history have modern humans, (*Homo sapiens*), lived on Earth?
    A. <1%
    B. 5%
    C. 20%
    D. 50%

20. A geologic map contains all of the following information EXCEPT?
    A. locations of various rock types
    B. geologic features such as folds and faults
    C. the ages of various rock types
    D. position of valleys and mountains

21. Which statement BEST explains why insects are poorly represented in the fossil record?
    A. insects do not have hard parts and are rarely preserved in the fossil record
    B. insects have only existed on Earth in the very recent geologic past
    C. insects are only found on land far away from depositional environments
    D. insect fossils form but are easily destroyed by geologic processes

Part C: Essay.
22. Describe an investigation from this module. In your description, include the following:
    A. the hypothesis you tested;
    B. any independent variable in the experiment;
    C. any dependent variable in the experiment;
    D. a description of how the experiment was a controlled experiment.

23. Consider the following scenario. Many years from now, after humans have become extinct, other life forms begin searching for traces of human life and activity. What do you think that they will find? Why? Describe what they would see.

Answers

1. H
2. D
3. I
4. E
5. C
6. B
7. C
8. B
9. C
10. C
11. A
12. A
13. B
14. D
15. C
16. C
17. A
18. D
19. A
20. D
21. A

22. Student responses will vary. In **Investigation 1**, we tried to find out the likelihood of fossilization of various materials. We hypothesized that everything but the shrimp and leaf would fossilize. An independent variable was the presence of hard parts and a dependent variable was the likelihood of fossilization. It was a controlled experiment because all of the organic materials were kept in the same kinds of bags and subjected to the same environmental conditions.

23. Student responses will vary. Students may discuss the possibility of life forms, finding roads, interstates, and train tracks. These transportation routes would provide information for understanding that humans moved about. These structures would be considered trace fossils of human existence. Other trace fossils that could be discovered include tombstones, building fountains, and some kinds of refuse left in landfills.

Investigating Earth Systems Assessment Tools

Assessing the Student *IES* Journal

- Journal-Entry Evaluation Sheet
- Journal-Entry Checklist
- Key-Question Evaluation Sheet
- Investigation Journal-Entry Evaluation Sheet
- Review and Reflect Journal-Entry Evaluation Sheet

Assisting Students with Self Evaluation

- Group-Participation Evaluation Sheet I
- Group-Participation Evaluation Sheet II

Assessing the Final Investigation

- Final-Investigation Evaluation Sheet
- Student-Presentation Evaluation Form

References

- Doran, R., Chan, F., and Tamir, P. (1998). *Science Educator's Guide to Assessment.*
- Leonard, W.H., and Penick, J.E. (1998). *Biology – A Community Context.* South-Western Educational Publishing. Cincinnati, Ohio.

Journal-Entry Evaluation Sheet

Name: _____ Date: _____ Module: _____

Explanation: The journal is an important component of each *IES* module. In using the journal as you investigate Earth science questions, you are mirroring what scientists do. The criteria, along with others that your teacher may add, will be used to evaluate the quality of your journal entries. Use these criteria, along with instructions within investigations, as a guide.

Criteria

1. Entry Made
       1   2   3   4   5   6   7   8   9   10   _____
   Blank   Nominal   Above average   Thorough

2. Detail
       1   2   3   4   5   6   7   8   9   10   _____
   Few dates   Half the time   Most days   Daily
   Little detail   Some detail   Good detail   Excellent detail

3. Clarity
       1   2   3   4   5   6   7   8   9   10   _____
   Vague   Becoming clearer   Clearly expressed
   Disorganized   well organized

4. Data Collection/Analysis
       1   2   3   4   5   6   7   8   9   10   _____
   Data collected   Data collected,   Data collected
   Not analyzed   some analyzed   and analyzed

5. Originality
       1   2   3   4   5   6   7   8   9   10   _____
   Little evidence   Some evidence   Strong evidence
   of originality   of originality   of originality

6. Reasoning/Higher-Order Thinking
       1   2   3   4   5   6   7   8   9   10   _____
   Little evidence   Some evidence   Strong evidence
   of thoughtfulness   of thoughtfulness   of thoughtfulness

7. Other
       1   2   3   4   5   6   7   8   9   10   _____

8. Other
       1   2   3   4   5   6   7   8   9   10   _____

Journal-Entry Checklist

Name: _____ Date: _____ Module: _____

Explanation: The journal is an important component of each *IES* module. In using the journal as you investigate Earth science questions, you are mirroring what scientists do. The criteria, along with others that your teacher may add, will be used to evaluate the quality of your journal entries. Use these criteria, along with instructions within investigations, as a guide.

Criteria

1. Makes entries _____

2. Provides dates and details _____

3. Entry is clear and organized _____

4. Shows data collected _____

5. Analyzes data collected _____

6. Shows originality in presentation _____

7. Shows evidence of higher-order thinking _____

8. Other _____

9. Other _____

Total Earned _____

Total Possible _____

Comments:

Key-Question Evaluation Sheet

Name: _____ Date: _____ Module: _____

	No Entry		Fair		Strong
Shows evidence of prior knowledge	0	1	2	3	4

	No Entry		Fair		Strong
Reflects discussion with classmates	0	1	2	3	4

Additional Comments

Key-Question Evaluation Sheet

Name: _____ Date: _____ Module: _____

	No Entry		Fair		Strong
Shows evidence of prior knowledge	0	1	2	3	4

	No Entry		Fair		Strong
Reflects discussion with classmates	0	1	2	3	4

Additional Comments

Key-Question Evaluation Sheet

Name: _____ Date: _____ Module: _____

	No Entry		Fair		Strong
Shows evidence of prior knowledge	0	1	2	3	4

	No Entry		Fair		Strong
Reflects discussion with classmates	0	1	2	3	4

Additional Comments

Investigation Journal-Entry Evaluation Sheet

Name: _____ Date: _____ Module: _____

Criteria

1. Completeness of written investigation
       1 2 3 4 5 6 7 8 9 10   _____
   Blank   Incomplete   Thorough

2. Participation in investigations
       1 2 3 4 5 6 7 8 9 10   _____
   None or little;   Needs minimal guidance, Leads, is inquisitive,
   unable to guide sometimes helping others persistent, focused
   self

3. Skills attained
       1 2 3 4 5 6 7 8 9 10   _____
   Few skills   Tends to use some   High degree of
   evident   appropriate skills   appropriate skills used

4. Investigation Design
       1 2 3 4 5 6 7 8 9 10   _____
   Variables not   Sometimes   Considers variables
   considered   considers variables, Sound rationale for
   techniques   uses logical techniques techniques
   illogical

5. Conceptual understanding of content
       1 2 3 4 5 6 7 8 9 10   _____
   No evidence   Approaches understanding Exceeds expectations
   of understanding of most concepts   for content attainment

6. Ability to explain/discuss inquiry
       1 2 3 4 5 6 7 8 9 10   _____
   Unable to   Some ability to   Uses scientific reasoning
   articulate   explain/discuss   to explain any
   scientific thought the inquiry   aspect of the inquiry

7. Other
       1 2 3 4 5 6 7 8 9 10   _____

8. Other
       1 2 3 4 5 6 7 8 9 10   _____

Review and Reflect Journal-Entry Evaluation Sheet

Name: _____ Date: _____ Module: _____

Criteria	Blank		Fair		Excellent	
Thoroughness of answers	0	1	2	3	4	5
Content of answers	0	1	2	3	4	5
Other	0	1	2	3	4	5

Review and Reflect Journal-Entry Evaluation Sheet

Name: _____ Date: _____ Module: _____

Criteria	Blank		Fair		Excellent	
Thoroughness of answers	0	1	2	3	4	5
Content of answers	0	1	2	3	4	5
Other	0	1	2	3	4	5

Review and Reflect Journal-Entry Evaluation Sheet

Name: _____ Date: _____ Module: _____

Criteria	Blank		Fair		Excellent	
Thoroughness of answers	0	1	2	3	4	5
Content of answers	0	1	2	3	4	5
Other	0	1	2	3	4	5

Group-Participation Evaluation Sheet I

Key:
4 = Worked on his/her part and assisted others
3 = Worked on his/her part
2 = Worked on part less than half the time
1 = Interfered with the work of others
0 = No work

My name is _____ .   I give myself a _____

The other people in my group are: I give each person:

A. _____   _____

B. _____   _____

C. _____   _____

D. _____   _____

Key:
4 = Worked on his/her part and assisted others
3 = Worked on his/her part
2 = Worked on part less than half the time
1 = Interfered with the work of others
0 = No work

My name is _____ .

The other people in my group are:

A. _____

B. _____

C. _____

D. _____

Group-Participation Evaluation Sheet II

Name: _____ Date: _____ Module: _____

Key:
Highest rating _____
Lowest rating _____

1. In the chart, rate each person in your group, including yourself.

	Names of Group Members				
Quality of Work					
Quantity of Work					
Cooperativeness					
Other Comments _____					

2. What went well in your investigation?

3. If you could repeat the investigation, how would you change it?

Investigating Fossils

Final-Investigation Evaluation Sheet

Alerting students

Before your students begin the final investigation, they must understand what is expected of them and how they will be evaluated on their performance. Review the task thoroughly, setting time guidelines and parameters (whom they may work with, what materials they can use, etc.). Spell out the evaluation criteria for each level of proficiency shown below. Use three categories for a 3-point scale (Achieved, Approaching, Attempting). If you prefer a 5-point scale, add the final two categories.

Name: _____ Date: _____ Module: _____

	Understanding of concepts and inquiry	Use of evidence to explain and support results	Communication of ideas	Thoroughness of work
Exceeding proficiency 5	Demonstrates complete and unambiguous understanding of the problem and inquiry processes used.	Uses all evidence from inquiry that is factually relevant, accurate, and consistent with explanations offered.	Communicates ideas clearly and in a compelling and elegant manner to the intended audience.	Goes beyond all deliverables agreed upon for the project and has extended the data collection and analysis.
Achieved proficiency 4	Demonstrates fairly complete and reasonably clear understanding of the problem and inquiry processes used.	Uses the major evidence from inquiry that is relevant and consistent with explanations offered.	Communicates ideas clearly and coherently to the intended audience.	Includes all of the deliverables agreed upon for the project.
Approaching proficiency 3	Demonstrates general, yet somewhat limited understanding of the problem and inquiry processes used.	Uses evidence from inquiry to support explanations but may mix fact with opinion, omit significant evidence, or use evidence that is not totally accurate.	Completes the task satisfactorily but communication of ideas is incomplete, muddled, or unclear.	Work largely complete but missing one of the deliverables agreed upon for the project.
Attempting proficiency 2	Demonstrates only a very general understanding of the problem and inquiry processes used.	Uses generalities or opinion more than evidence from inquiry to support explanations.	Communication of ideas is difficult to understand or unclear.	Work missing several of the deliverables agreed upon for the project.
Non-proficient 1	Demonstrates vague or little understanding of the problem and inquiry processes used.	Uses limited evidence to support explanations or does not attempt to support explanations.	Communication of ideas is brief, vague, and/or not understandable.	Work largely incomplete; missing many of the deliverables agreed upon for the project.

Student-Presentation Evaluation Form

Student Name_____ Date_____

Topic_____

	Excellent		Fair		Poor
Quality of ideas	4	3	2	1
Ability to answer questions	4	3	2	1
Overall comprehension	4	3	2	1

COMMENTS _____
_____
_____
_____

Student-Presentation Evaluation Form

Student Name_____ Date_____

Topic_____

	Excellent		Fair		Poor
Quality of ideas	4	3	2	1
Ability to answer questions	4	3	2	1
Overall comprehension	4	3	2	1

COMMENTS _____
_____
_____
_____

Blackline Master *Fossils* P.1

Questions about Fossils

- What is a fossil?

- How are fossils formed?

- How can we find out how old a fossil is?

- What can fossils tell you about how life changed through time?

- What are some things that you want to understand better about fossils and changes in life through time?

Use with *Fossils* Pre-assessment.

Blackline Master *Fossils* P.2

Student Journal Cover Sheet
Investigating Fossils

Name: _____

Group Members:

1. _____

2. _____

3. _____

4. _____

Teacher: _____

Class: _____

Dates of Investigation:

Start _____ Complete _____

Keep this journal with you at all times during your study of
Investigating Fossils.

Use with *Fossils* Pre-assessment.

Blackline Master *Fossils* I.1

Name: _____

Earth System Connection Sheet   Fossils

When you finish an investigation, use this sheet to record any links you can make with the Earth System. By the end of the module you should have as complete a diagram as possible.

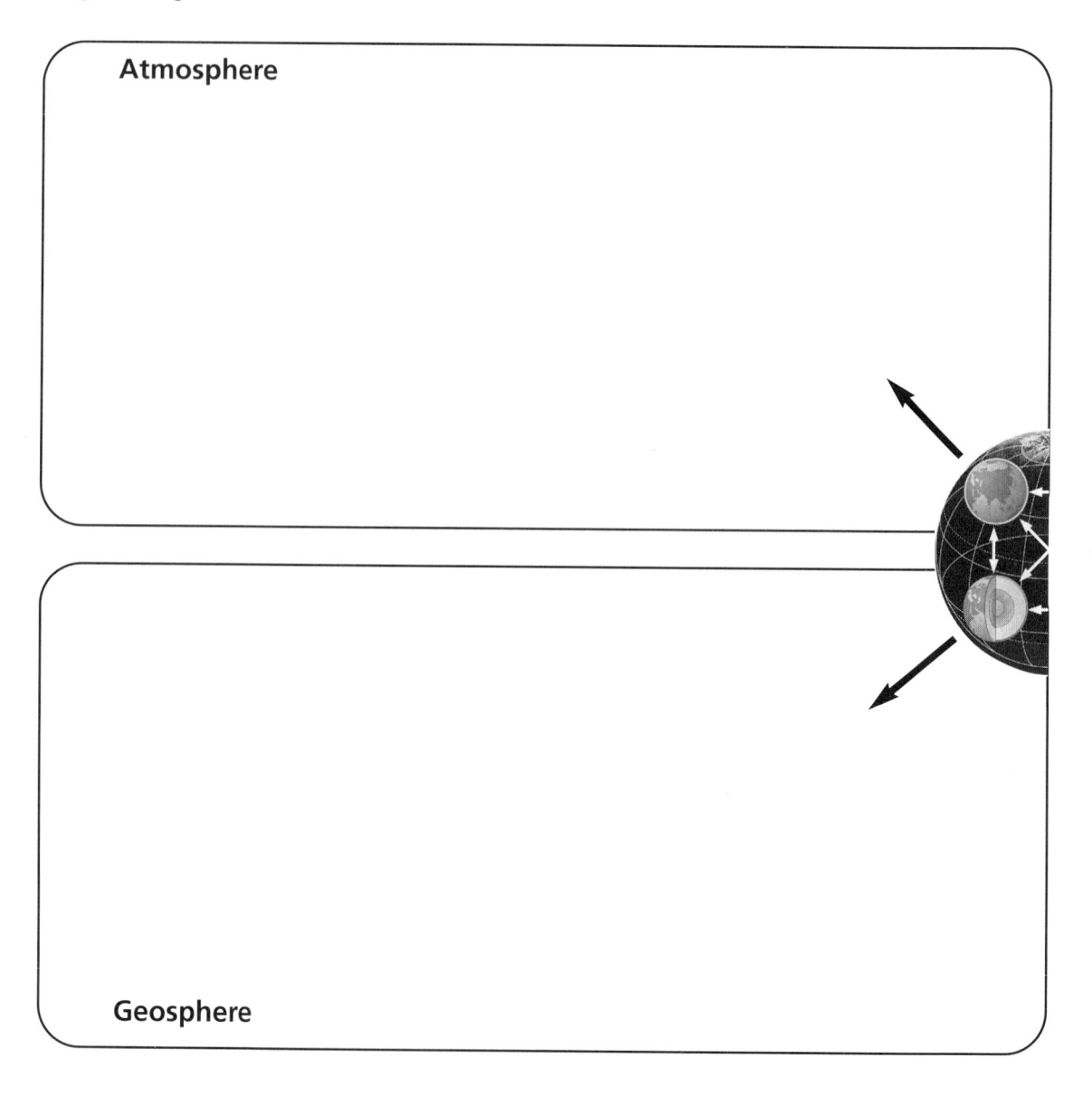

Atmosphere

Geosphere

Use with *Fossils* Introducing the Earth System.

Biosphere

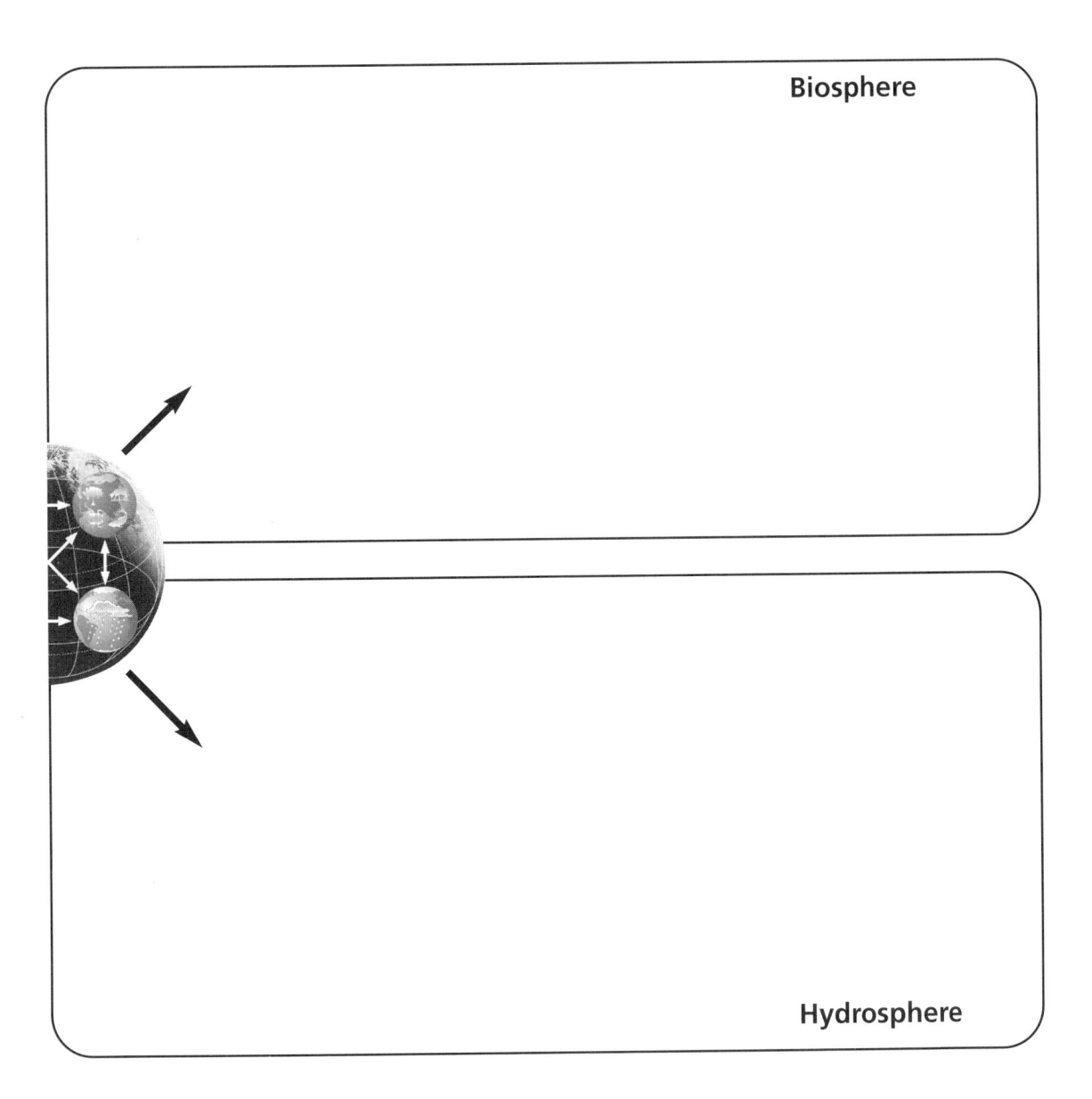

Hydrosphere

Investigating Fossils

Blackline Master *Fossils* I.2

Inquiry Processes

- Explore questions to answer by inquiry.

- Design an investigation.

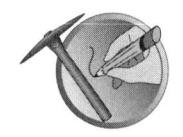

- Conduct an investigation.

- Collect and review data using tools.

- Use evidence to develop ideas.

- Consider evidence for explanations.

- Seek alternative explanations.

- Show evidence and reasons to others.

- Use mathematics for science inquiry.

Use with *Fossils* Introducing the Earth System.

Blackline Master *Fossils* 1.1

Data Table for Fossil Formation of Dead Organisms

Item	Observations	Prediction (Can it become a fossil?)	Reason (Use an analogy if possible.)
Unpeeled shrimp			
chicken wing			
clamshell			
green leaf			
small twig			

Use with *Fossils* Investigation 1: The Properties of Fossils

Blackline Master *Fossils* 2.1

Data Table for Class Results from Measurements for Sizes of Spheres

Object	Class's Average Measurement (include units)	Comparison
basketball		
soccer ball		
volleyball		
softball		
tennis ball		
table-tennis ball		
marble		
other		

Use with *Fossils* Investigation 2: Sediment Size and Fossil Formation

Blackline Master *Fossils* 2.2

Data Table for Size of Different Sediment Types

Sediment Type	Size Range (particle diameter)	Comparison
Very Coarse Sand	1.0–2.0 mm	
Coarse Sand	0.5–1.0 mm	
Medium Sand	0.25–0.50 mm	
Fine Sand	0.125–0.250 mm	
Very Fine Sand	0.0625–0.1250 mm	
Silt	0.0040–0.0625 mm	
Clay	<0.004	

Use with *Fossils* Investigation 2: Sediment Size and Fossil Formation

Blackline Master *Fossils* 3.1

Wheel of Fossilization

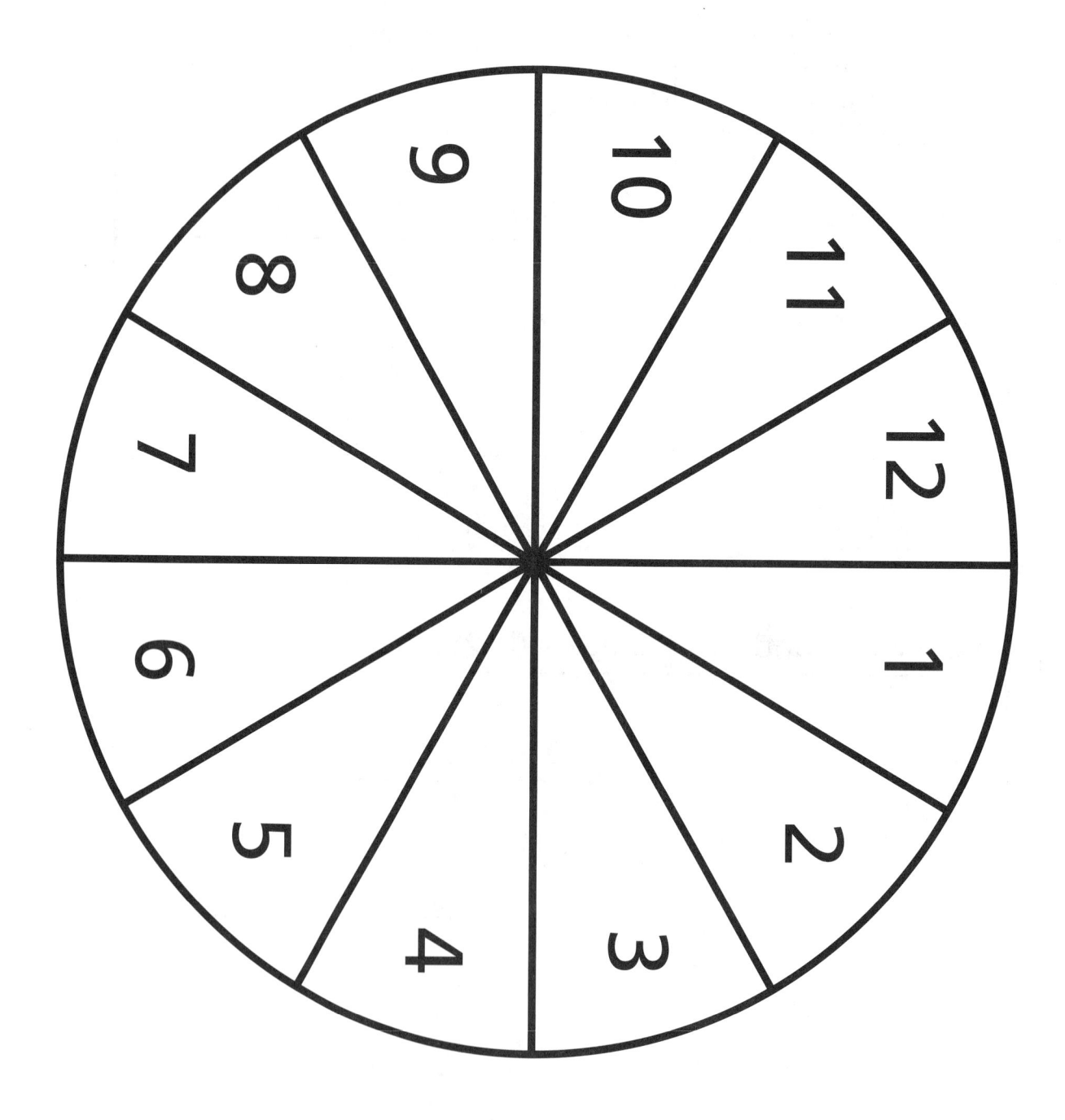

Use with *Fossils* Investigation 3: Conditions for Fossil Formation

Blackline Master *Fossils* 3.2

Possible Fates on the Wheel of Fossilization

1. You are a saber-toothed cat. Your body decomposes and your bones disintegrate in a field—NO FOSSIL
2. You are a shelled protozoan (a foraminiferan). Your body decomposes and your shell dissolves in the deep sea—NO FOSSIL
3. You are an oak tree. Your wood and leaves all decompose in a forest—NO FOSSIL
4. You are a snail. Your shell is preserved as a fossil, but rock erosion later destroys it—NO FOSSIL
5. You are a clam. Your shell is buried by mud in a quiet water setting—YOUR SHELL FOSSILIZES
6. You are a barnacle. Your body and shell are metamorphosed in an undersea lava flow—NO FOSSIL
7. You are a jellyfish. You have no hard skeleton, and your soft body decomposes —NO FOSSIL
8. You are a crab. You get eaten and your shell gets broken down into tiny bits in the process—NO FOSSIL
9. You are a tree fern. Your leaves are buried and preserved in swamp mud—YOUR TISSUES FOSSILIZE
10. You are a clamshell. Your body decomposes and your shell is broken to bits by waves—NO FOSSIL
11. You are a snail shell. Your body decomposes and your shell is recrystallized during mountain-building—NO FOSSIL
12. You are a *Tyrannosaurus rex*. Your footprint in mud is buried by sand along a river—YOUR TRACK FOSSILIZES.

Use with *Fossils* Investigation 3: Conditions for Fossil Formation

Blackline Master Fossils 3.3

Environments of Sediment Deposition

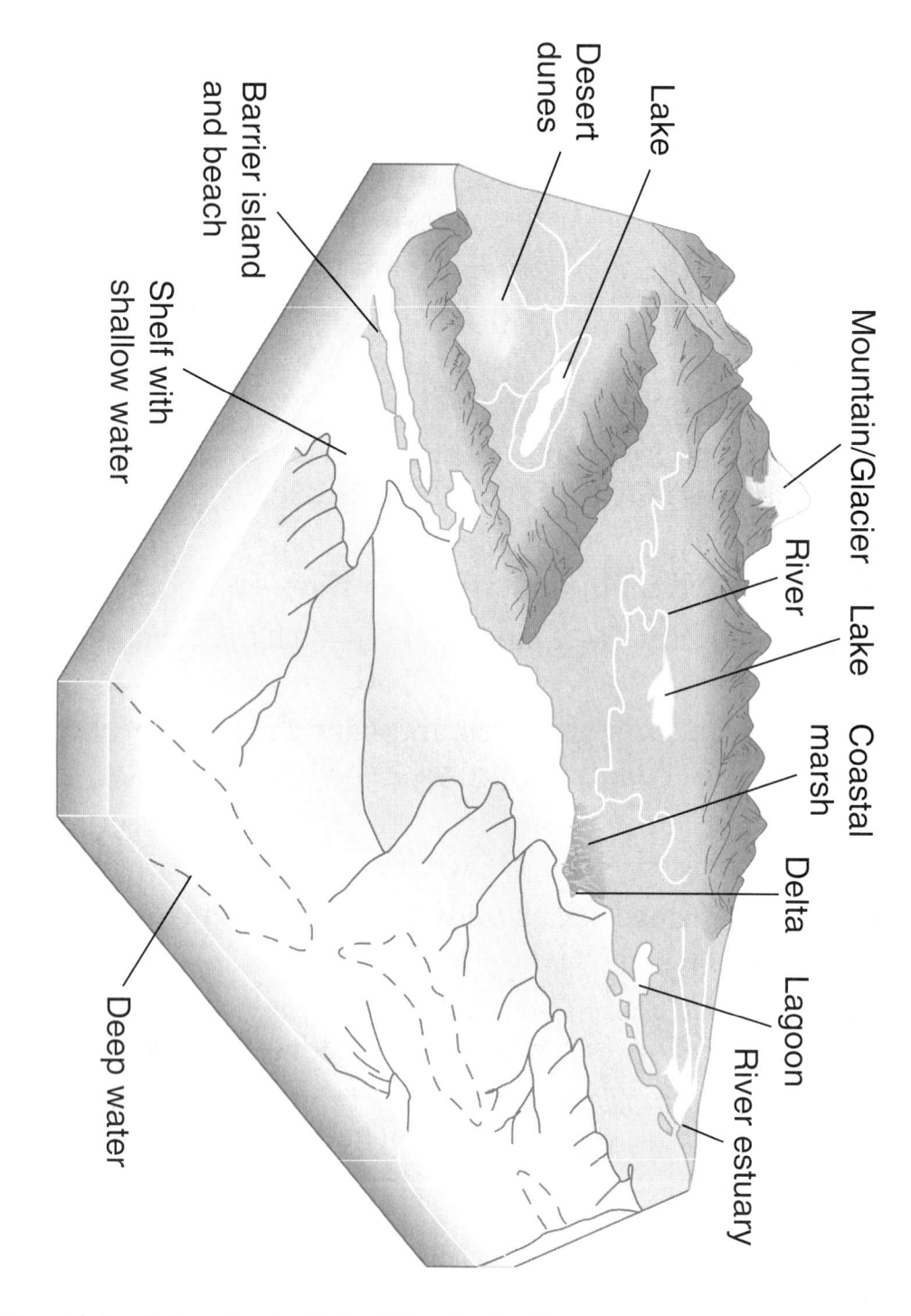

Labels: Barrier island and beach; Desert dunes; Lake; Mountain/Glacier; River; Lake; Coastal marsh; Delta; Lagoon; River estuary; Shelf with shallow water; Deep water

Use with Fossils Investigation 3: Conditions for Fossil Formation

Blackline Master *Fossils* **4.1**

Major Divisions of Geologic Time

Major Divisions of Geologic Time
(boundaries in millions of years before present)

Era	Period	Event	
Cenozoic	Quaternary	modern humans	
			1.8
	Tertiary	abundant mammals	
			65
Mesozoic	Cretaceous	flowering plants; dinosaur and ammonoid extinctions	
			145
	Jurassic	first birds and mammals; abundant dinosaurs	
			213
	Triassic	abundant coniferous trees	
			248
Paleozoic	Permian	extinction of trilobites and other marine animals	
			286
	Pennsylvanian	fern forests; abundant insects; first reptiles	
			325
	Mississippian	sharks; large primitive trees	
			360
	Devonian	amphibians and ammonoids	
			410
	Silurian	early plants and animals on land	
			440
	Ordovician	first fish	
			505
	Cambrian	abundant marine invertebrates; trilobites dominant	
			544
Proterozoic		primitive aquatic plants	
			2500
Archean		oldest fossils; bacteria and algae	

Use with *Fossils* Investigation 4: Fossils through Geologic Time

Blackline Master *Fossils* **4.2**

Data Table on Average Length of Steps

Names of Group Members	Distance of Steps (in meters and centimeters)	Average Step (total distance for each person divided by 10)
Total for Your Group (add each person's average)		T =
Average Group Step (divide total by number of persons in your group)		AGS =

Use with *Fossils* Investigation 4: Fossils through Geologic Time

Blackline Master *Fossils* 4.3

Stratigraphic Notebook

Group 1 Location
- Layer 1   0-60 meters below surface
  Z fossils
- Layer 2   60-120 meters below surface
  No fossils
- Layer 3   120-180 meters below surface
  D fossils
- Layer 4   180-240 meters below surface
  No fossils
- Layer 5   240-300 meters below surface
  S fossils

Group 2 Location
- Layer 1   0-50 meters below surface
  B fossils
- Layer 2   50-100 meters below surface
  No fossils
- Layer 3   100-150 meters below surface
  N fossils
- Layer 4   150-200 meters below surface
  No fossils
- Layer 5   200-250 meters below surface
  A fossils
- Layer 6   250-300 meters below surface
  S fossils

Group 3 Location
- Layer 1   0-75 meters below surface
  B fossils
- Layer 2   75-150 meters below surface
  Z fossils
  N fossils
- Layer 3   150-225 meters below surface
  D fossils
- Layer 4   225-300 meters below surface
  A fossils

Group 4 Location
- Layer 1   0-50 meters below surface
  B fossils
- Layer 2   50-100 meters below surface
  Z fossils
- Layer 3   100-150 meters below surface
  No fossils
- Layer 4   150-200 meters below surface
  D fossils
- Layer 5   200-250 meters below surface
  No fossils
- Layer 6   250-300 meters below surface
  S fossils

Group 5 Location
- Layer 1   0-75 meters below surface
  Z fossils
- Layer 2   75-150 meters below surface
  N fossils
- Layer 3   150-225 meters below surface
  D fossils
  A fossils
- Layer 4   225-300 meters below surface
  S fossils

Group 6 Location
- Layer 1   0-60 meters below surface
  B fossils
- Layer 2   60-120 meters below surface
  N fossils
- Layer 3   120-180 meters below surface
  D fossils
- Layer 4   180-240 meters below surface
  A fossils
- Layer 5   240-300 meters below surface
  S fossils

Use with *Fossils* Investigation 4: Fossils through Geologic Time

Investigating Fossils

Blackline Master *Fossils* 4.4

Stratigraphic Correlation

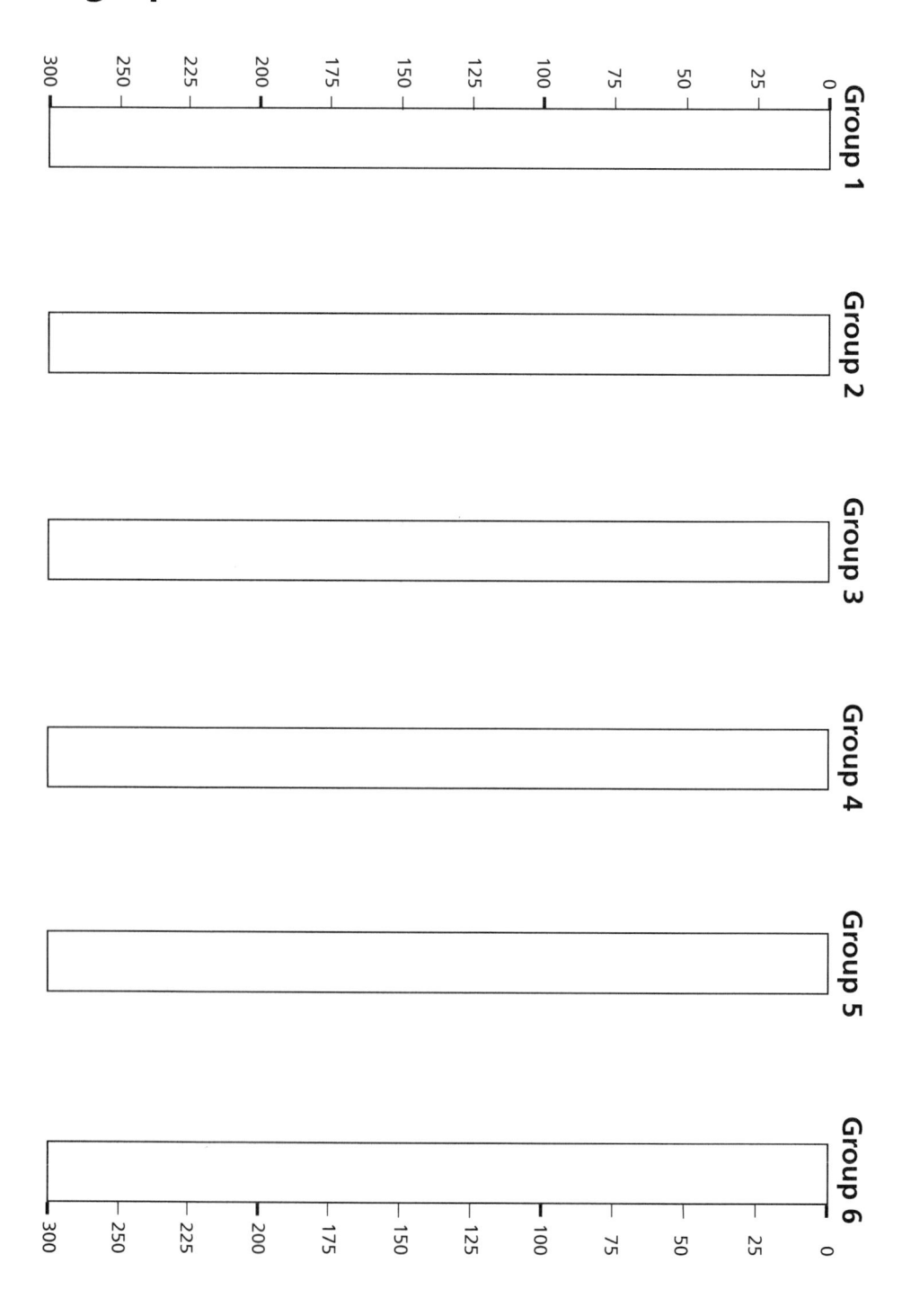

	300	250	225	200	175	150	125	100	75	50	25	0	
													Group 1
													Group 2
													Group 3
													Group 4
													Group 5
	300	250	225	200	175	150	125	100	75	50	25	0	Group 6

Use with *Fossils* Investigation 4: Fossils through Geologic Time

Blackline Master *Fossils* 5.1

Sample Illustrations of Fossils

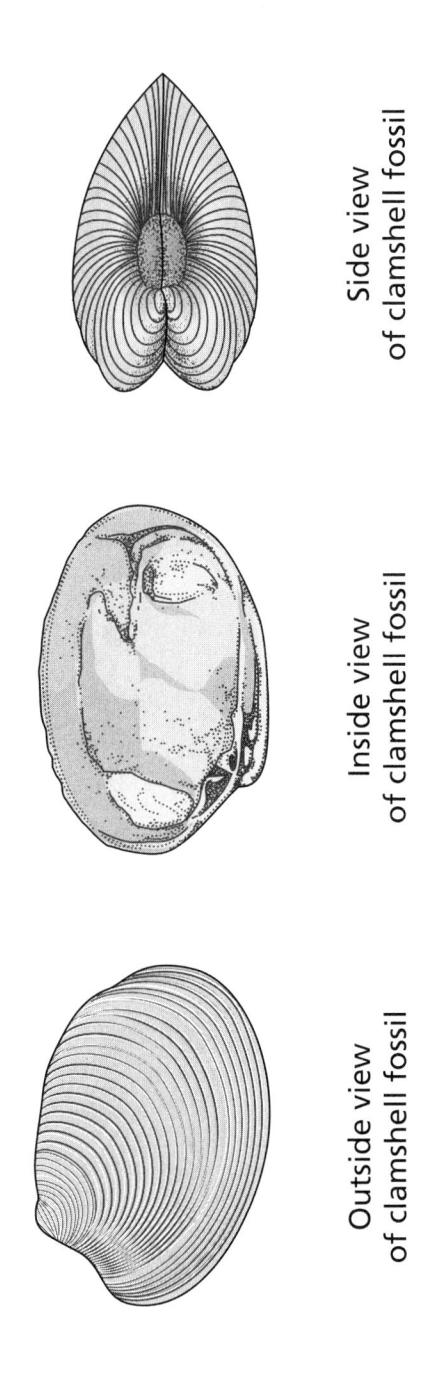

Side view of clamshell fossil

Inside view of clamshell fossil

Outside view of clamshell fossil

Use with *Fossils* Investigation 5: Comparing Fossils Over Time

Blackline Master *Fossils* 5.2

Diagram of Parts of a Clamshell

Outside of the Shell

- Dorsal
- umbo
- lanule
- growth ridges
- Anterior
- Posterior
- Ventral

Inside of the Shell

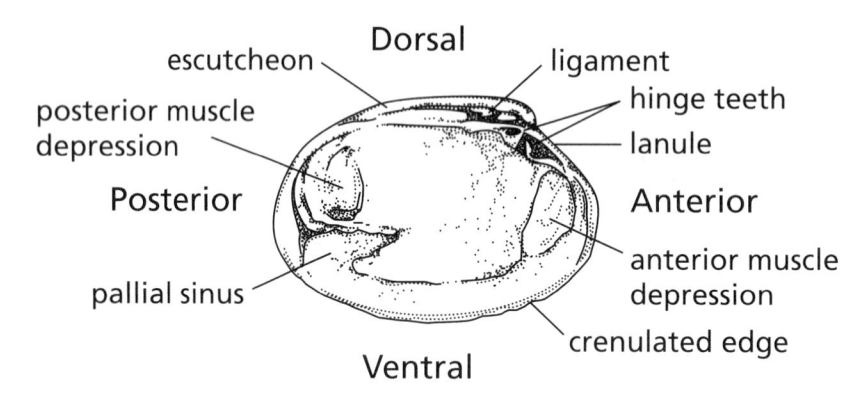

- Dorsal
- escutcheon
- ligament
- posterior muscle depression
- hinge teeth
- lanule
- Posterior
- Anterior
- pallial sinus
- anterior muscle depression
- crenulated edge
- Ventral

Use with *Fossils* Investigation 5: Comparing Fossils Over Time

Blackline Master *Fossils* 6.1

Animal Characteristics

Eyes Forward in head On sides of head **Feet** Webbed Clawed Padded Hooved **Mouth** Beak Tearing teeth Grinding teeth Cutting teeth	**Covering** Fur Feathers Scales Skin Shell **Coloration** Camouflage Bright **Movement** Running Flying Climbing Swinging Leaping	**Homes** Trees Caves Underground Water **When Animals Eat** Day Night Dawn or Dusk **Dealing with Heat and Cold** Body Covering Active/Feeding Times Homes **Other Defenses** Bad Smell or Taste Size

Use with *Fossils* Investigation 6: Adaptations to a Changing Environment

Blackline Master *Fossils* 6.2

The Modern Horse and Some of Its Ancestors

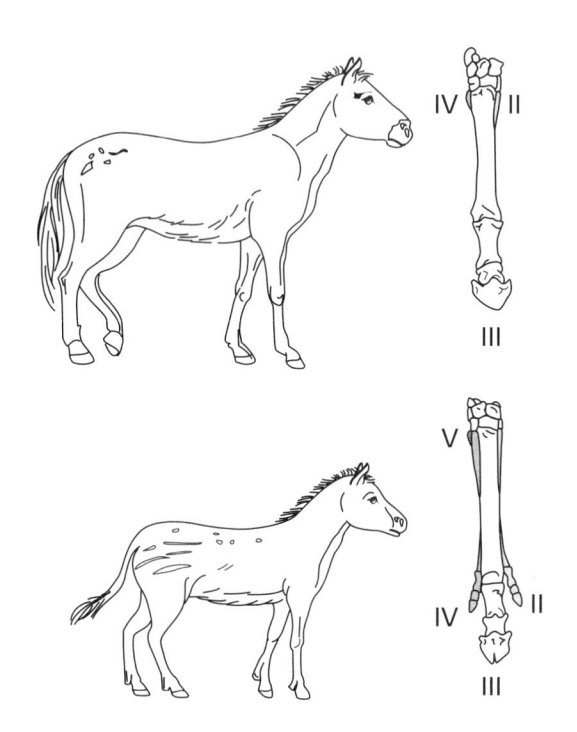

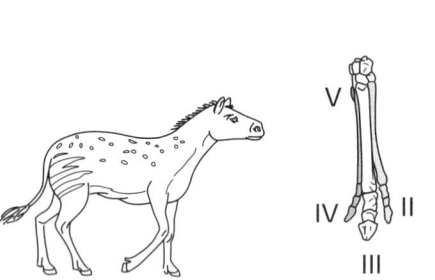

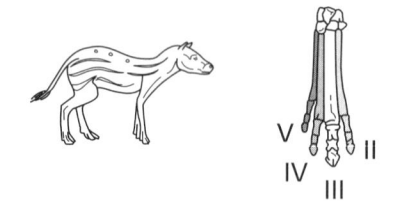

Equus (modern horse)
- Lived from about 5 million years ago to the present
- Lives in areas of the grassy plains
- Eats grasses and is classified as a grazer
- Is about 1.6 m tall at the shoulder
- Has 1 hoofed toe on each of its front and rear limbs.

Merychippus
- Lived from about 17 to 11 million years ago
- Lived in areas with shrubs and on the grassy plains
- Ate leafy vegetation and grasses and is classified as a grazer (the first in the line of horses)
- Was about 1.0 m tall at the shoulder and had a long face and legs making it appear much like a modern horse.
- Had 3 hoofed toes on each of its front and rear limbs. The central toe was much larger than the others.

Miohippus
- Lived from about 32 to 25 million years ago
- Lived in less thickly wooded areas
- Ate leafy vegetation and is classified as a browser
- Was about 0.6 m tall at the shoulder (about the size of a German shepherd dog) and had padded feet.
- Had 3 toes on each of its front and rear limbs.

Hyracotherium-Oldest known horse
- Lived from about 55 to 45 million years ago
- Lived in thickly wooded areas
- Ate leafy vegetation and is classified as a browser
- Was about 0.4 m tall at the shoulder (about the size of a small dog) and had padded feet.
- Had 4 toes on each of its front limbs and three on each of its rear limbs.

Use with *Fossils* Investigation 6: Adaptations to a Changing Environment

Blackline Master *Fossils* 7.1

Geologic Map and Cross-Section

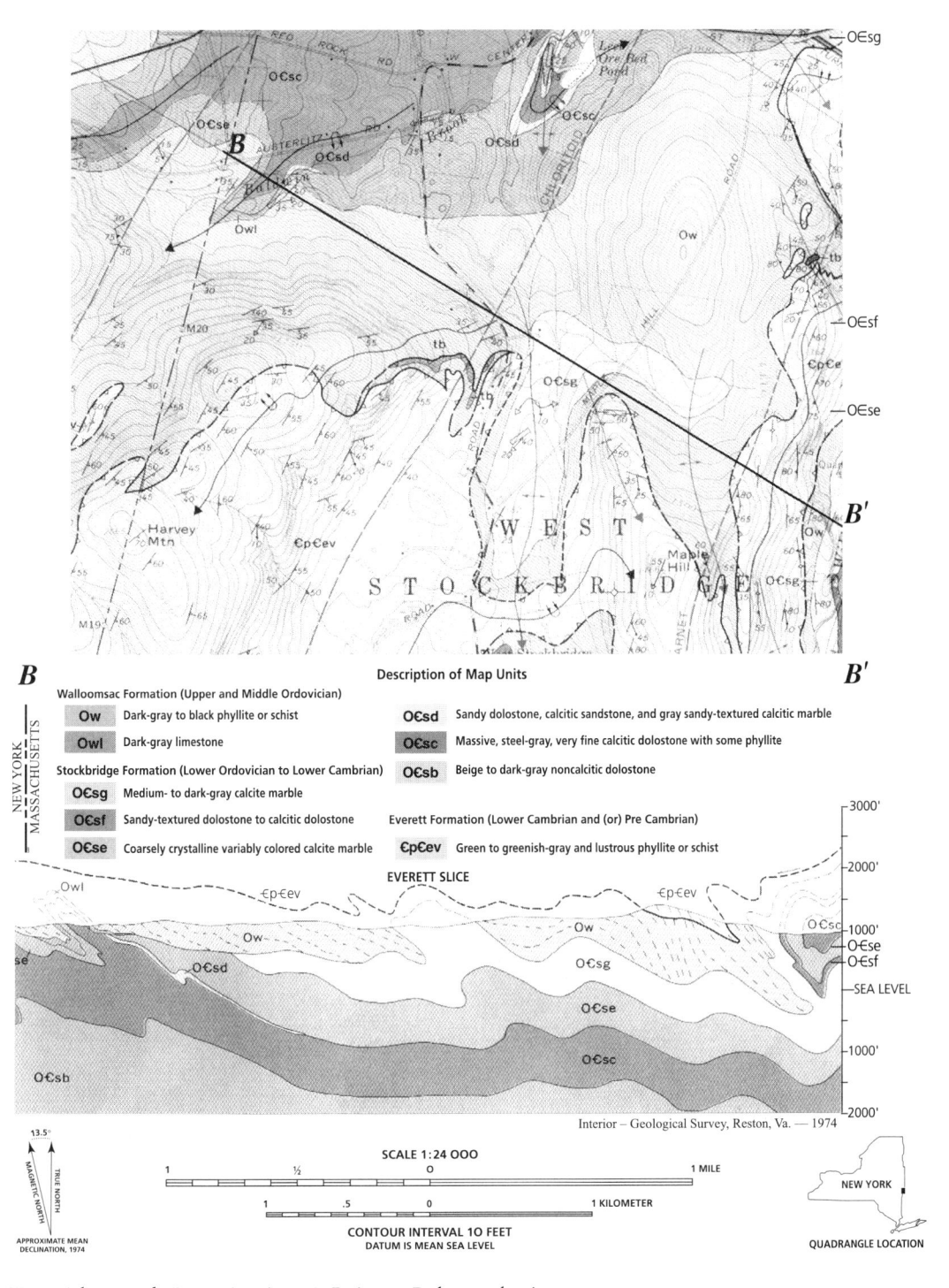

Description of Map Units

Walloomsac Formation (Upper and Middle Ordovician)
- Ow — Dark-gray to black phyllite or schist
- Owl — Dark-gray limestone

Stockbridge Formation (Lower Ordovician to Lower Cambrian)
- O€sg — Medium- to dark-gray calcite marble
- O€sf — Sandy-textured dolostone to calcitic dolostone
- O€se — Coarsely crystalline variably colored calcite marble
- O€sd — Sandy dolostone, calcitic sandstone, and gray sandy-textured calcitic marble
- O€sc — Massive, steel-gray, very fine calcitic dolostone with some phyllite
- O€sb — Beige to dark-gray noncalcitic dolostone

Everett Formation (Lower Cambrian and (or) Pre Cambrian)
- €p€ev — Green to greenish-gray and lustrous phyllite or schist

EVERETT SLICE

Interior – Geological Survey, Reston, Va. — 1974

SCALE 1:24 000

CONTOUR INTERVAL 10 FEET
DATUM IS MEAN SEA LEVEL

APPROXIMATE MEAN DECLINATION, 1974

QUADRANGLE LOCATION

Use with *Fossils* Investigation 7: Being a Paleontologist

Investigating Fossils 303

NOTES

NOTES

NOTES

NOTES

NOTES

NOTES

NOTES